LEGENDARY LOCALS

OF

MONROE

LOUISIANA

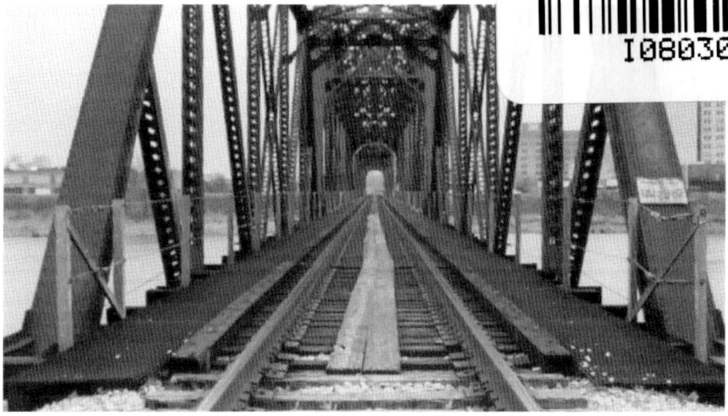

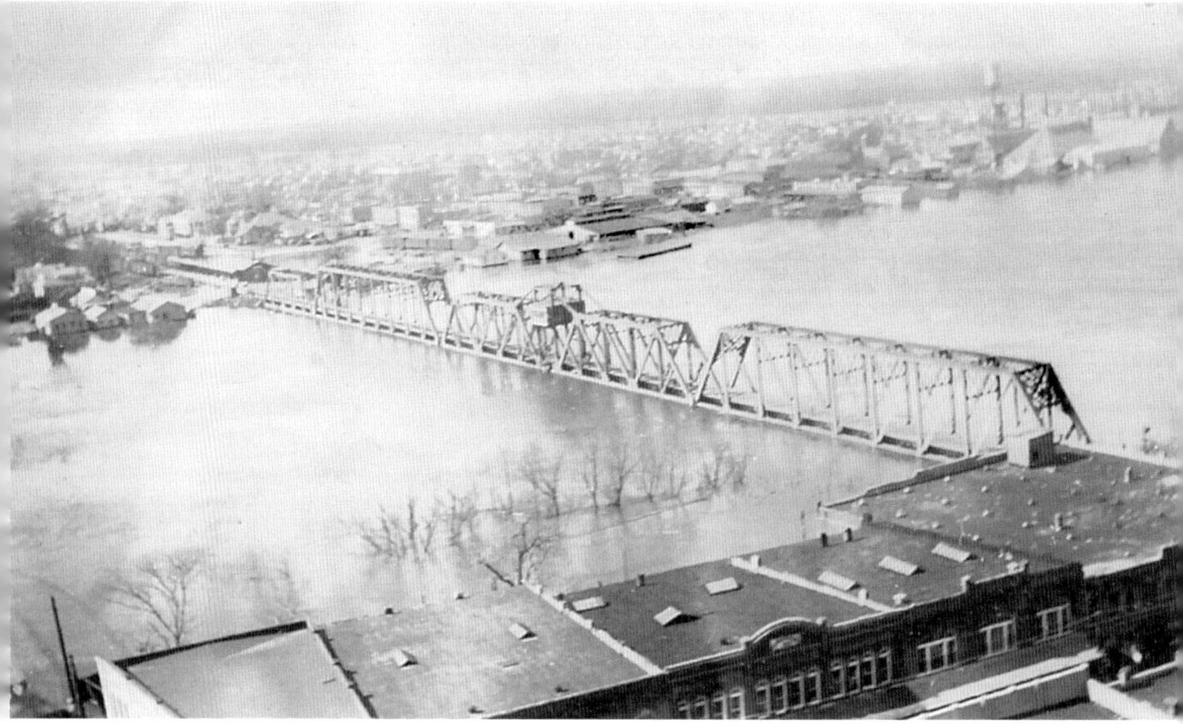

River City
Pictured is an aerial view of Monroe, Louisiana, during the so-called "Great Flood" of 1932, considered by many residents of the day to be the "Flood of the Century." (Courtesy of Louise Khoury and the family of Mary Savana.)

Page 1: **Downtown Railroad Bridge**
The Downtown Railroad Bridge spans the Ouachita River, connecting the Twin Cities. (Photograph by Griffin Scott.)

LEGENDARY LOCALS

OF

MONROE

LOUISIANA

GRIFFIN SCOTT AND AMY SLIGER

LEGENDARY LOCALS

Copyright © 2014 by Griffin Scott and Amy Sliger
ISBN 978-1-4671-0163-9

Legendary Locals is an imprint of Arcadia Publishing
Charleston, South Carolina

Printed in the United States of America

Library of Congress Control Number: 2014932574

For all general information, please contact Arcadia Publishing:
Telephone 843-853-2070
Fax 843-853-0044
E-mail sales@arcadiapublishing.com
For customer service and orders:
Toll-Free 1-888-313-2665

Visit us on the Internet at www.arcadiapublishing.com

Dedication
To our families, collaborators, friends, and coworkers, for without your infinite patience and support, this project would not have been possible.

On the Front Cover: Clockwise from top left:
Claire Lee Chennault, World War II hero, founder of the famous "Flying Tigers" (photograph by United States Armed Services; see page 38), Hamid Drake, internationally renowned jazz musician (courtesy of Michael Hoefner; see page 70), Bill Russell, basketball star, civil rights advocate (photograph by *New York World-Telegram* and the *Sun* staff photographer; see page 106), Sidney Saunders, infamous businessman (courtesy of Griffin Scott; see page 122), Rev. Lea Joyner, spiritual and community leader (courtesy of Mike Takewell; see page 26), Phil Robertson, star of A&E's *Duck Dynasty* (photograph by Edward Vantine Studios Inc., courtesy of Louisiana Tech University; see page 22), Edmund Williamson, noted multimedia artist and community advocate (photograph by Brad Arender, courtesy of Arender Studio + Gallery; see page 50), Kitty DeGree, philanthropist and education advocate (courtesy of Daphne Terral; see page 33), Emy Lou Biedenharn, opera singer and daughter of Joseph Biedenharn, first bottler of Coca-Cola (courtesy of the Biedenharn Museum & Gardens; see page 66).

On the Back Cover: From left to right:
John Denison and Judy Wagoner, longtime KNOE-TV news anchors (courtesy of Pete Battaglia; see page 44), James A. Noe, governor, founder of KNOE-TV (courtesy of Louise Khoury and the family of Mary Savana; see page 84).

CONTENTS

ACKNOWLEDGMENTS

Legendary Locals of Monroe would not have been possible without the assistance of the Ouachita Parish Public Library, Larry Foreman, the City of Monroe, Mayor Jamie Mayo, Rod Washington, Elisabeth Grant-Gibson, Susan Allain, Cindy Ingram, Kay Knight LaFrance, Pete Battalgia, John Denison, Rhonda Counselman, Mike Takewell, Louise Khoury, Chuck Khoury, Doug Tarver, Katie Tarver, Taylor Kaitlin Sliger, Lennon Sliger, Brenda Sliger Brown, Joshua Brown, Jeremy Brown, Brennan Brown, Jordan Brown, James "Big Jim" Elliott, Toby Otero, John Reynolds, Greg Guylas, Arabella Moore, Teresine Tarver, Brad Arender, Joey Cruse, Amanda McMullen, the family of Sol Rosenberg, the Biedenharn Museum & Gardens, Ralph Calhoun, CenturyLink, the Big Whit 77 Foundation, Andrew Whitworth, Melissa Clark Whitworth, the Strauss Theatre Center, Donna Branson, the Radio People, Susan Cox, the United Way of Northeast Louisiana, Joey Cruse, Mark Sanders, Jessica Bennett Vandervoort, Sebastian Vandervoort, Johnny's Pizza House, Kenneth Masters, Veronica Dickey, Greg Hilburn, Bob Holladay, Swanberg Ministries, the C.E. Byrd High School Alumni Association, Ron Downing, Eleanor Brown, Ken Booth, Cory Bahr, Restaurant Cotton, Meaghan Donohoe, Clay Norman, Kim Lowrey, Janet Durden, Audrey Hester, Jason Grisham, Joli Livaudais Grisham, Doug Duffey, Katie Taylor, Frank Ticheli, the Louisiana Folklife Center, P.C. Paul Hamerlinck, Dr. Shane Rasmussen, Edwards Barham, the Louisiana Department of Wildlife Fisheries, Robert J. Barham, John C. Ensminger, Mike Walsworth, Charlynn Cicero Leehy, Amey Crousillac, Rudy Niswanger, and Cassidy Riley.

INTRODUCTION

First and foremost, Monroe is a river town. The city's western border is the Ouachita River, the 25th-longest river in America, beginning in western Arkansas, in the heart of the Ouachita Mountain Range. The river that splits Monroe and West Monroe runs 605 miles on its course before an eventual rendezvous with the Gulf of Mexico.

When Spanish explorers arrived in the 16th century, they encountered the Ouachita people, a Native American tribe living in present-day Monroe. The name Ouachita finds it origins in the word "Washita," which translates to "good hunting grounds," a fitting name for the northeast corner of Sportsman's Paradise. Don Juan Filhiol, a Frenchman in the service of the king of Spain, established Fort Miro on the good hunting grounds in 1785.

A few decades later, after the Louisiana Purchase, when the region became part of the United States of America, a technological wonder arrived in Fort Miro. The modern marvel was a steamboat, named the *James Monroe* after America's fifth president and founding father. It was the first steam-powered paddle-wheeler, or "steamer" to reach the area.

The *James Monroe* was built on the East Coast, and, incredibly, the boat actually sank upon arrival in New Orleans and had to be raised to make its record-breaking journey north to Fort Miro. The effect was so transformative that, soon after, the developing community was renamed Monroe. It was a fitting tribute, as the steamboat era, which lasted almost 100 years, saw Monroe evolve into a bustling Southern town. Commerce, it seemed, literally flowed through the city, along the commercial highway of the Ouachita River.

Gilbert Brian "G.B." Cooley was deeply connected to Monroe and the river that runs through it. The waterway itself for two reasons: one, his brother L.V. Cooley was one of the country's last great riverboat captains, and two, Cooley loved spending time cruising the Ouachita on his yacht, the *Weto*.

Cooley's connection to the city goes back to 1894, when he opened a steam laundry in Monroe. He did quite well, and his success enabled him to turn his greatest efforts towards philanthropy. The G.B. Cooley Hospital opened in 1939 and continues to serve developmentally disabled individuals today. But Cooley's connection to Monroe goes even deeper than a love of the water and a community spirit.

Standing sentinel over the Ouachita River, on the southern side of the city's downtown, is one of the most unique homes in America, custom built for Cooley and his family. The Cooley House, as it became known, is a two-story concrete structure, one of the last original examples of Prairie School residential architecture in the South.

Joseph Biedenharn also had a historic home, which, much like Cooley's, still stands on the eastern banks of the Ouachita. Today, that grand Southern home is a museum that shares the grounds with two other museums: the Bible Museum, exhibiting the family's collection of religious relics, and a Coca-Cola museum, as it was the beverage Biedenharn famously helped introduce to the rest of the world when he developed a bottling technique that propelled mass distribution of the fizzy favorite. Each is a testament to the historical footprint left by the Biedenharn family, both in the city and beyond.

A pair of local aviation pioneers, Augustus James Selman and Claire Lee Chennault, served the United States, and Monroe has remembered two of its favorite sons accordingly. The city's first airport was called Selman Field in honor of the Navy pilot who died while on duty in 1921. Today near the site of that airport stands the Chennault Aviation and Military Museum, named for the World War II hero immortalized on film by John Wayne.

Monroe is a long way from the Big Easy and Louisiana's only professional sports teams: the New Orleans Saints and the New Orleans Pelicans. The northeast corner of "the boot" is also a long way from

Louisiana State University's famed Tiger Stadium in Baton Rouge, as well as the Pete Maravich Assembly Center, home court for the LSU basketball team, which Dick Vitale dubbed "the Deaf Dome."

But the region's legendary high school football programs, at Richwood High School, West Monroe High School, Ouachita Parish High School, and Neville School, just to name a few, and the universities strung along Interstate 20, Grambling State, Louisiana Tech, and, of course, the University of Louisiana at Monroe, have produced a long list of world champions and all-stars, a list to rival American cities of every size.

Bill Russell, one of the greatest players in National Basketball Association history, was born in Monroe in 1934. After high school, Russell went on to the University of San Francisco and led the team to consecutive NCAA titles. He joined the Boston Celtics in 1956 and, over the next 13 seasons, led the team to a record 11 NBA championships.

Professional football scouts jokingly refer to Monroe and West Monroe as the National Football League's farm team. Andrew Whitworth, Bradie James, Billy Joe Dupree, Bubby Brister, and Stan Humphries are just a few of the NFL aces who honed their gridiron skills on football fields just a stone's throw from the Ouachita River.

Baseball has been called the American pastime, and Monroe has given many baseball fans a reason to cheer from the bleachers around the diamond. Ralph "Road Runner" Garr, Chuck Finley, and Ben Sheets are all major parts of Monroe's sports history.

A few of the famous women to have left a lasting mark on our city include former Louisiana first lady Anna Gray Noe, pioneering businessperson Ruth Davis Cooley, and philanthropist and education advocate "Miss" Kitty DeGree. Included among these strong female community leaders is the incredibly inspiring yet ultimately tragic story of Rev. Lea Joyner, a Monroe minister who in the 1940s defied the odds and became one of the only female ministers to be officially ordained by the Methodist Church. The despair that gripped Monroe after the brutal murder of Reverend Joyner in 1985 is one of the sadder notes in the city's recent history.

The slain reverend is only one of the many who have helped continue a long history of faith and religion in Monroe. Dennis Swanberg is another notable member of local clergy. Swanberg launched a worldwide ministry from the First Baptist Church of West Monroe, located about four blocks from the river in downtown West Monroe.

Baptism is an important part of the Christian faith, and Phil Robertson, the patriarch on the television show *Duck Dynasty*, has baptized dozens of people in the muddy waters of the Ouachita.

The days when Monroe and northeast Louisiana depended on the river for commerce are long gone, as public roads, particularly the interstate highway system, ended that era. The Ouachita River is still an important, albeit smaller, part of local commerce. Monroe traffic near the river routinely pauses when the city's bridges are opened to allow tugboats and barges to pass through the Twin Cities.

Agriculture is still a major economic driver for the region, as cotton, soybean, rice, grain, and cattle farms abound in northeast Louisiana.

As important as the waterways and the fertile fields in and around Monroe are to the local economy, so, too, are the skies over northeastern Louisiana. In 1909, while still a young man, Collete Woolman traveled to Paris to attend the world's very first aviation airshow. The seeds for a grand idea were planted on that trip. Woolman went on to help develop the world's first commercial crop-dusting service, and expanded that business in June 1929 when a small airplane lifted off from Dallas and flew to Monroe carrying five passengers. It was the first flight of Delta Airlines. Today, the airline started in Monroe operates 5,000 flights daily, with service on six continents, and employs over 80,000 worldwide.

CenturyLink, the third-largest telecommunications business in America, started and is still headquartered right here in Monroe, and, believe it or not, the origins of this technology titan are rooted in romance. When he was only eight years old, Clarke M. Williams started delivering handwritten bills on his bicycle for the rural telephone company his parents ran from their northeast Louisiana home. When young Clarke later married, his parents gifted him and his new bride with the telephone company. The rest is Monroe history.

Some members of the Monroe business community are connected to history in truly amazing ways.

Sol Rosenberg survived no less than four Nazi labor camps and the famous Warsaw Ghetto Uprising in World War II. He came to America and embraced his new home, building Sol's Pipe & Steel into a thriving Monroe business, which was one of the very first to bring desperately needed supplies to New York City after the terrorist attacks of September 11, 2001, and to New Orleans following Hurricane Katrina.

The bright lights and stages of Broadway and the belching smokestacks of the massive West Monroe paper mill are worlds apart, yet these two places are intricately connected. Luther "L." Slade Brown was president of the company that built the West Monroe paper mill and was also a Broadway producer, part of the team that delighted audiences with hit shows like *All American*, *A Joyful Noise*, and the Tony Award–winning smash *Bye Bye Birdie*.

William Congreve, a 15th-century playwright, once said, "Music has charms to soothe a savage breast." The musical history of Monroe is a tapestry of talents that includes bluesman Pee Wee Whitaker, jazz drummer Hamid Drake, rocker Kevin Griffin of Better than Ezra, and composer Frank Ticheli, who has conducted orchestras all over the globe. Equally impressive are the actors of stage and screen who claim roots in the Twin Cities, including indie movie queen Parker Posey, who hails from Monroe.

No profile of Louisiana people would be complete without a chapter on the Bayou State's notorious political scene, and in the following pages, we take a look at the good, the bad, and the ugly of Louisiana politics as it relates to Monroe and northeast Louisiana. Like any other city, Monroe has had its share of questionable characters; Huey P. Newton, the founder of the Black Panthers and a convicted killer, is only one of ours.

Monroe has come a long way from the days of the original Native American inhabitants, the Ouachita tribe, who first settled the good hunting grounds near the river named after them. Those long-ago people, as well as founding father Don Juan Filhiol, would no doubt marvel at the modern city on the river we see today, but one thing remains, and it is one thing Filhiol and the Ouachita people would recognize instantly. In addition to good hunting grounds, the word Washita was also a Native American expression used to describe the river, loosely translated to "sparkling silver water."

These are the stories of the legends of Monroe, a sparkling Louisiana city on the banks of the Ouachita River.

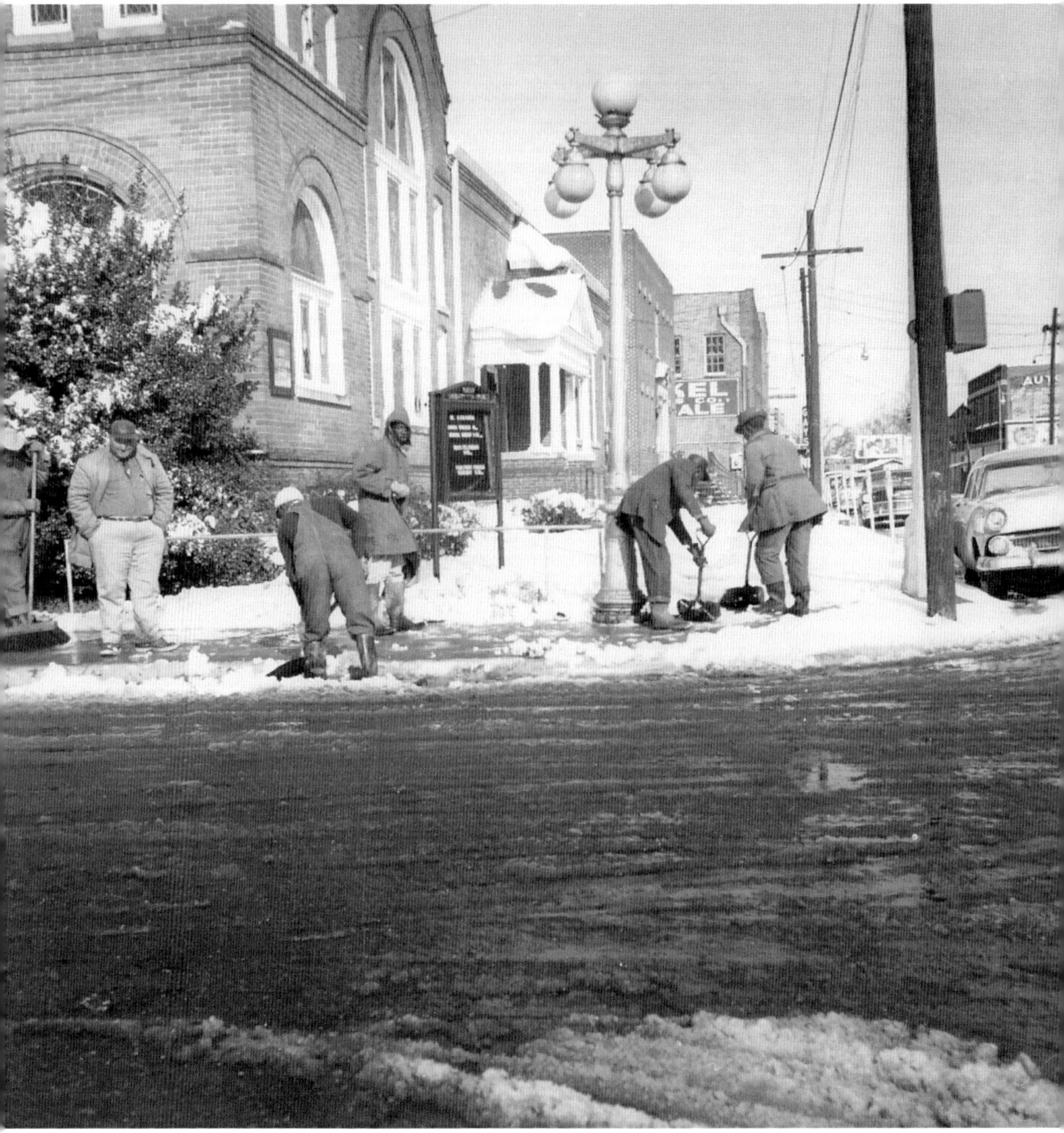

Community Teamwork

Monroe residents shovel a rare snow accumulation in front of St. Matthews Cathedral, downtown, around 1940. (Courtesy of Louise Khoury and the family of Mary Savana.)

CHAPTER ONE

Business Leaders and Innovators

Monroe and its smaller cousin, West Monroe, are located at the center of northeast Louisiana.

Divided by the Ouachita River, the "Twin Cities," as the neighboring municipalities are collectively known, are the birthplace to some notable titans of modern American industry, including one of the largest airlines in the world and a top-three telecommunications company.

The family that first bottled Coca-Cola, the most popular soft drink on the planet, hails from Monroe, as does one of the biggest clans in reality television history.

Also found here is the inspiring story of a Holocaust survivor who built one of Monroe's most successful businesses, a company that stepped up when America desperately needed construction supplies in the terrible aftermaths of the September 11, 2001, terrorist attacks and Hurricane Katrina.

There is also the story of a pioneering businesswoman who started her professional career as a secretary right after World War II, went on to become a teacher, and later started her own successful business before becoming the first female mayoral candidate in the city's history.

Another local legend was a political wunderkind whose too-brief career burnt out like a comet, a teenage political activist who grew up to become a talk radio host and political consultant, wielding a powerful influence that could be felt from Baton Rouge to the halls of Washington, DC, before dying tragically at a young age.

There are also giants of local media in this collection of influential northeast Louisiana citizens, including a newspaper editor born into the publishing business, a radio dynamo who holds the collective attention of the people via a group of powerhouse radio stations, and a 1960s civil rights activist who went on to become a minister, influential newspaper owner, educator, and community advocate.

The legends profiled here, some from days long gone and others who continue to make local history, are the business leaders and innovators of Monroe.

Collett Everman "C.E." Woolman

The son of a physics professor, aviation pioneer and Monroe legend Collett Everman "C.E." Woolman made his mark on the world first as general manager and vice president of Huff Daland Dusters. In 1925, Dusters was the world's largest private aircraft fleet, and the beginnings of what would eventually become Delta Airlines.

In 1909, a 20-year-old Woolman fell in love with airplanes when he attended the world's first aviation meet, held in Paris. Years later, he graduated college with a degree in agricultural engineering. Combining his love of aviation and agriculture, Woolman, himself an aviator by this time, helped lead a team of pilots, engineers, and entomologists to develop the modern-day crop-duster, a plane that eradicates crop-threatening bugs quickly by spraying, or "dusting," fields with powder insecticides, an innovation that revolutionized modern agriculture.

Woolman came to northeast Louisiana to fight insects, specifically the boll weevil, a pesky critter vilified to this day for threatening the local cotton industry. Huff Daland Airplanes Inc. was successful, but crews could only work during growing season, so Woolman expanded the business into Mexico and Peru, where warmer weather meant crops needed insect protection year-round.

In Peru, Huff Daland Dusters began taking on passengers, but, after a South American revolution threatened the fledgling business, Woolman returned to northeast Louisiana and, along with a group of Monroe businessmen, formed Delta Air Service.

On June 17, 1929, a five-passenger plane lifted off from Dallas and made stops in Shreveport and then at Selman Field in Monroe, where the new airline service was headquartered, before ending the 427-mile journey in Jackson, Mississippi. Delta Airlines was born.

Woolman was not just a brilliant engineer and businessman, he was also much beloved by his employees. On the company's 25th birthday, they presented him with a brand new Cadillac, a car he kept until his death in 1966.

After his passing, a group from Delta Airlines restored an original 1925 Huff Daland crop duster and presented it to the Smithsonian Institution as a tribute and memorial to the beloved Woolman.

Designed and built by Delta employees, the plane greets visitors and employees today at the entrance of the company's Technical Operations Center in Atlanta. (Photograph by Griffin Scott.)

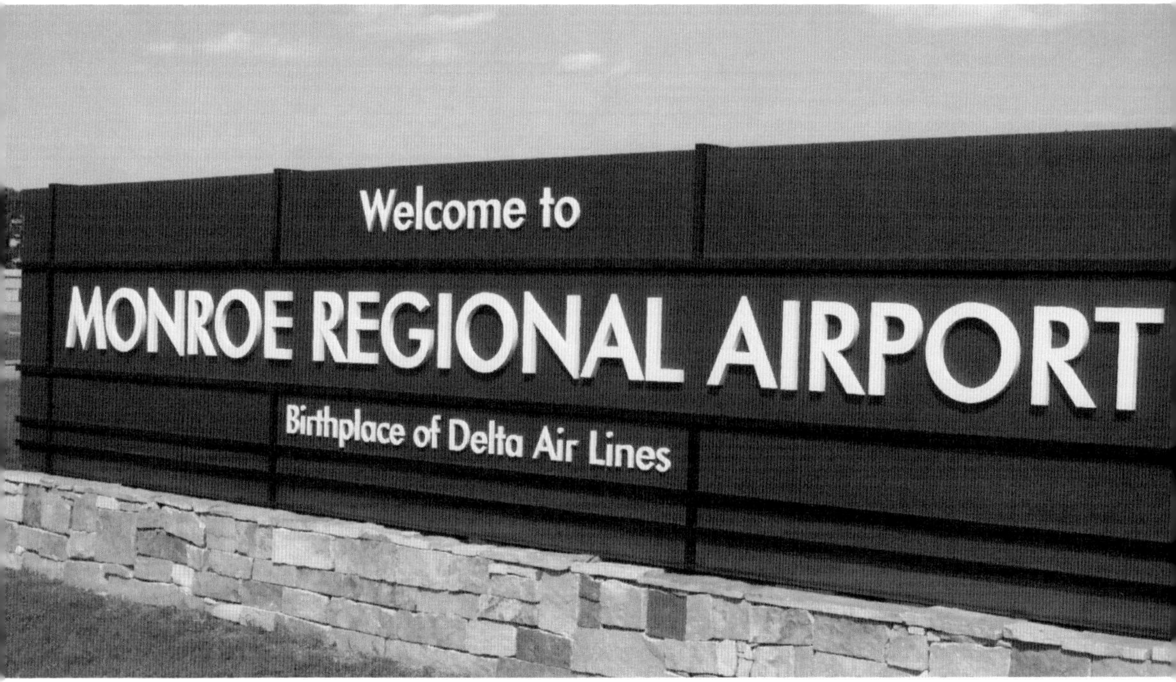

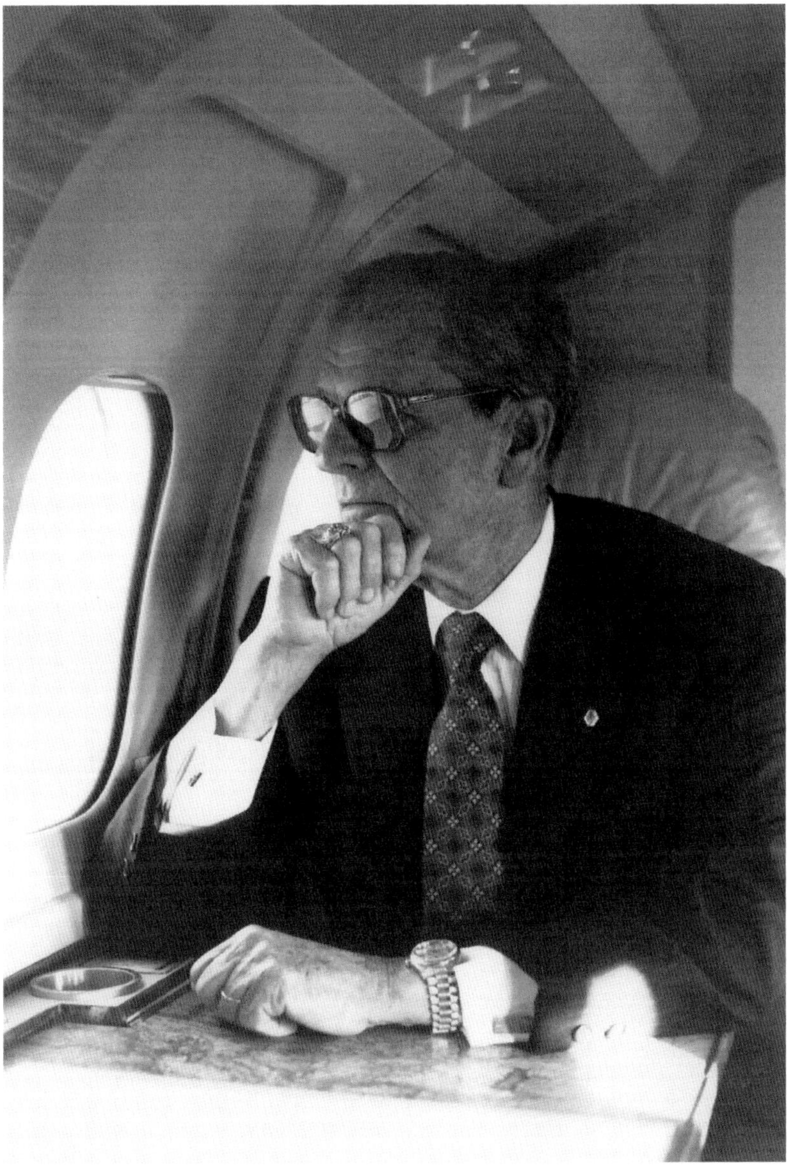

Clarke M. Williams

The origins of CenturyLink, the third-largest telecommunications company in America, can be traced back to 1930. That year, a young couple with three small children purchased the Oak Ridge Telephone Company, a small outfit with less than 100 subscribers. William Clarke Williams and his wife, Marie, set up a switchboard in the parlor of their home.

Their son Clarke McRae Williams started out in the family business at the age of eight, delivering handwritten bills on his bicycle. When he returned from service in World War II and married, William and Marie gave the Oak Ridge Telephone Company to the young couple.

Under the leadership of Williams, the small organization grew through strategic acquisitions. By 1968, the company had 10,000 customers. Just 10 years later, its shares were listed on the New York Stock Exchange. Today, that tiny rural telephone company is called CenturyLink, an industry leader and one of the largest telecommunications companies in the world. (Courtesy of CenturyLink.)

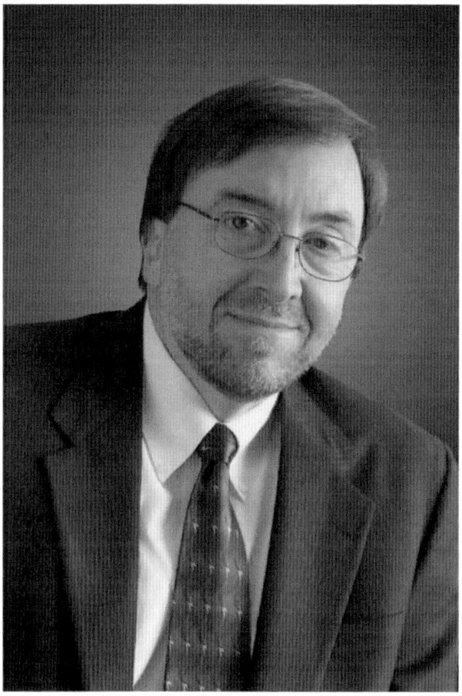

Glen Post

When northeast Louisiana native and Louisiana Tech University graduate Glen Post began his career at Century Telephone Enterprises in 1976, the rural local exchange carrier operated in nine states. Post's dedication, hard work, and keen business sense eventually led to his promotion to CEO in 1992. At that time, the company's annual revenues were $360 million.

Since that time, Post has directed all of the company's acquisitions and divestitures, leading the transformation of Century Telephone Enterprises into CenturyLink, the third-largest telecommunications company in the United States, with 2013 annual revenues of $18 billion.

The business is now global in scope, and is Louisiana's only home-based Fortune 500 company. Post recently signed a contract to keep CenturyLink headquartered in Monroe through 2022, continuing his commitment to the people of northeast Louisiana. (Left, photograph by Brad Arender, Arender Studio + Gallery, courtesy of CenturyLink; below, photograph by Griffin Scott.)

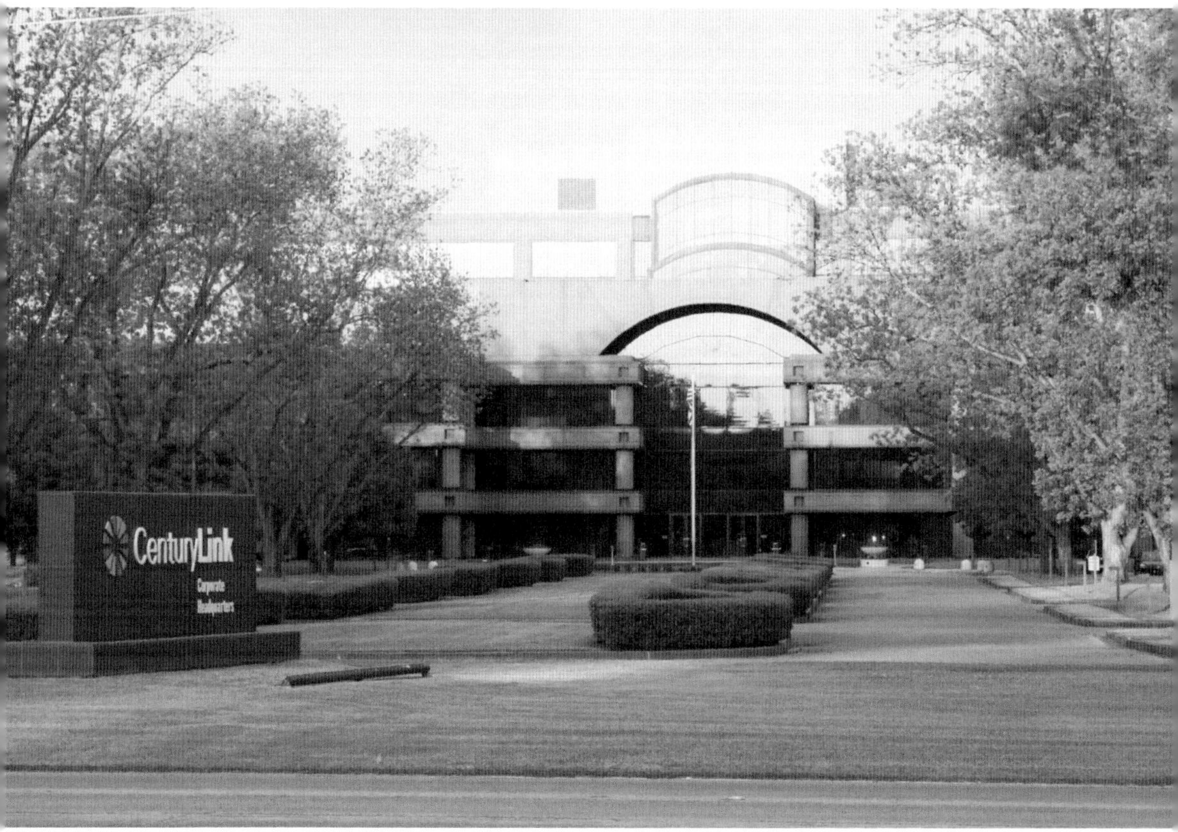

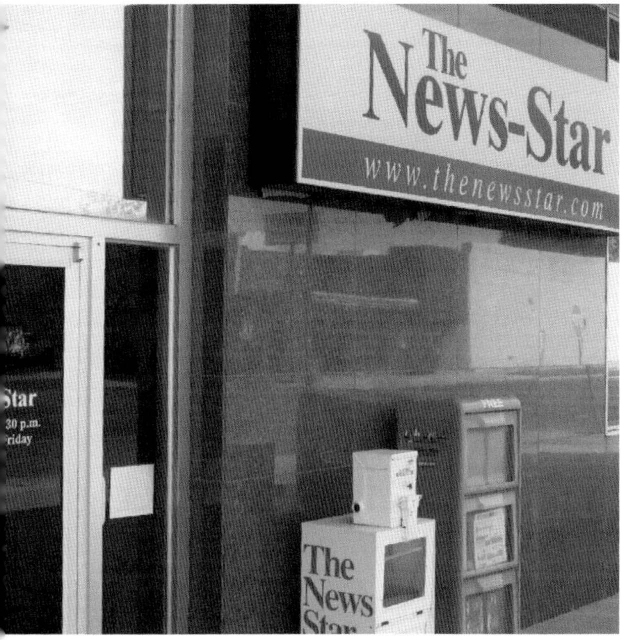

Edmund Graves Brown

Despite being born and raised in the Big Easy and beginning his newspaper career at the *New Orleans Times-Picayune*, Edmund Graves Brown Jr. left an indelible print on northeast Louisiana.

After serving in World War II, where he saw action at the Battle of the Bulge, a young Brown returned home to attend Tulane University. In 1952, he joined the *Monroe News-Star-World* (now the *News-Star*), a daily newspaper owned by his family, and remained there until his retirement in 1977.

After leaving the newspaper business, Brown remained active in the Monroe community, serving on various civic boards and community organizations until his death in 2008 at the age of 87. (Photograph by Griffin Scott.)

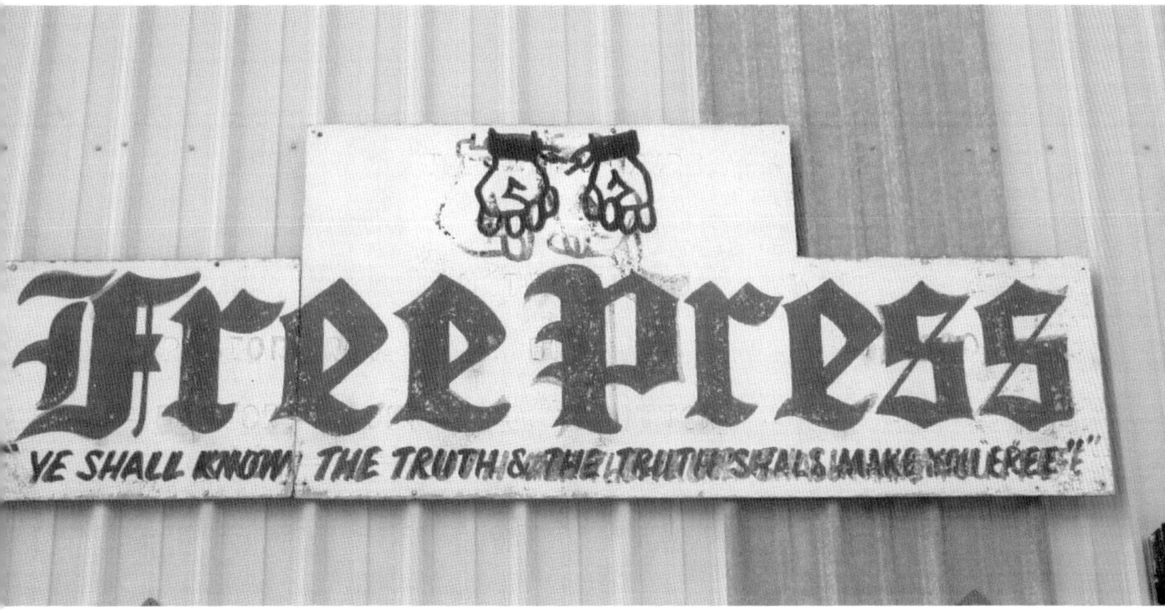

Roosevelt Wright Jr.

In 1969, Roosevelt Wright Jr., a 20-year-old civil rights activist, launched a journalism career by publishing *Rapping Black*, a one-sheet newsletter distributed in Monroe's African American communities detailing reports of discrimination experienced in retail outlets and covering local civil rights movement news.

Today, the *Monroe Free Press*, a weekly newspaper run by Wright and his family, is one of America's very few remaining family-owned newspapers.

In addition to a long career as a journalist, publisher, and activist, Wright is also a reverend, leading the New Tabernacle Baptist Church in Monroe, and serves as executive director at Excellence Academy, a junior high charter school launched in 2013. (Photograph by Griffin Scott.)

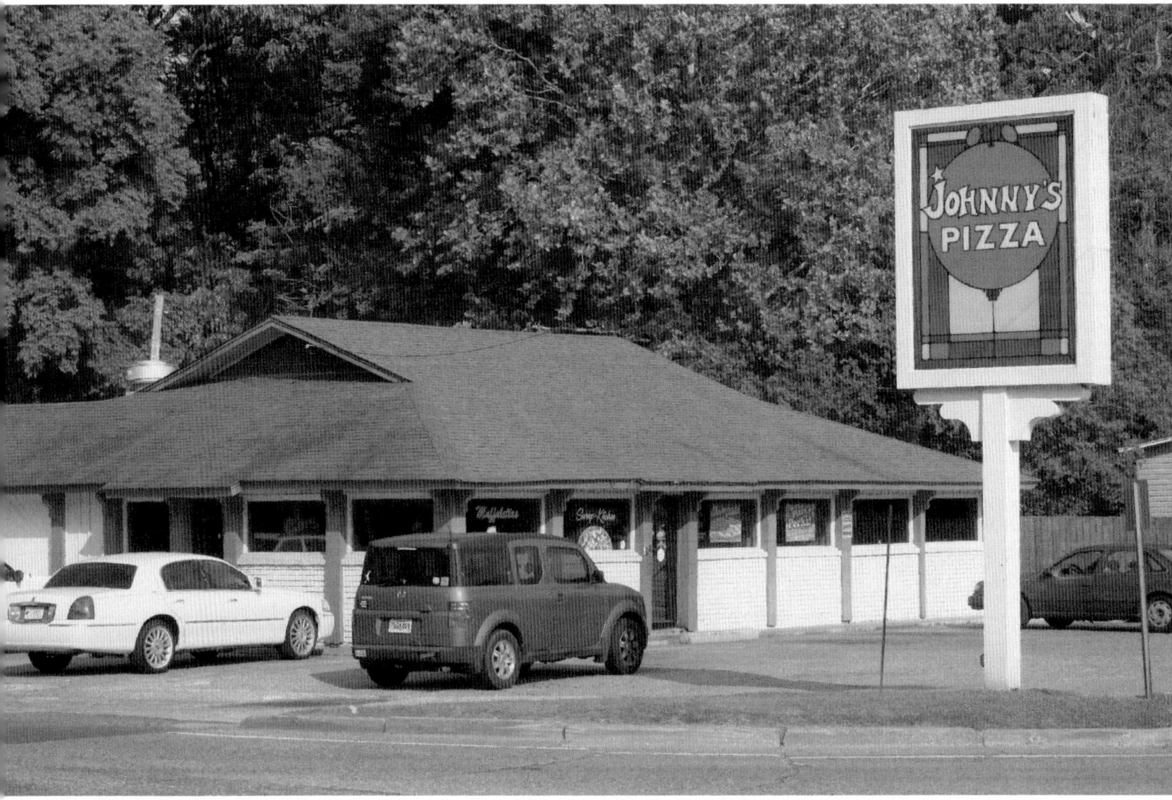

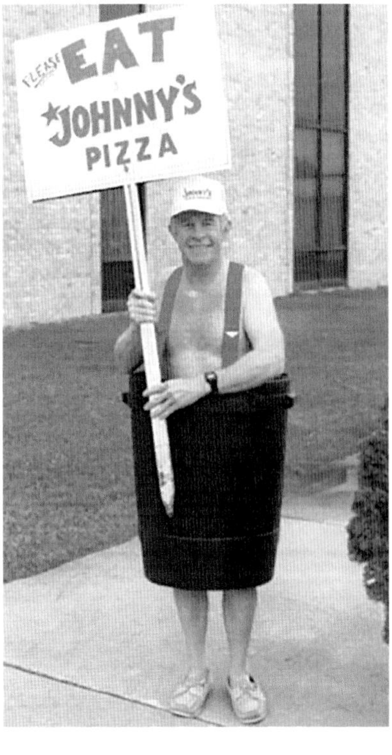

Johnny Huntsman

It was 1967 when Johnny Huntsman noticed a small building for rent and was compelled to stop and investigate. After opening the first location of Johnny's Pizza House, dubbed "the only link in the world's smallest pizza chain," Huntsman's pizzas were so loved by the locals that word soon spread, and the small pizza joint on DeSiard Street eventually grew into what is now an impressive regional chain of over 40 restaurants across Louisiana and Texas.

Huntsman is also active in the community via multiple area civic organizations and has an endowed scholarship at the University of Louisiana at Monroe. (Above, photograph by Griffin Scott; right, courtesy of Johnny's Pizza House.)

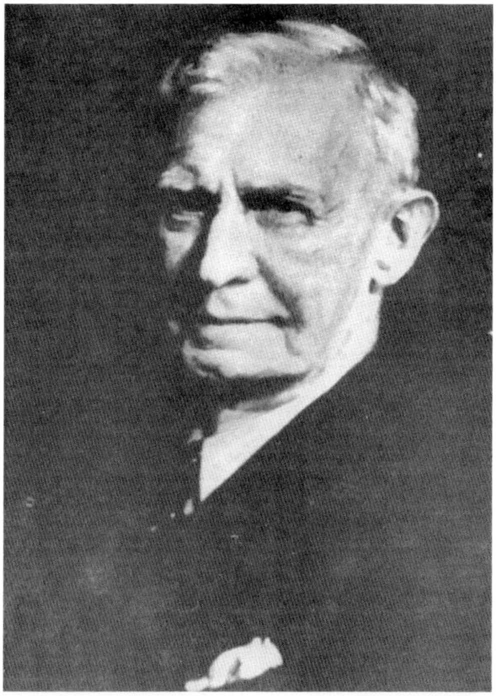

Joseph Biedenharn

Of all of Monroe's favorite sons, none have had quite the effect on the world at large as Joseph Augustus Biedenharn, the first person to bottle Coca-Cola, the most popular soft drink in the world.

Decades after his death in 1952 at the age of 85, the Biedenharn legacy is still strong, with three museums standing as testament to the family's endless contributions to both the community and the world. The Coca-Cola Museum, the Beidenharn Museum & Botanical Gardens, and the Biedenharn Bible Museum are all located adjacent to each other on the original Biedenharn family estate. (Left, courtesy of the Biedenharn Museum & Gardens; below, photograph by Griffin Scott.)

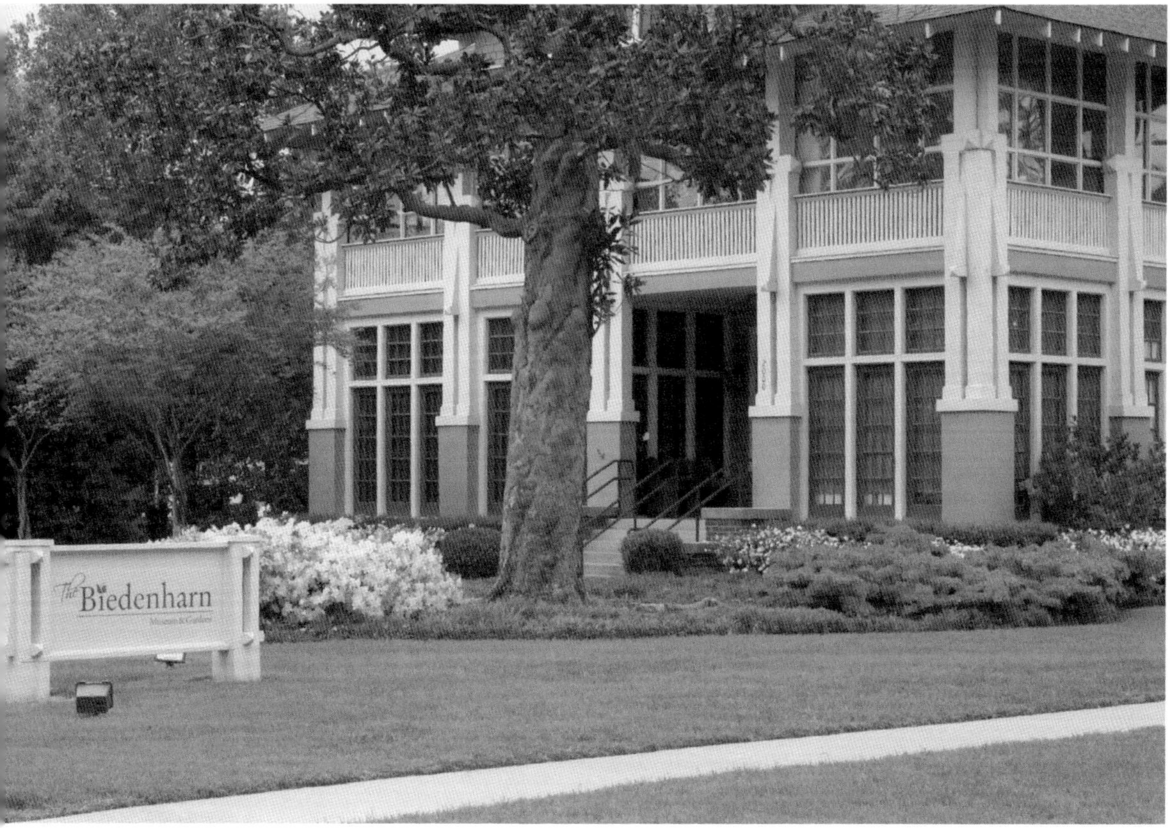

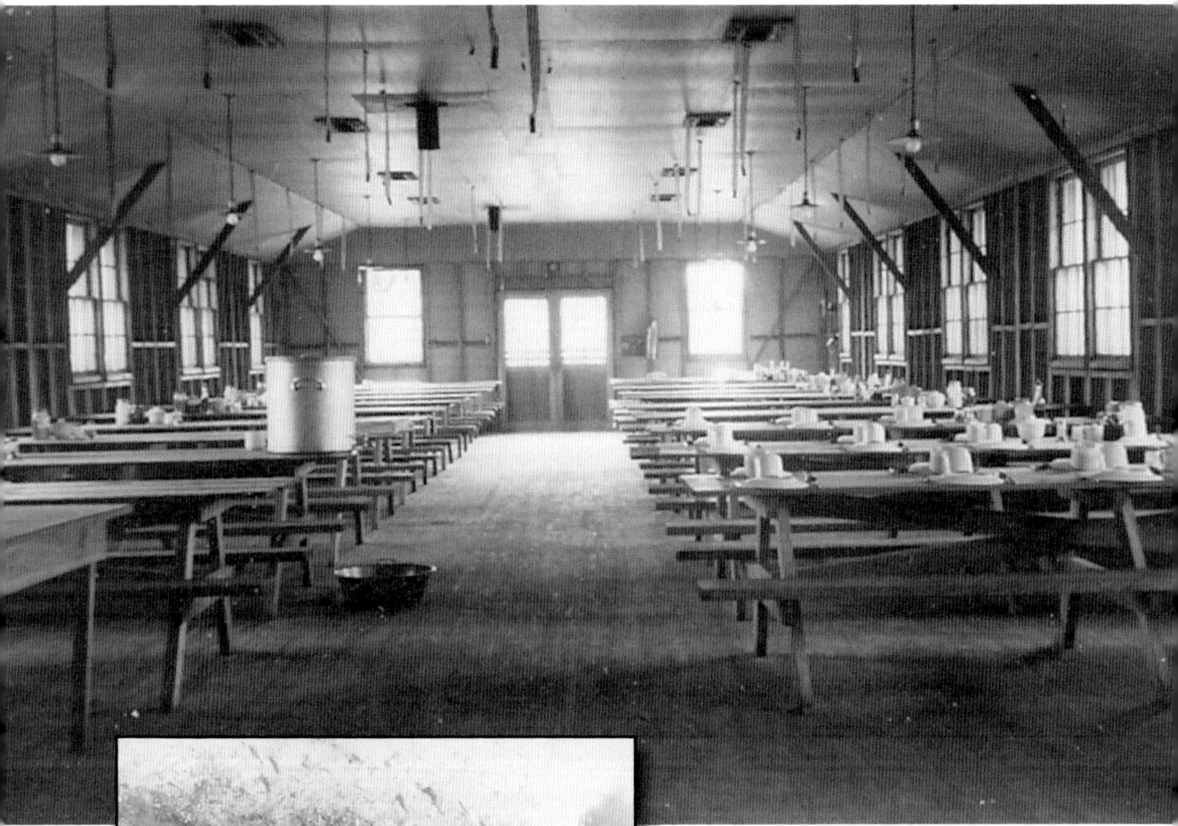

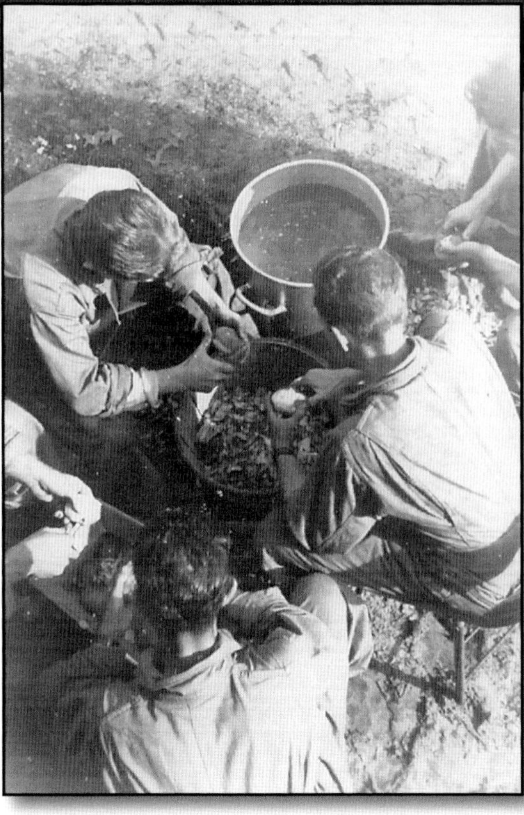

Augustus James Selman

Lt. Augustus James Selman joined the Navy in 1912 and earned his wings, becoming a Navy pilot when the country's air defense was in its infancy. Selman served as one of America's first naval aviators, dying nine years into his service on November 28, 1921, from injuries sustained in an airplane crash. Selman Field, Monroe's first airport, was named in his honor. Pictured above ia a mess hall at Selman Field; at left, soldiers prepare a meal at Selman Field during World War II. (Both, courtesy of Louise Khoury and the family of Mary Savana.)

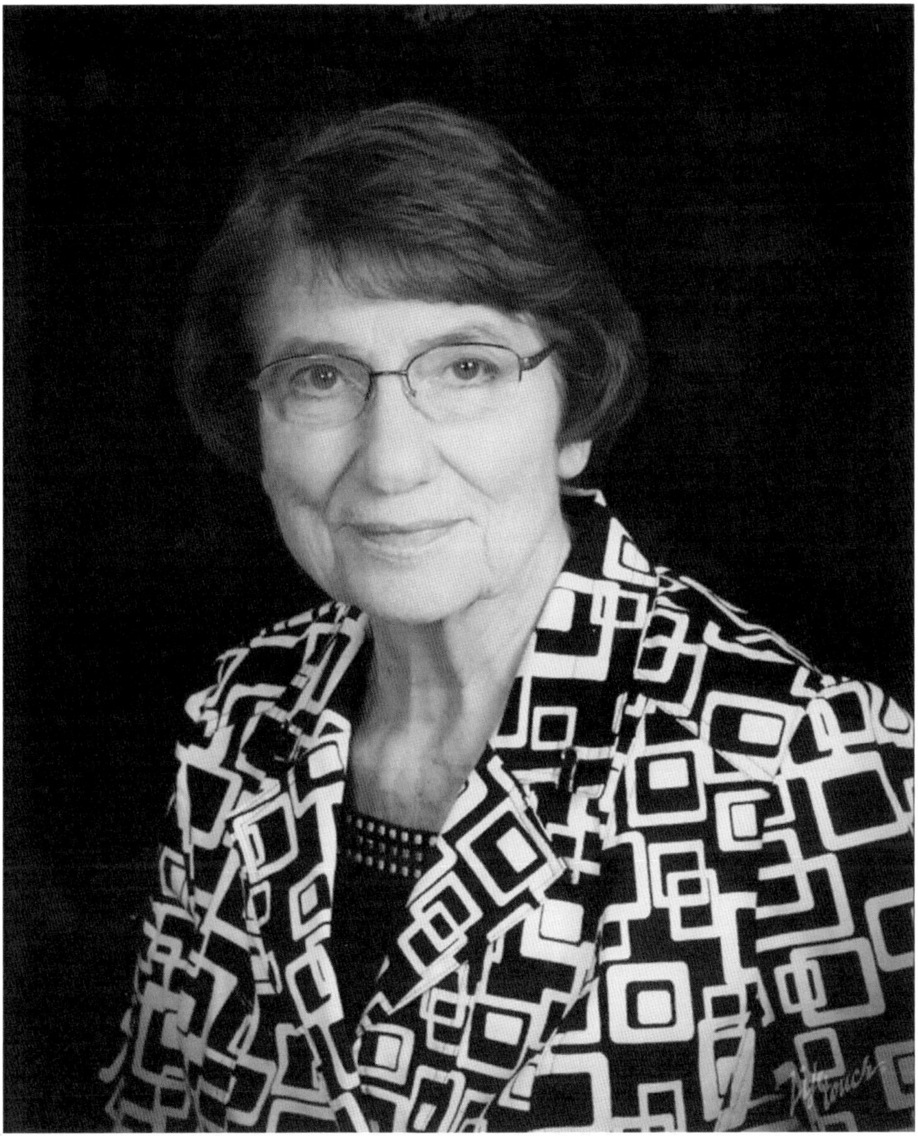

Ruth Davis Cooley
A pioneering businessperson and community leader, Ruth Cooley was one of Monroe's first female business owners, as well as the first serious female candidate in city history to run for mayor.

After marrying her high school sweetheart, Malcolm "Mal" Cooley, the former Ruth Davis and her husband moved to Monroe in 1946, where she worked as a secretary and also taught accounting at the local college. Cooley eventually branched out on her own, starting the Monroe Letter Shop in 1948, a typing and mimeographing service for business clients, attorneys, and churches. Today, Cooley Printers is still flourishing as a family-owned-and-operated business in Monroe.

Cooley died in March 2014. Along with her late husband, Mal, her life and legacy in the business community are honored through the Mal and Ruth Cooley Scholarship, awarded annually to exceptional advertising and marketing students through the Advertising Club of Northeast Louisiana, a trade organization that Cooley herself helped form and was a lifelong member of. (Courtesy of Rhonda Counselman and the family of Ruth Davis Cooley.)

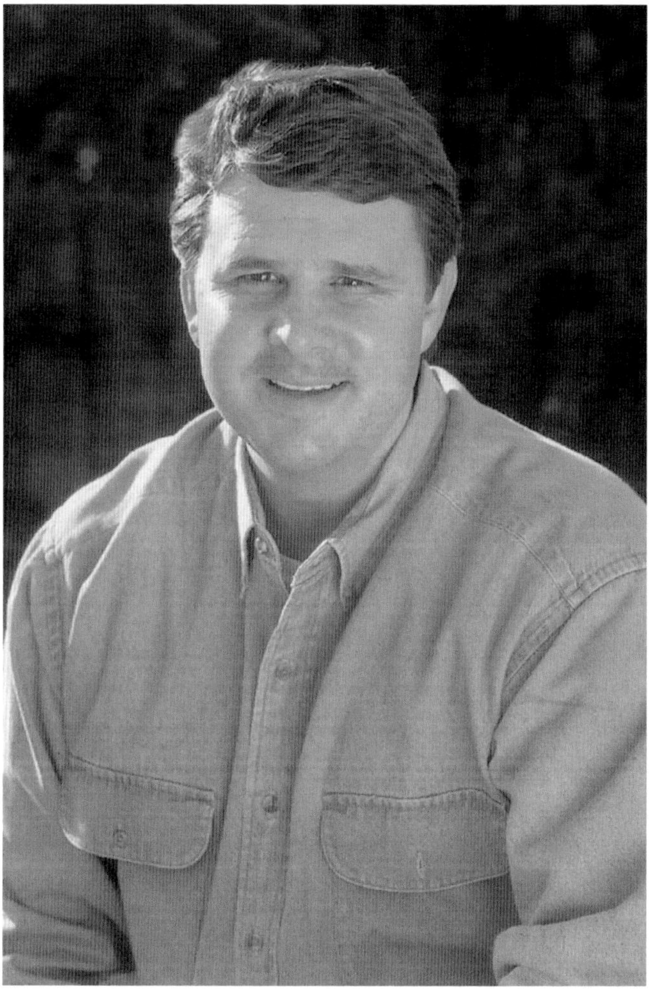

Lee Fletcher

Looking back on Lee Fletcher's brief yet impressive resume, it is clear why many felt this son of a West Carroll Parish farmer was destined for bigger things before tragically dying in his early 40s.

The conservative Republican was passionate about politics from a young age. He campaigned for Pres. Ronald Reagan as a teenager, and after graduating from Louisiana Tech University in 1988, went to work for Pres. George H.W. Bush.

Progressing quickly through the Washington, DC, ranks, Fletcher worked first for the Office of Presidential Personnel at the White House, and later as deputy white house liaison for two successive secretaries of agriculture.

After serving as district manager for one Louisiana congressman, and later as chief of staff for another, Fletcher came home to northeast Louisiana, and from Monroe started the Fletcher Group, a full-service advertising firm.

Following a stint substitute-hosting on a local political talk show, Fletcher launched his own radio station and began broadcasting his own daily talk show.

Although an avowed Republican, Fletcher worked for Democrats as well, and was considered to be one of Louisiana's top political consultants.

Sadly, this political comet burned out quickly. Fletcher was diagnosed with cancer in February 2009 and died in Monroe a few months later, at the age of 43. (Courtesy of Amanda McMullen.)

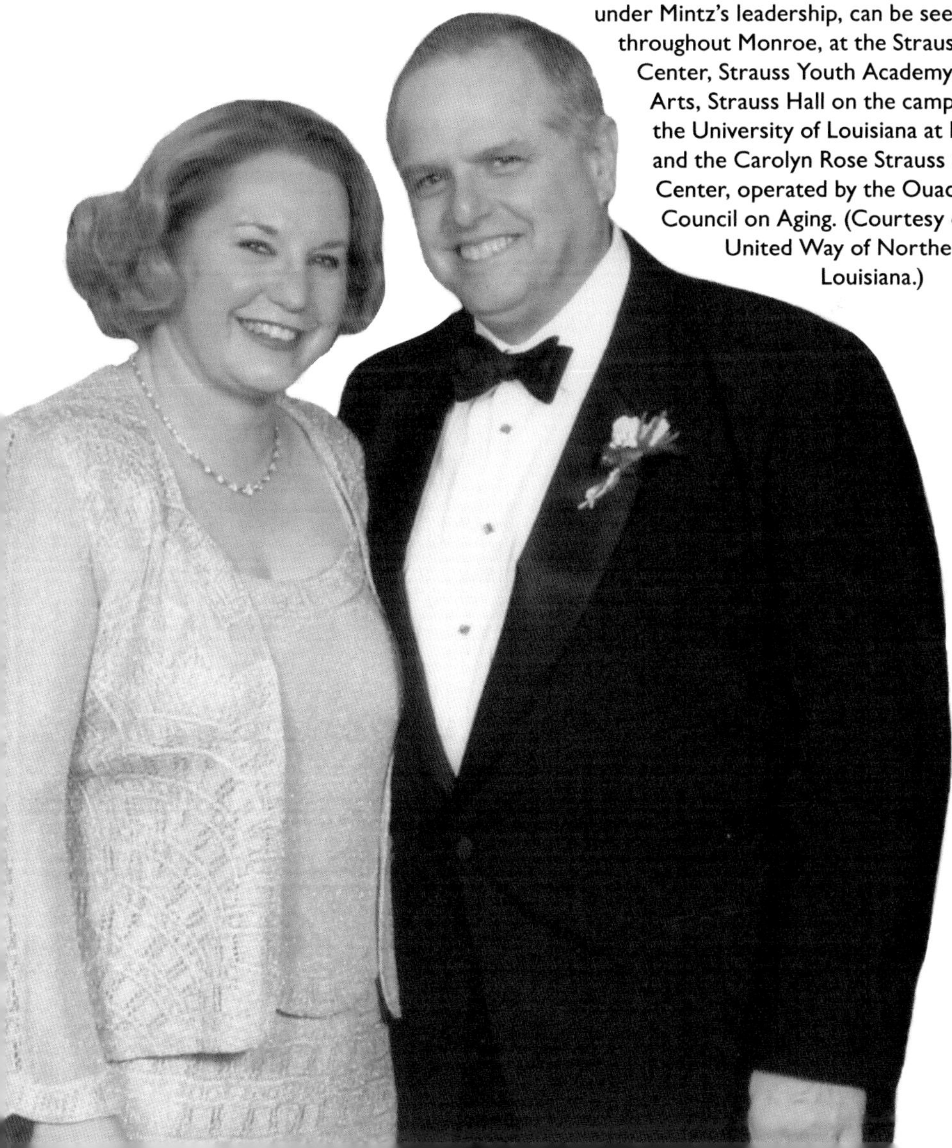

Morris F. Mintz
As principal owner and managing director of Strauss Interests LLC, a company with holdings in commercial real estate, investments, manufacturing, and banking, as well as a host of other interests, Morris F. Mintz became a successful businessman. Highly regarded in business circles, Mintz is also known for his volunteerism and community spirit, serving as past board chair of both the United Way of Northeast Louisiana and the City of Monroe Air Industrial Park Advisory Board, among others. The influence of Strauss Interests, under Mintz's leadership, can be seen throughout Monroe, at the Strauss Theatre Center, Strauss Youth Academy for the Arts, Strauss Hall on the campus of the University of Louisiana at Monroe, and the Carolyn Rose Strauss Senior Center, operated by the Ouachita Council on Aging. (Courtesy of the United Way of Northeast Louisiana.)

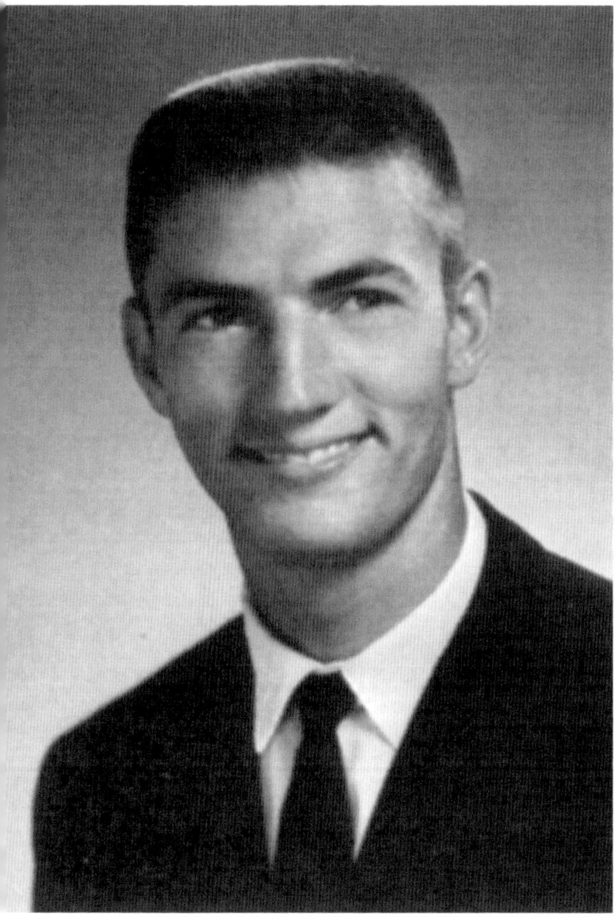

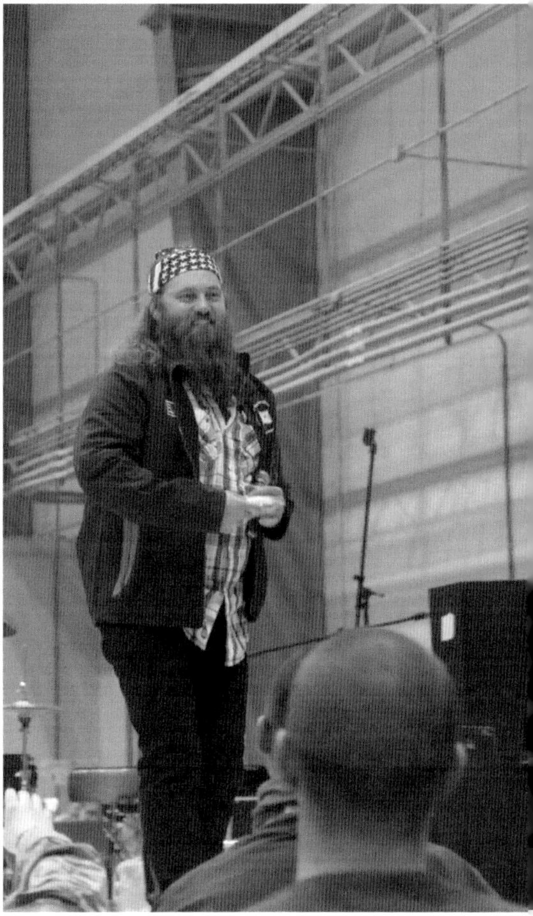

The Robertsons of A&E's *Duck Dynasty* and Duck Commander
Phil, Willie, Si, and Jase Robertson and family shot to international fame as the stars of A&E's wildly successful reality television series *Duck Dynasty*, a program that follows the close-knit rural family, documenting their adventures in northeast Louisiana. In hunting circles, however, Robertson and his motley crew of lovable, bearded family members were already long considered rock stars due to the popularity of their industry-leading Duck Commander duck calls.

In March 2012, *Duck Dynasty* premiered on A&E and immediately became a smash hit, eventually becoming one of the most watched television programs in cable television history. (Left, photograph by Edward Vantine Studios Inc.; right, photograph by S.Sgt. Rachel Copeland.)

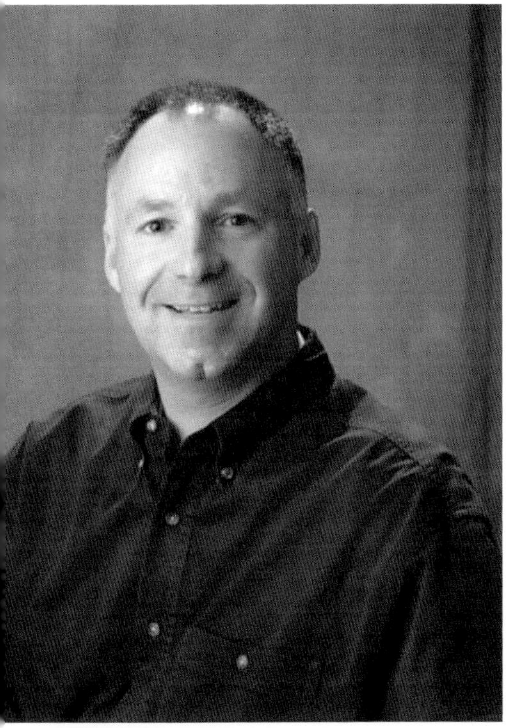

Bob Holladay
Long before Facebook and YouTube, even before Google and Amazon, Bob Holladay saw the future of digital media on the horizon.

A graduate of the University of Alabama and the Wharton School of Business, Holladay is a successful radio broadcaster with stations in Florida, Texas, Alabama, and Louisiana. He also founded Bayou Internet, one of the very first internet service providers in northeast Louisiana. Pictured below is one of Holladay's stations, KMLB, the oldest radio station in northeast Louisiana. (Both courtesy of the Radio People.)

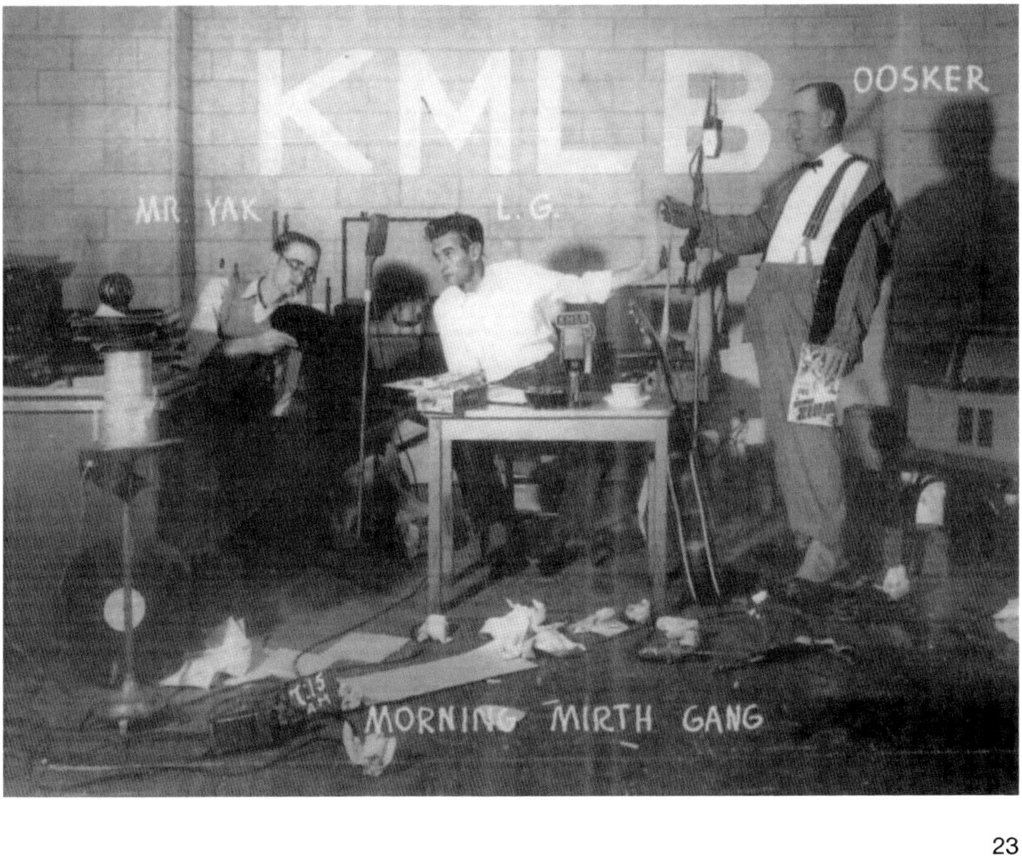

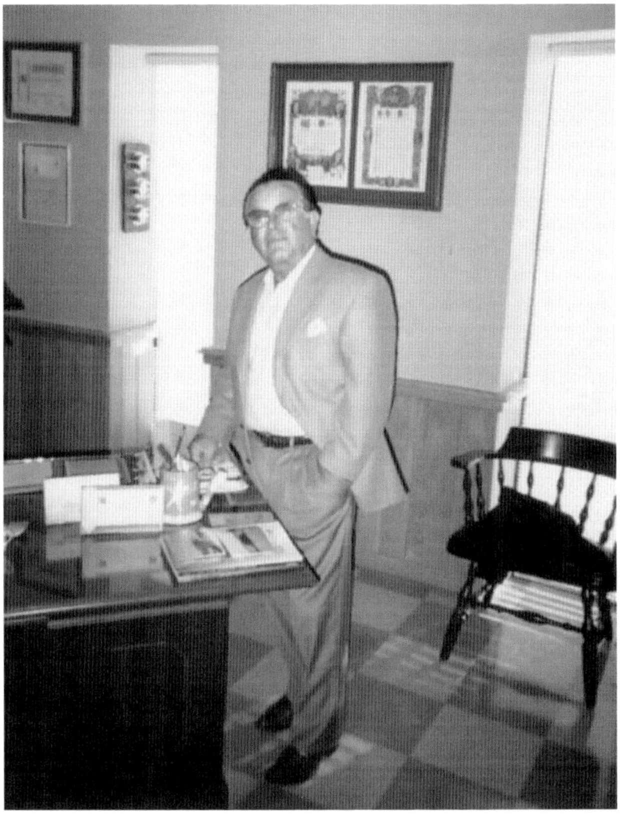

Sol Rosenberg

In 1926, Sol Rosenberg was born a world away from Louisiana, in pre–World War II Warsaw, Poland, but he passed away in Monroe in 2009, a city he fell in love with after settling here in 1949.

As a young man, Rosenberg saw the horrors of war firsthand, losing both parents, two sisters, and more than 50 aunts, uncles, cousins, and extended family members to the Holocaust.

According to his official biography, *Sol's Story: A Triumph of the Human Spirit*, by Richard Chardkoff, Rosenberg survived four labor camps before escaping the notorious concentration camp Treblinka, making his way home and taking part in the Warsaw Ghetto Uprising before falling into Nazi hands again.

Young Sol then survived the infamous Dachau Death March to the concentration camp of the same name, where he managed to survive until Allied forces liberated the camp following the death of Hitler and the fall of the Third Reich.

After the war, Sol met his wife, Tola. In 1949 they came to Monroe, where they raised five children. In 1952, they started a scrap iron and used pipe business. Sol's Pipe & Steel grew quickly, and is one of Monroe's top employers today, supplying local, national, and international companies with pipes of every size and description, including the huge pipes used in bridge pilings and offshore platforms.

On September 11, 2001, the terrorist attacks on New York City's World Trade Center left an immense amount of debris that proved too much for dump trucks, so a barge terminal had to be built near the site. Sol's Pipe & Steel supplied the massive pipes required to build pilings on the East River.

Four years later, in the wake of Hurricane Katrina, New Orleans was underwater and the Army Corps of Engineers needed drainage pipes, fast. Trucks with the Sol's Pipe & Steel logo were among the first to ride into the Big Easy, bringing with them desperately needed 50-foot sections of 42-inch pipe to drain the flooded city.

Following his death in 2009, the US Congress recognized Rosenberg as a "local titan in industry, philanthropy and civic affairs." (Courtesy of the family of Sol Rosenberg.)

CHAPTER TWO

Community and Spiritual Leaders

The area's abundance of congregations, representing seemingly every faith, are a standing testament to the spiritual roots of the region. Religion plays such an important role in the culture and lifestyle of northeast Louisiana that, for many, spirituality combined with a community spirit is just a natural-born way of life.

The legends profiled in this chapter are quite different from one another, although they are connected through their faith in a higher power.

This chapter takes a look at the life, and tragic death, of a revolutionary female reverend, as well as a Christian comedian who uses the power of humor to profess and share his faith with devoted followers around the globe.

Rev. Lea Joyner was an inspirational figure, overcoming incredible odds from very humble beginnings to lead what was, at the time of her tragic death, one of Monroe's largest churches.

Christian comedian and "Minister of Encouragement" Dennis Swanberg grew up enjoying classic 1960s television programming like the *Andy Griffith Show*, *Green Acres*, and *Hee-Haw*. He learned to imitate the characters from those shows, along with a host of other iconic figures, including Howard Cosell, Muhammad Ali, Ronald Reagan, and dozens of real and fictional characters, incorporating them into a performance that is part sermon, part standup comedy. The preacher and humorist, affectionately known by fans as the "Swan," has also authored several books and makes hundreds of appearances spreading the word of God to audiences worldwide, using his unique blend of positivity combined with an upbeat sense of humor.

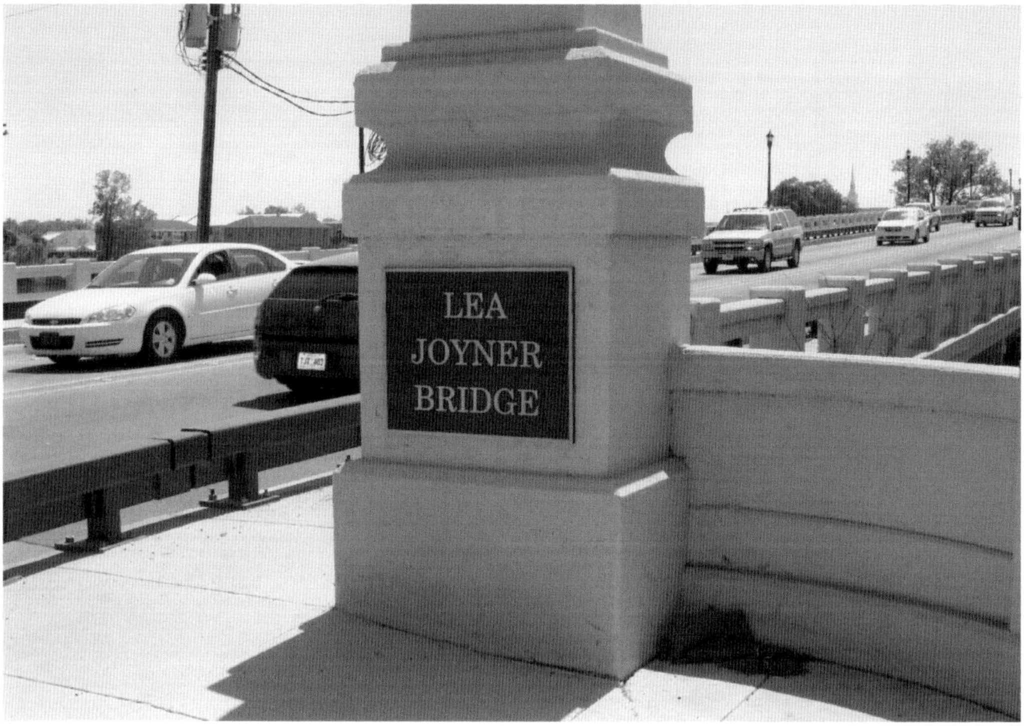

Rev. Lea Joyner (ABOVE AND OPPOSITE PAGE)
Although she was born in Franklin parish, Rev. Lea Joyner was deeply connected to Monroe, perhaps even more so after her tragic death.

After attending Westminster College in Texas, Joyner graduated from High Point College in North Carolina and then returned home to northeast Louisiana. Dreaming of becoming a minister since childhood, Joyner was one of only five women ordained by the Methodist Church in 1939, the year she was officially anointed.

Led by Joyner, Southside United Methodist Church was founded as a last resort. In 1952, after serving eight years as an associate pastor at a Monroe congregation, Joyner lost her job when a replacement senior preacher refused to work with a woman. The Methodist ministry could not fire her, so they devised a plan to give her a $5,000 nest egg and three vacant lots of land owned by the church on the city's south side. From those humble beginnings, Southside United Methodist, at one time the largest Methodist congregation helmed by a woman in the United States, was formed. At the time of the reverend's death, the church had over 2,200 members.

Joyner is remembered as a tireless pastor who attended to her flock as well as to the poor residents of the surrounding community. A relentless worker, Joyner kept long hours and was known for her acts of kindness toward the troubled souls of Monroe. Her seemingly unyielding compassion sadly led to her shocking death. It was late at night on Tuesday, March 12, 1985, when Joyner was brutally killed as she was leaving the church that now bears her name. Her murderer was a young neighborhood man and petty criminal she had attempted to mentor.

In spite of its senseless, heartbreaking end, this pioneering Monroe minister's life remains an inspiration. Her incredible story is detailed in the book *Standing in the Gap: The Life and Ministry of the Reverend Lea Joyner*, by Dr. Harry Hale.

Today, her name is memorialized across Monroe, as a major thoroughfare, a bridge crossing the Ouachita River, and the church she founded in 1952 (now the Lea Joyner United Methodist Church) are named in honor of the late, beloved reverend. (Above, photograph by Griffin Scott; opposite page, courtesy of Mike Takewell.)

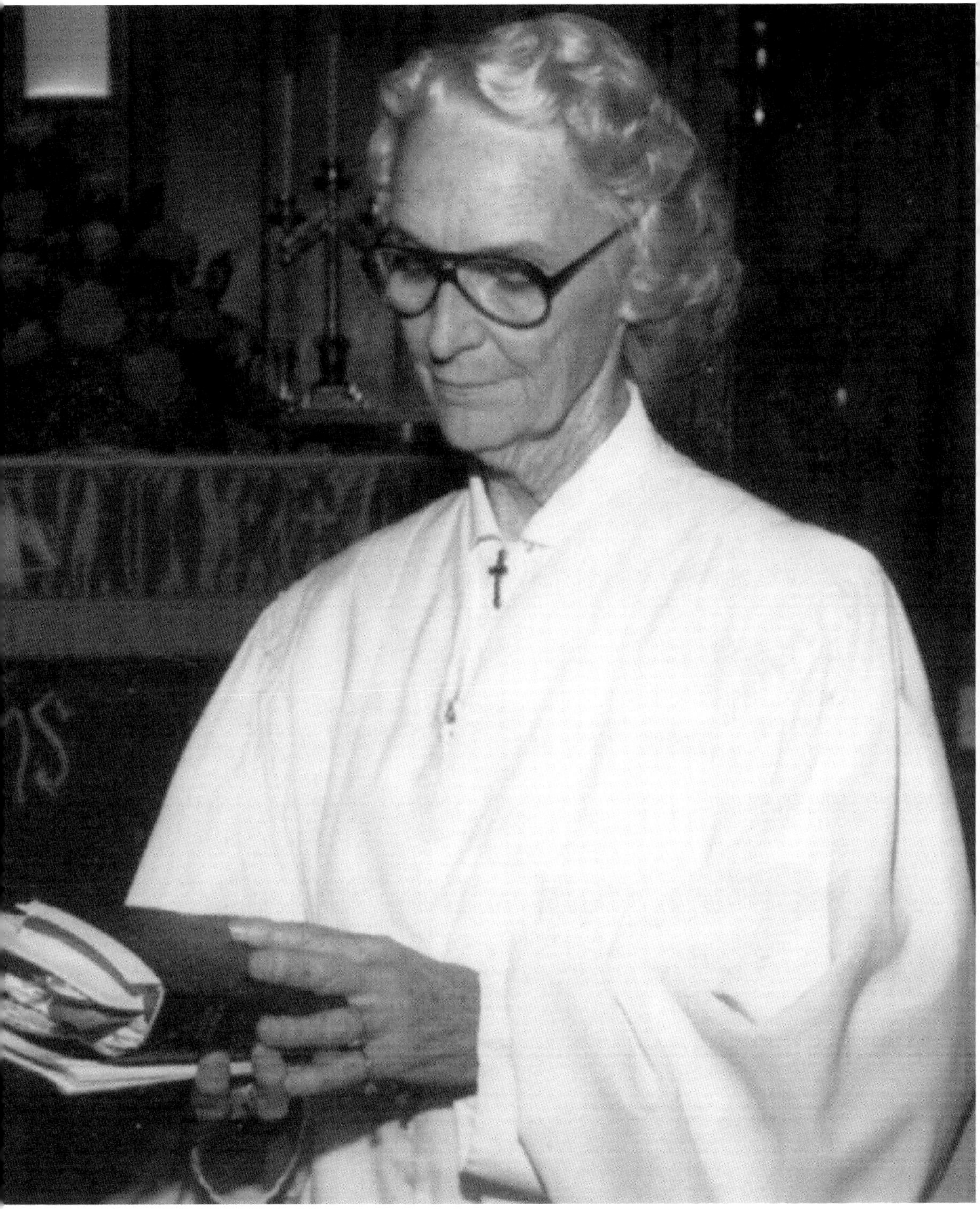

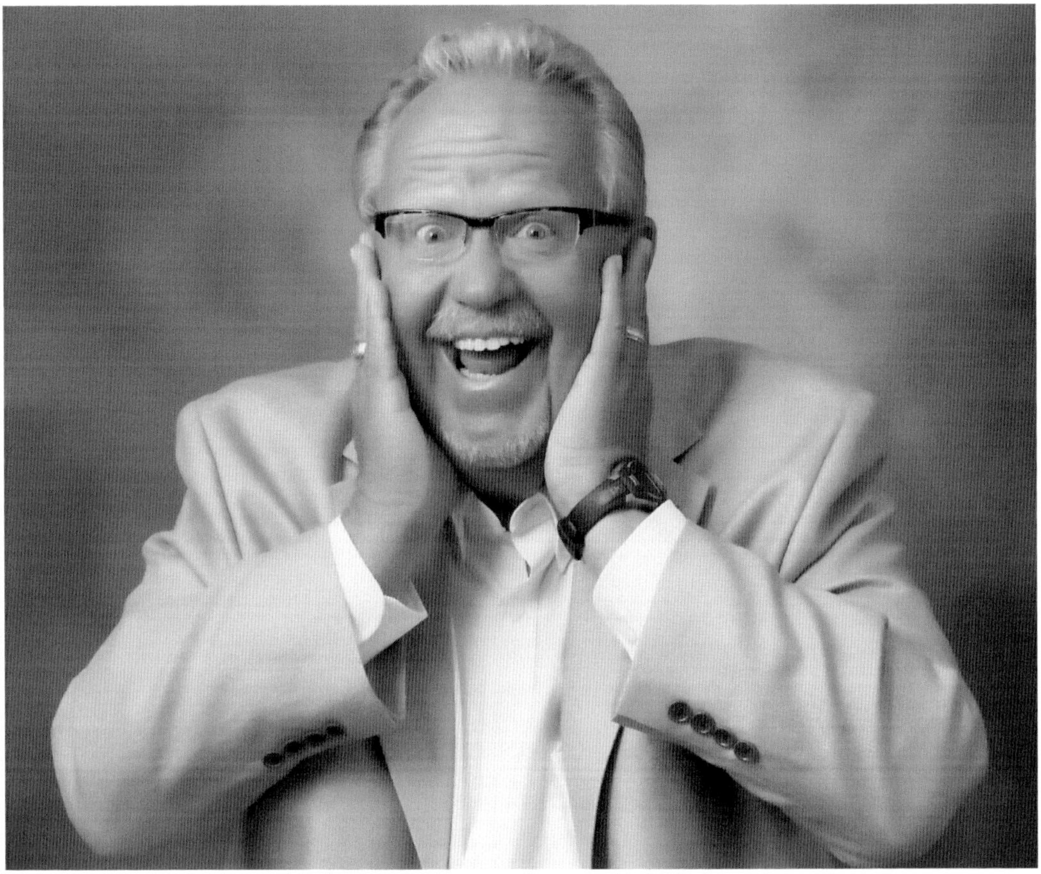

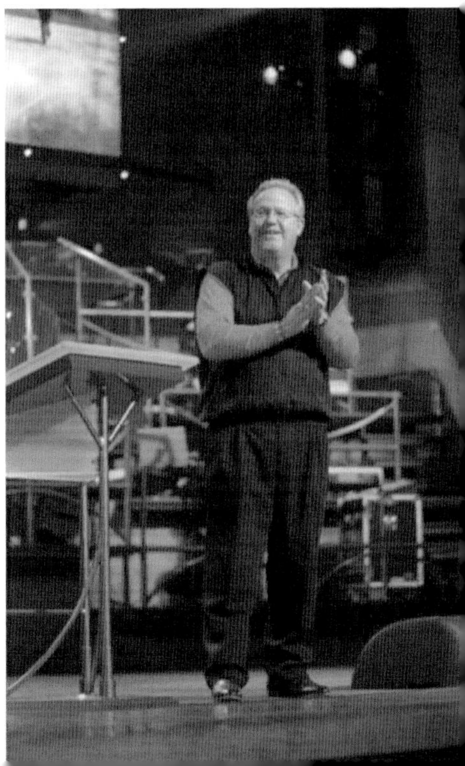

Dennis Swanberg

Monroe-based Christian comedian, motivational speaker, and pastor Dennis Swanberg bills himself as "America's Minister of Encouragement."

Swanberg, who holds a doctorate in theology, is a self-described class clown who thought he would grow up to be a crazy disc jockey or a wacky weatherman but instead became a full-time minister.

Affectionately known by fans as the "Swan," Swanberg has authored nine books and also hosts two nationally televised programs, *Swan's Place* and the *Dennis Swanberg Show*. (Both courtesy of Swanberg Ministries and Dennis Swanberg.)

CHAPTER THREE

Educators and Community Advocates

Teachers, principals, and mentors have the power to make a lasting impression on the young, impressionable minds they are tasked with helping develop. It is those exceptional, spirited educators who inspire change in the community and make it possible for area youth to grow into successful college students, businesspeople, public servants, performers, civic volunteers, professional athletes, and more.

Among these outstanding educators are two trailblazing women, both of whom left a lasting legacy of philanthropy across the community. One is a business dynamo and former Coast Guard yeoman turned benevolent champion of higher education, and the other is a Louisiana first lady and former schoolteacher who helped organize the Monroe League of Women Voters.

This chapter also features a bombardier who became a teacher, then a writer, and later a distinguished scholar.

Another, a businessman, elected official, and farmer, was a true renaissance man, spending 50 years in the telecommunications field, serving on the city school board, and heading a scholarship foundation at the University of Louisiana at Monroe.

Yet another lifelong educator spent several decades as principal of a Monroe high school that now bears his name.

Another notable local, hailing from rural Jackson Parish, went on to become a dean at Monroe's only college, later taking the helm as president when it became Northeast Louisiana University in 1970.

At the heart of every legendary local's story is the tale of one of these inspiring men and women.

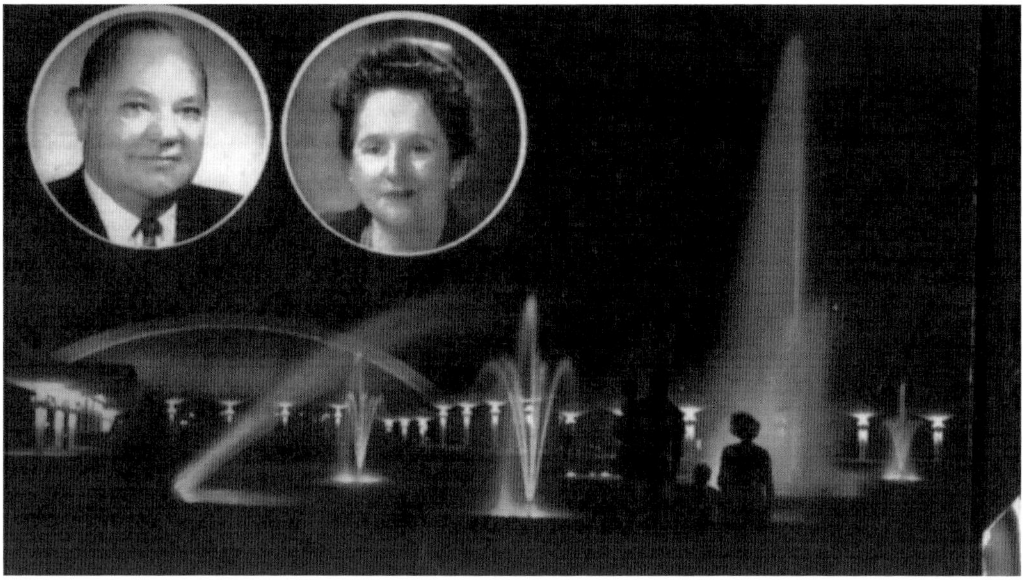

Anna Gray Sweeney Noe

Although she was Louisiana's first lady for only three months, Anna Gray Noe left a lasting legacy. The wife of fellow notable James A. Noe, who briefly served as Louisiana's 43rd governor, Noe attended Louisiana State University before working as a schoolteacher and later serving as a member of the city school board.

Active in the community, Noe is credited with helping organize the Monroe League of Women Voters. Today, her impact on the city is evidenced by the alumni center at the University of Louisiana at Monroe and a downtown park, which both bear her name. (Above, courtesy of the Ouachita Parish Public Library; below, photograph by Griffin Scott.)

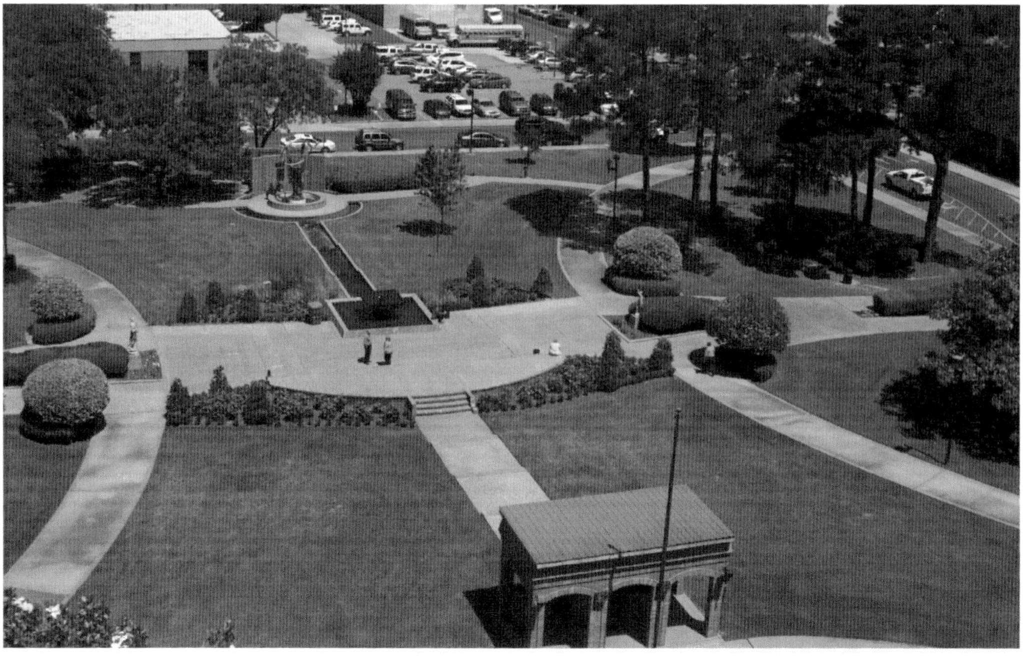

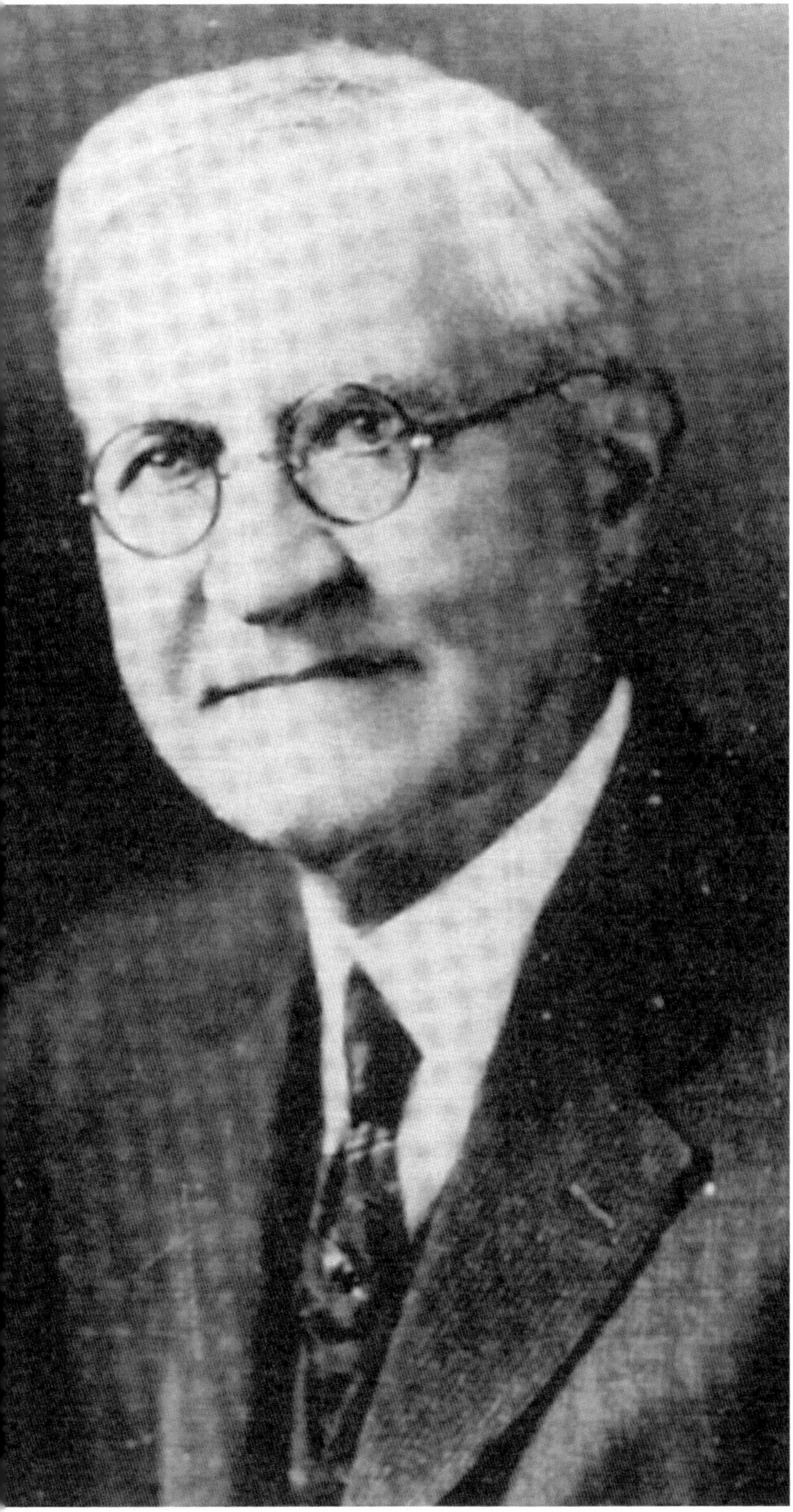

C.E. Byrd
In the early 20th century, professor Clifton Ellis "C.E." Byrd was one of Louisiana's top educators. A West Virginia native, Byrd came to Monroe in 1889 to fill his first role as a principal, following several years in the classroom as an instructor.

Byrd left Monroe in 1892 to become principal of the first public high school in Shreveport, where he remained for 33 years until his death in 1926. Thousands came to pay their respects at his funeral. Soon afterward, the school was renamed C.E. Byrd High School in his honor. (Courtesy of the C.E. Byrd High School Alumni Association.)

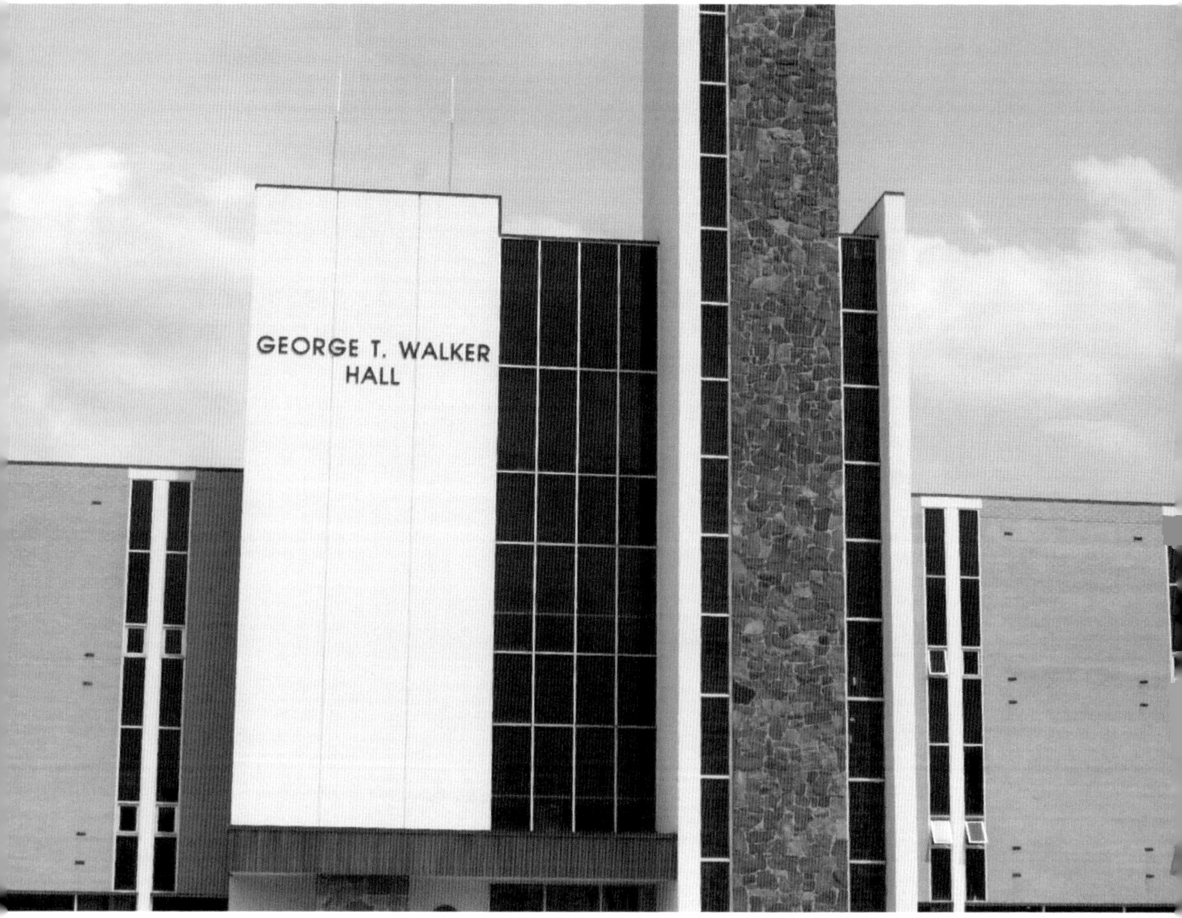

George T. Walker

George T. Walker served as president of the University of Louisiana at Monroe (formerly Northeast Louisiana University), leading the school through an era of expansion and growth, with enrollment at the school more than tripling during his tenure.

The Jackson Parish native earned a business degree from Louisiana State University in 1948 and transitioned from student to teacher quickly, working at several Louisiana colleges before assuming the presidency of what was then known as Northeast Louisiana State College in 1958.

In 1970, Walker oversaw the renaming of the college to Northeast Louisiana University. He retired in 1976. (Photograph by Griffin Scott.)

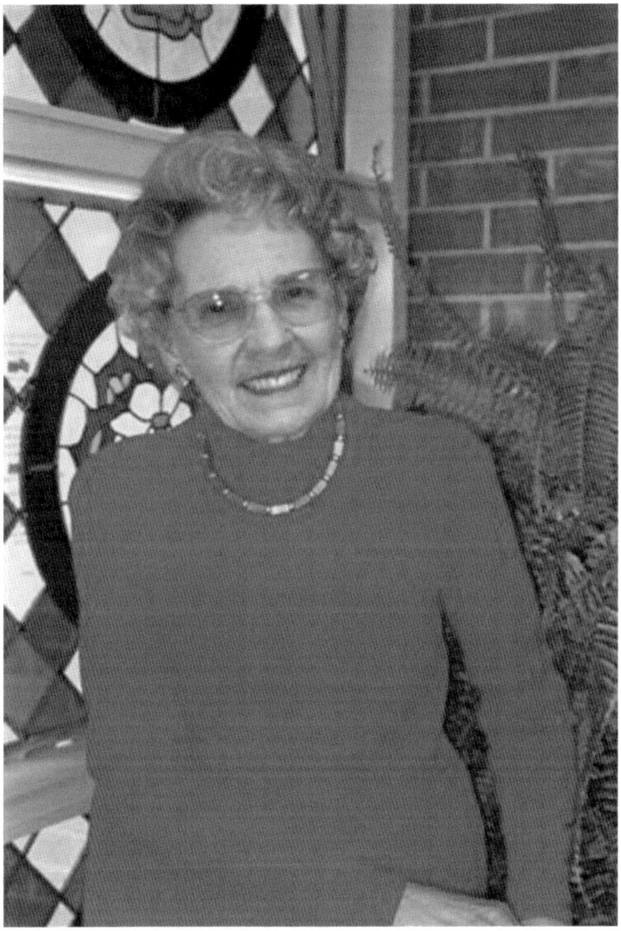

Kitty DeGree

During World War II, Kitty DeGree served as a yeoman in the Coast Guard. In the decades that followed, DeGree would build a legacy as a trailblazing businesswoman, tireless advocate for education, and, most notably, benevolent philanthropist. Her generous and significant contributions to northeast Louisiana, particularly in the areas of education and health care, will continue to serve generations across the area for decades to come.

In 1949, following the end of her Coast Guard service, DeGree, a New Hampshire native, and her husband, Joseph, moved to Monroe, a town she referred to as her "home by choice and love," where she lived until her death at age 90.

DeGree's business acumen and penchant for real estate proved fruitful in the local market, and, by the end of her 70-year career, she had accumulated a multimillion-dollar fortune.

In retirement, DeGree donated millions from her estate to benefit local colleges, hospitals, and other nonprofit and civic organizations. In 1999, DeGree set up a foundation so she could continue giving to the community she so loved, even after her death.

As a result, "Ms. Kitty" (as this gentle lady insisted everyone call her) and her name and legacy adorn the walls of university halls, libraries, and medical centers across the region.

In winter 2012, thousands of mourners from across the region attended her memorial, a public event held in a building at the Kitty DeGree School of Nursing on the University of Louisiana at Monroe campus, which was renamed in her honor, as she was ULM's all-time greatest individual supporter. (Photograph by Daphne Terral.)

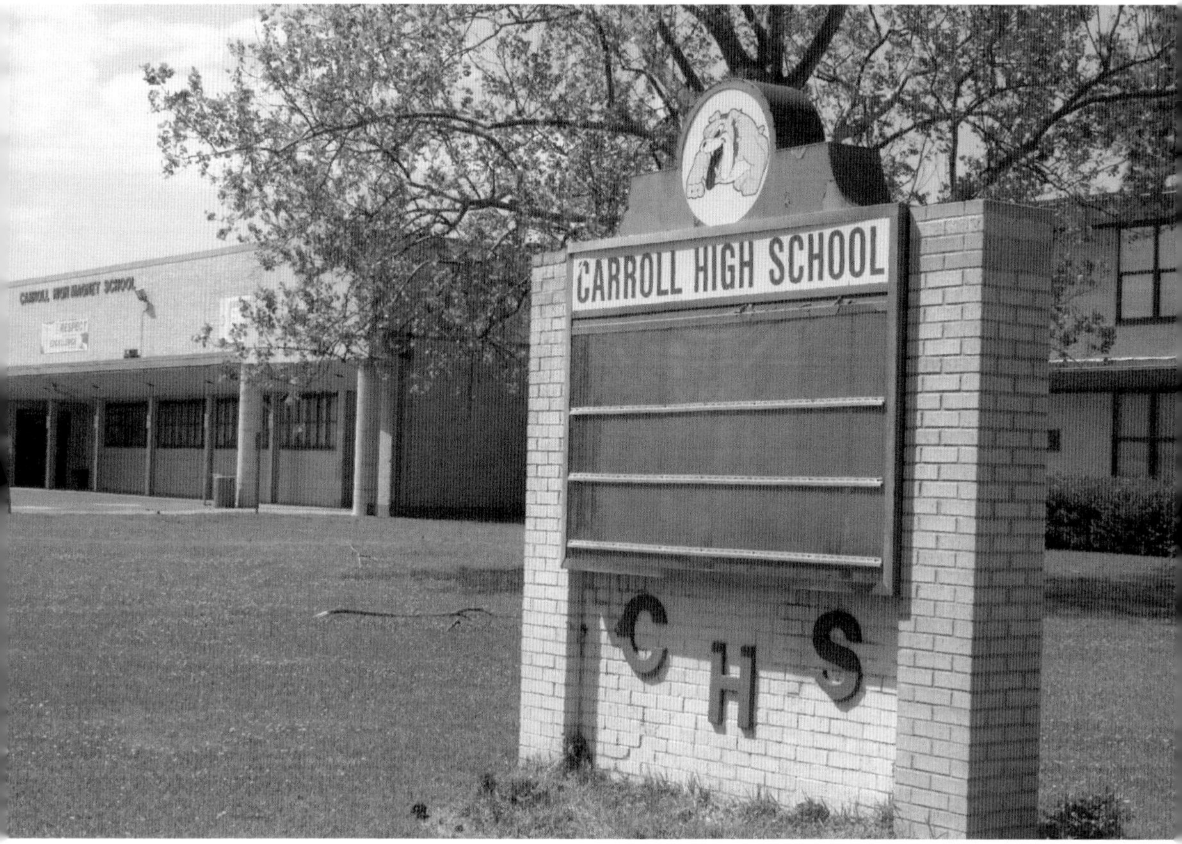

M.H. Carroll

Constructed in 1953, Carroll High School was named after Morris Henry "M.H." Carroll, the last principal of the Monroe Colored High School and the first principal of the school that bears his name to this day.

Carroll helmed the high school named in his honor for 20 years before retiring in 1972. More than an educator, he also hosted a local radio show and owned Carroll's Twin City Gymnasium.

Northeast Louisiana students still benefit from the legacy of this pioneering black educator through the M.H. Carroll Foundation, an organization that endows scholarships for high school graduates who aspire to be teachers. (Photograph by Griffin Scott.)

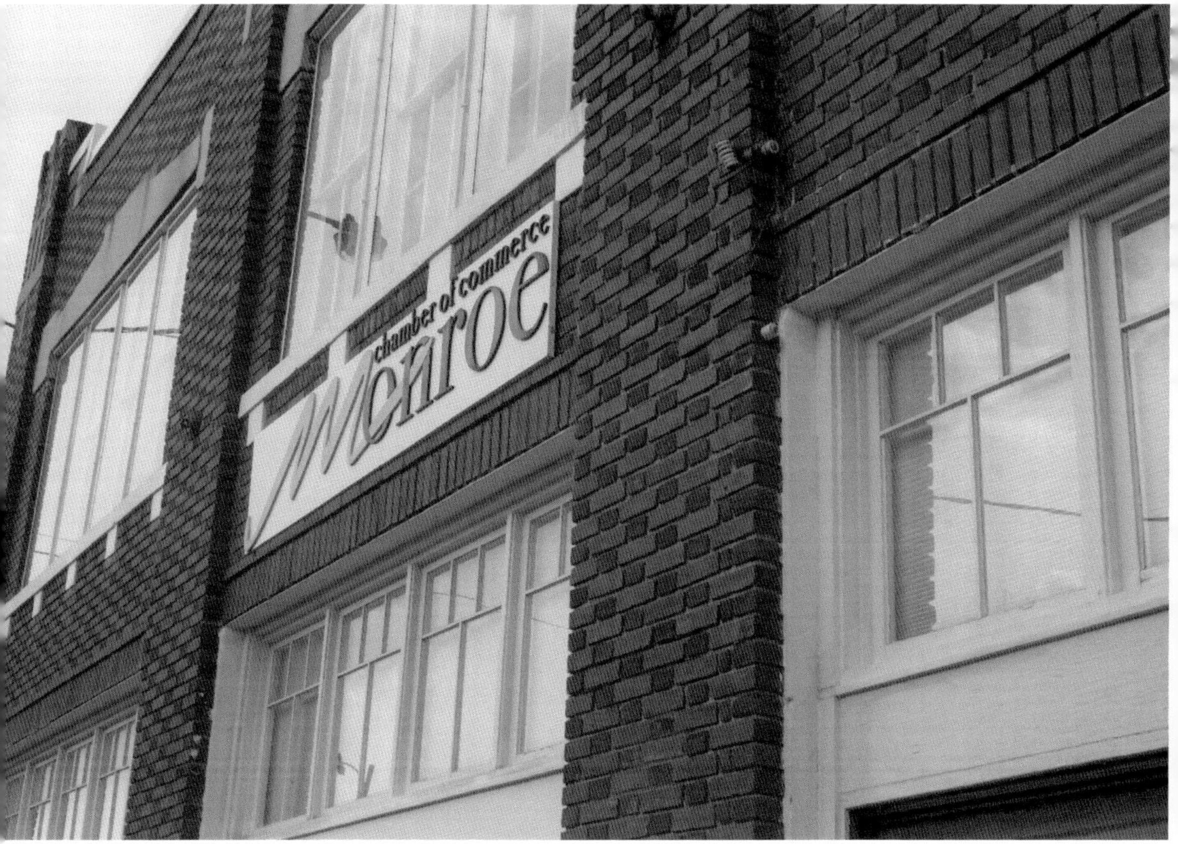

W.E. Whetstone

A businessman, elected official, and farmer, W.E. Whetstone wore many hats in life. Whetstone worked for the former South Central Bell Company for almost 50 years, from 1928 to 1977. He also served as vice president and then president of the 11-member Louisiana State Board of Education.

First elected to the position in 1962, Whetstone spent 16 years on the Board of Trustees for State Colleges and Universities, served two terms on the Monroe City School Board as well as the Louisiana Educational Television Authority, and was also president of the University of Louisiana at Monroe (then Northeast Louisiana University) Scholarship Foundation.

His dedication to community was equally impressive. Whetstone was a member of multiple civic and charitable organizations, including the Monroe Chamber of Commerce, Rotary International, the United Way of Northeast Louisiana, and the American Red Cross.

In his later years, Whetstone, like his father, Will, farmed in nearby Morehouse Parish. (Photograph by Griffin Scott.)

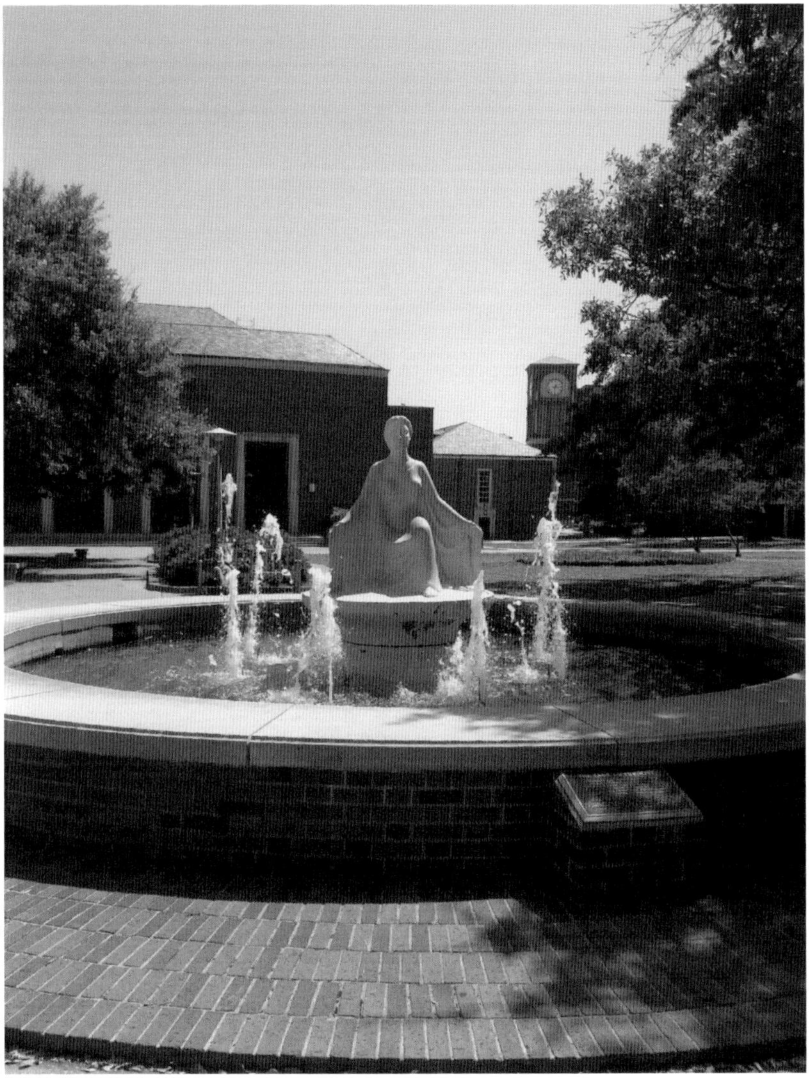

William Y. Thompson

The son of a Presbyterian minister, William Y. Thompson was born in Baton Rouge and was educated in New York, Tennessee, North Carolina, and Alabama. As a young man, Thompson went on a European tour as a bombardier on 50 World War II combat missions in a B-24. The aerial warrior went on to became a college professor who lived in Monroe until his death in 2013.

Thompson was a professor at Louisiana Tech University (Tech) in nearby Ruston from 1955 to 1988, serving as the president of the history department for 23 years. Upon his retirement, the university designated him professor emeritus.

He was also a distinguished writer with three biographies to his name, one about a Georgia veteran of the Civil War, another featuring a northeast Louisiana teacher turned attorney, and a third profiling the father of Shreveport's namesake, Capt. Henry Shreve.

For many years, Thompson also penned a weekly column, "As I Am," for the *News-Star* daily newspaper in Monroe. In 1982, the Daughters of the American Revolution named him Outstanding College Professor of American History. Thompson's name is also on an endowed scholarship at Tech. (Photograph by Larkin Culpepper.)

CHAPTER FOUR

Historical Figures and Founding Fathers

Monroe has a history almost as old as America itself. Throughout the centuries, many have played a role in that history, and none more than the larger-than-life figures who helped shape this tiny river town into a small metropolitan hub for the 12 parishes that encompass northeast Louisiana.

This chapter features profiles of these historical builders, including an 18th-century Spanish commandant who helped found Monroe, a businessman and boat enthusiast who contracted a world-famous architect to plan and build a celebrated river-view home, and a World War II hero who was portrayed on the big screen by "the Duke" himself, actor John Wayne.

Although French settlers had been in the region around the Ouachita River, present-day Monroe, for decades, it was Don Juan Fihiol who established Fort Miro, the region's first true settlement. Years later, Fihiol watched as Fort Miro became a part of a new nation, the United States of America, established only nine years after he, his wife, and the rest of his party first set foot on Louisiana soil.

Gilbert Brian "G.B." Cooley was a successful Monroe business owner and philanthropist who loved to cruise the river named after the Ouachita people. While the 20th century was still young, Cooley commissioned the design and construction of a family home to overlook his cherished waterway.

Walter Burley Griffin, today considered one of the greatest architects in history, was the man Cooley called upon to bring his stately visions to life. Griffin, a protégé of famed architect Frank Lloyd Wright, had made a name for himself when he won an international design contest to redesign Canberra, the capital city of Australia. When it was completed in 1926, the house, a two-story, Prairie Style home, gained the distinction of being the final Griffin-designed structure constructed in the United States.

Revered Hollywood star John Wayne played the male lead in 142 Hollywood films. In four of those pictures, Wayne portrayed a World War II aviator, including the 1942 film *Flying Tigers*, in which he played a character inspired by Monroe war hero Gen. Claire Lee Chennault. Chennault was the leader of a group of American pilots who helped bring the Chinese air force into the modern era and turn back the dreaded Japanese war machine.

A trio of titans, Fihiol, Cooley, and Chennault are among the most interesting historically significant figures from Monroe's past.

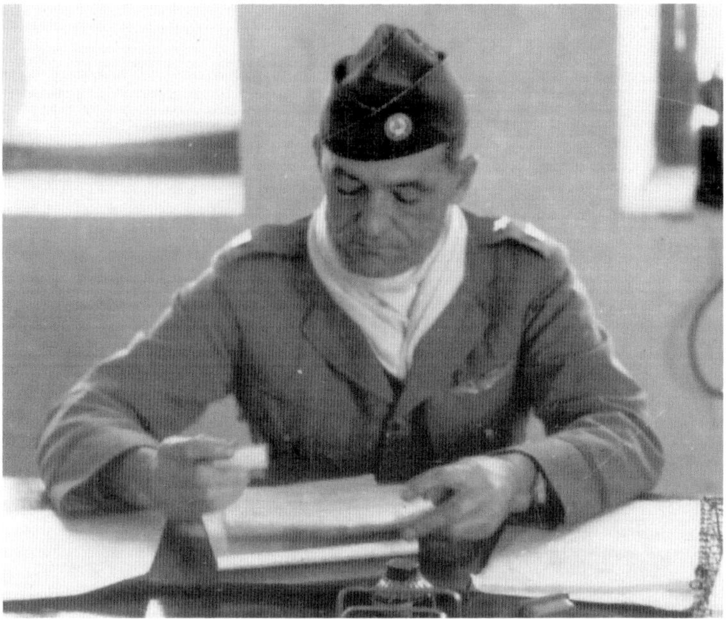

Gen. Claire Lee Chennault

Although born in Texas in 1893, Claire Lee Chennault spent the majority of his childhood in northeast Louisiana before joining the Army at the outset of World War I.

Operating in China, Chennault's American volunteer group, better known as the "Flying Tigers," brought down four Japanese bombers on December 20, 1941, the first American military strike against Japanese military forces following the sneak attack on Pearl Harbor days before.

Today, Monroe is home to the Chennault Aviation Museum, located near the entrance to Chennault Park, both of which are named in his honor. Chennault is pictured above and below on the left. (Above, photograph by US Army, courtesy of Daniel Ford; below, courtesy of the National Archives and Records Administration.)

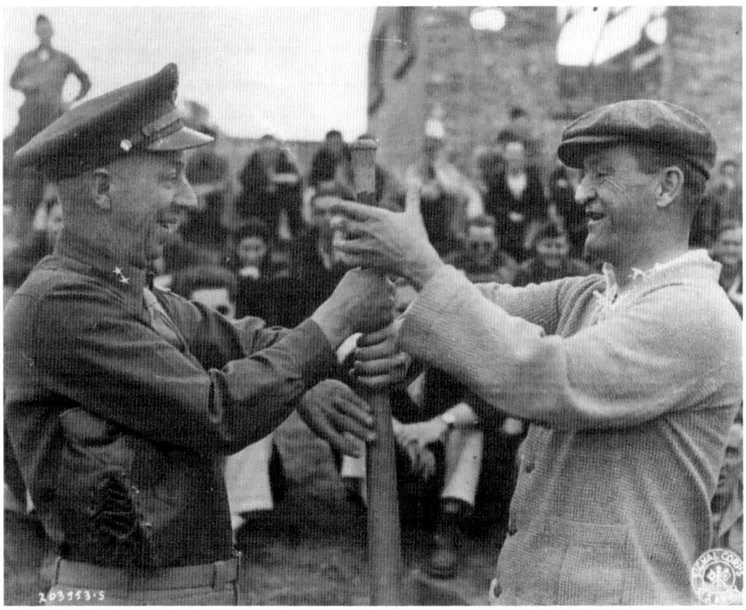

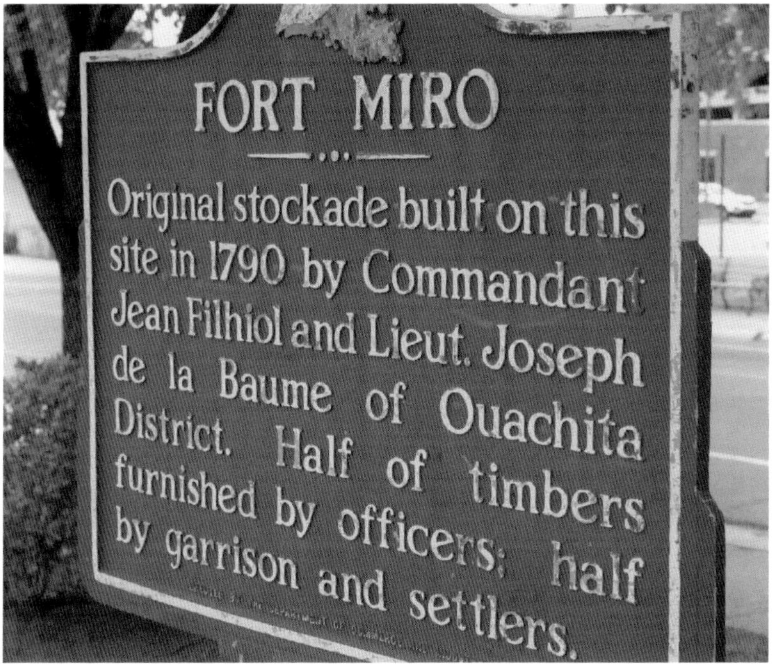

Don Juan Fihiol

Don Juan Filhiol was born in Eymet, France, and eventually settled in what is now Monroe–West Monroe, where he established the first European outpost in Louisiana, a trading post, fort, and small settlement on the banks of the Ouachita River, in 1785. He claimed the land on both sides of the Ouachita River as his own, establishing himself as commandant of a fort he named after Governor Miro. Within a few years, a village grew up around the fort, eventually becoming a small town, which was eventually named Monroe. (Both photographs by Griffin Scott.)

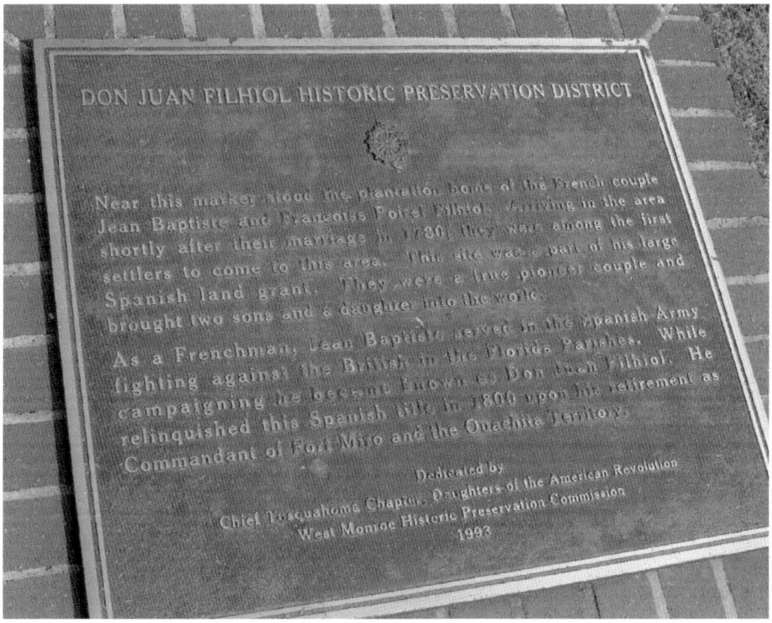

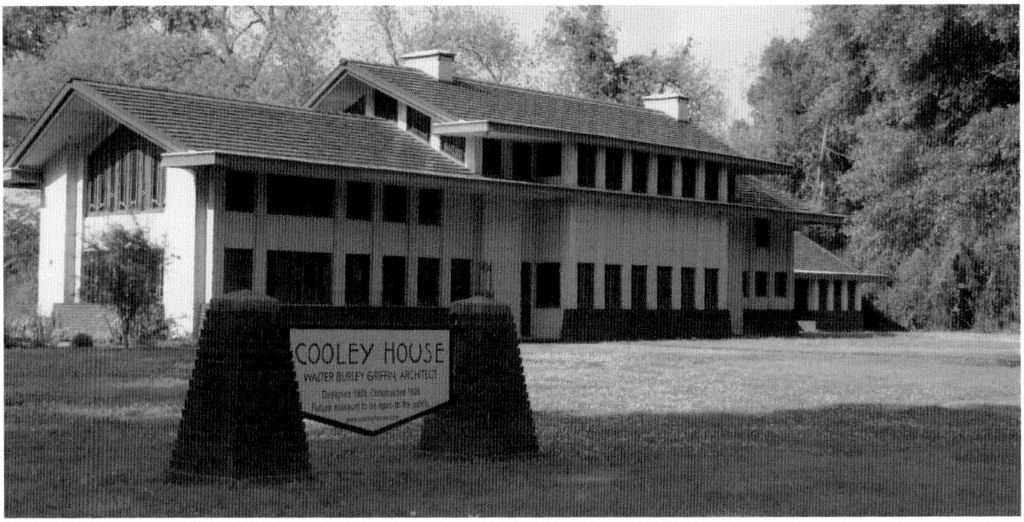

Gilbert Brian G.B. Cooley

A native of Illinois, Gilbert Brian "G.B." Cooley arrived in Monroe in 1894, founded the Monroe Steam Laundry, and soon set out to build a new home for his wife, Selena, envisioning a grand abode perched on the banks of the scenic Ouachita River.

Cooley turned to architect Walter Burley Griffin, an employee in the studio of famed architect Frank Lloyd Wright, to design the home. Although Griffin delivered his plans to Cooley in 1908, the project lay idle for years.

Finally completed in 1926, it is among the last surviving examples of Prairie School residential architecture in the South. (Above, photograph by Griffin Scott; below, courtesy of the Ouachita Parish Public Library.)

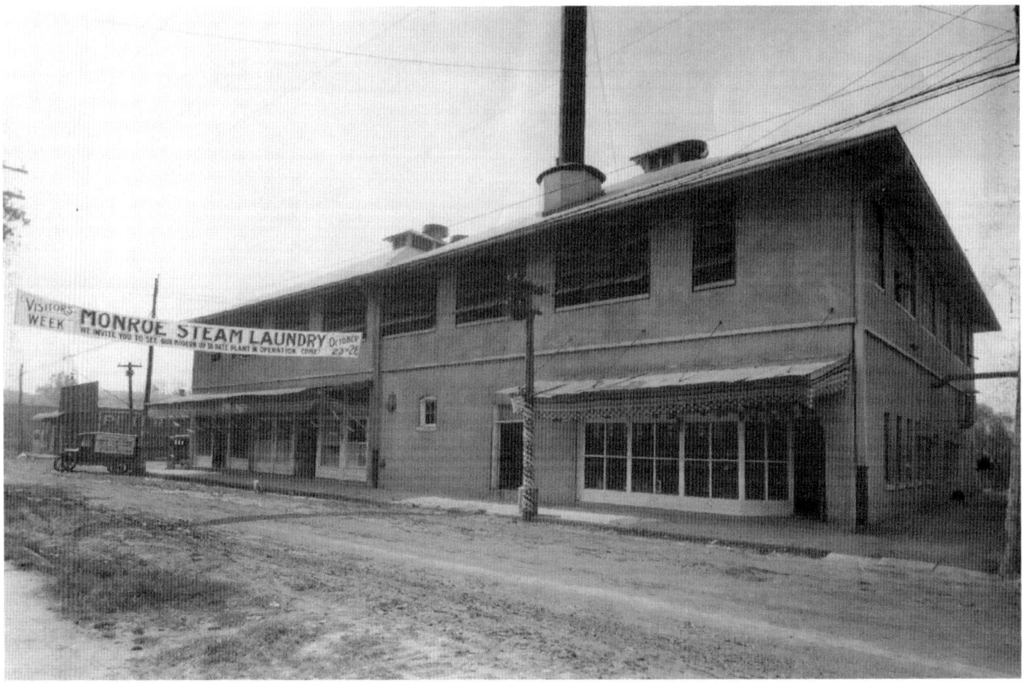

CHAPTER FIVE

Journalists and Broadcasters

Over the years, many have made up Monroe's collective news media, including the hundreds of newspaper writers, radio hosts, and television reporters who have covered the region.

From that list, several members of the "Fourth Estate" stand out. One is a television reporter who, for decades, made crooked businesspeople and dirty politicians cower just at the mention of his name. The worst of the bunch found themselves on the wrong side of prison bars thanks to his award-winning investigative reports on KNOE-TV8.

This chapter also profiles the powerhouse anchor-desk duo, each with a decades-long history in Monroe television and media, that became synonymous with broadcast news in the region.

Another was an influential radio reporter who went on to become a founding member of the staff of KEDM, Monroe's only public radio station. An award-winning news director and newspaper writer, she was also a poet, and briefly co-hosted a news talk radio show with Griffin Scott, one of the coauthors of this book.

Also in this chapter is a respected newspaper reporter who branched out on his own, buying and publishing three northeast Louisiana newspapers, including the *Ouachita Citizen* in West Monroe. His weekly column was a staple in newspapers all over the Bayou State. Almost a decade after his death, his family publishing dynasty is still thriving today.

A conservative radio talk show host and former caterer armed with a thick Cajun accent has a syndicated radio talk show heard across Louisiana airwaves from Beekman to Belle Chasse and Vivian to Vidalia, and also in parts of Mississippi.

Journalists and broadcasters have the important task of bringing the world into the homes of area residents, keeping residents informed and aware of what is going on in northeast Louisiana and beyond. This chapter focuses on their stories, triumphs, and accomplishments.

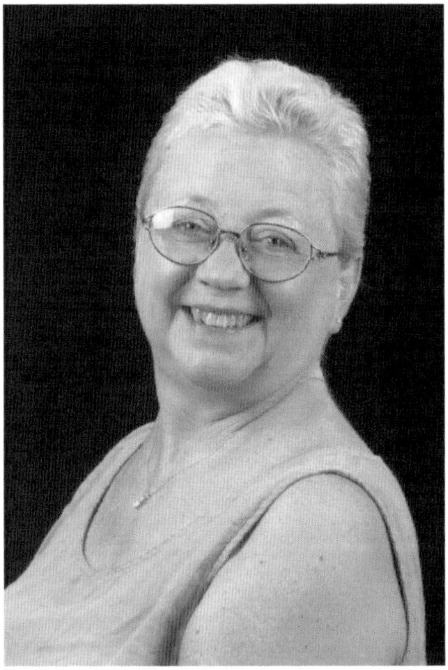

Sunny Meriwether

Any time Sunny Meriwether is mentioned, it puts a smile on the faces of people from the Arkansas-Louisiana-Mississippi region. Meriwether was a broadcast legend who added flavor, spice, and beauty to the community.

Born in Monroe, the Neville graduate became known as a singer and actor. She appeared in many plays in the 1960s and 1970s at the Children's Theatre School and the new Strauss Children's Theatre. As a student at Northeast Louisiana University (NLU; now the University of Louisiana at Monroe), she played the lead in *No, No, Nanette* with veteran Hollywood actor Virginia Mayo and performed roles in *Jesus Christ Superstar* and *Cabaret*. While still a student, she directed vanities both for NLU and for a dinner theater at the Monroe Civic Center.

Known as a crack reporter, Meriwether earned the respect of her audience and of her colleagues, as her scores of Associated Press awards attest. From 1988 to 1991, Meriwether worked in Little Rock as a legislative reporter for the KARN radio station. Never afraid to ask the hard questions, she developed a strong working relationship with Gov. Bill Clinton. The fact that their daughters went to school together personalized that relationship. On Meriwether's mantle today is a photograph of her interviewing the future president, who signed and inscribed it, "Sunny, I know you've heard it all before, but I wish you could put up a better front!"

As one of the original members of national public radio station KEDM, Meriwether created a top-flight news department, which she directed for 18 years. Her work brought state and national recognition. She developed *Lagniappe*, a local interview program that gave a voice to local arts organizations, nonprofits, and other community groups. Many authors had their first introduction to Monroe through an interview on *Lagniappe*, and, on occasion, Meriwether and her husband, Joe Saunders, opened their home and hospitality to these visiting authors.

Perhaps the most lasting legacy of Sunny Meriwether is her love for plants, many of them native to Louisiana, which she shared with friends and acquaintances across the South. These plants will bloom for generations. One friend calls her the Johnny Appleseed of flowers; another says that she grew friendships and bloomed people, too.

Sunny Meriwether died on April 19, 2014, in her home on the bayou, on a sunny day with her flowers in full bloom. (Courtesy of the family of Sunny Meriwether and Elisabeth Grant-Gibson.)

Sam Hanna Sr.

Through his weekly column "One Man's Opinion," Samuel Andrew Hanna Sr. appeared in newspapers all over Louisiana.

When the journalist and newspaper owner died in 2006, Kathy Spurlock, executive editor of the *News-Star*, Monroe's daily newspaper, referred to him as "The dean of the state's newspaper publishers, the most knowledgeable about state politics, certainly the one with the most institutional knowledge."

Hanna had his start in the newspaper business while still in college, as editor of the Louisiana State University campus paper.

He spent several years with the *News-Star* before purchasing his own newspaper. Hanna went on to own several papers, including the *Ouachita Citizen*, a weekly publication based out of West Monroe. (Photograph by Griffin Scott.)

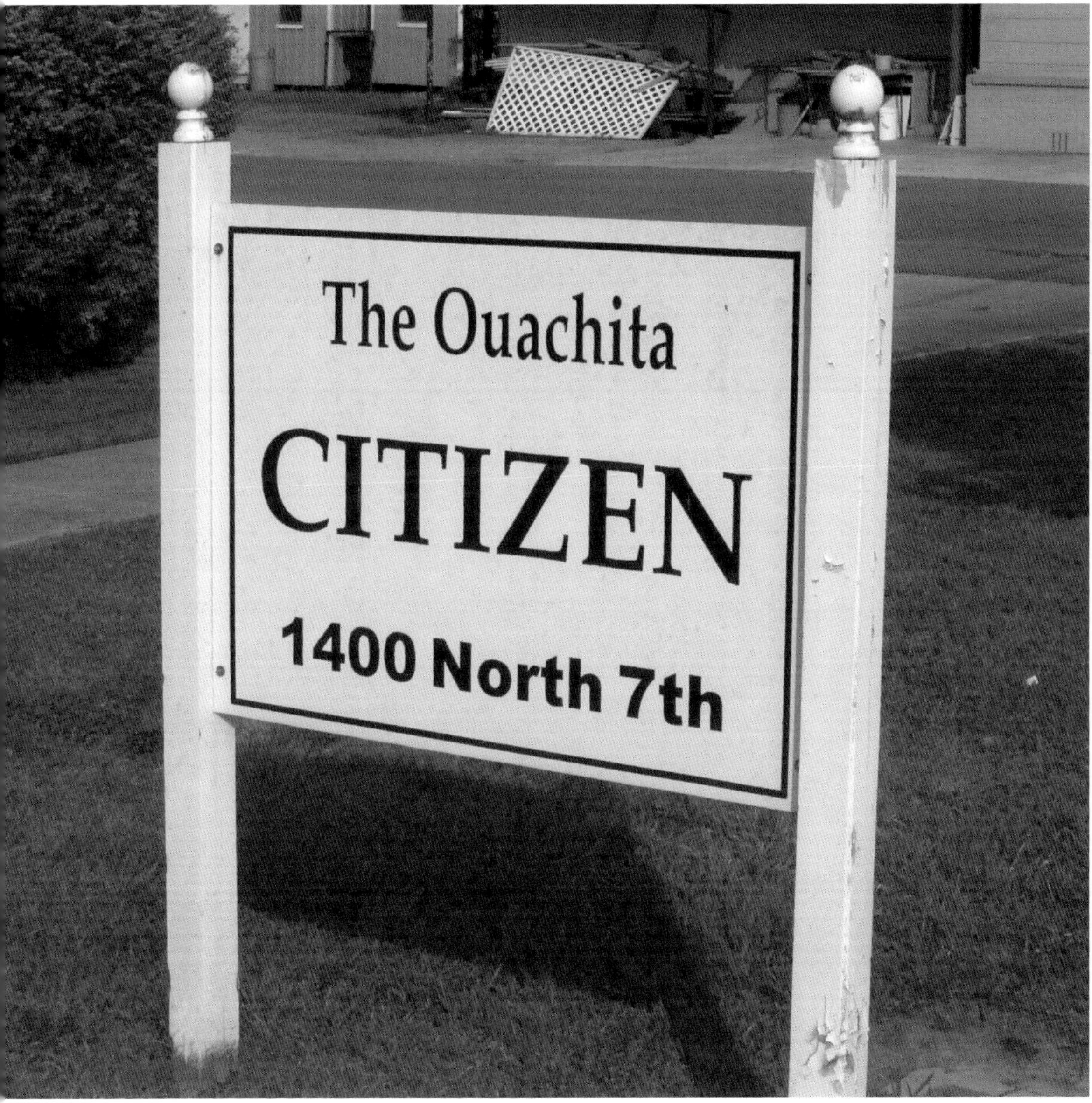

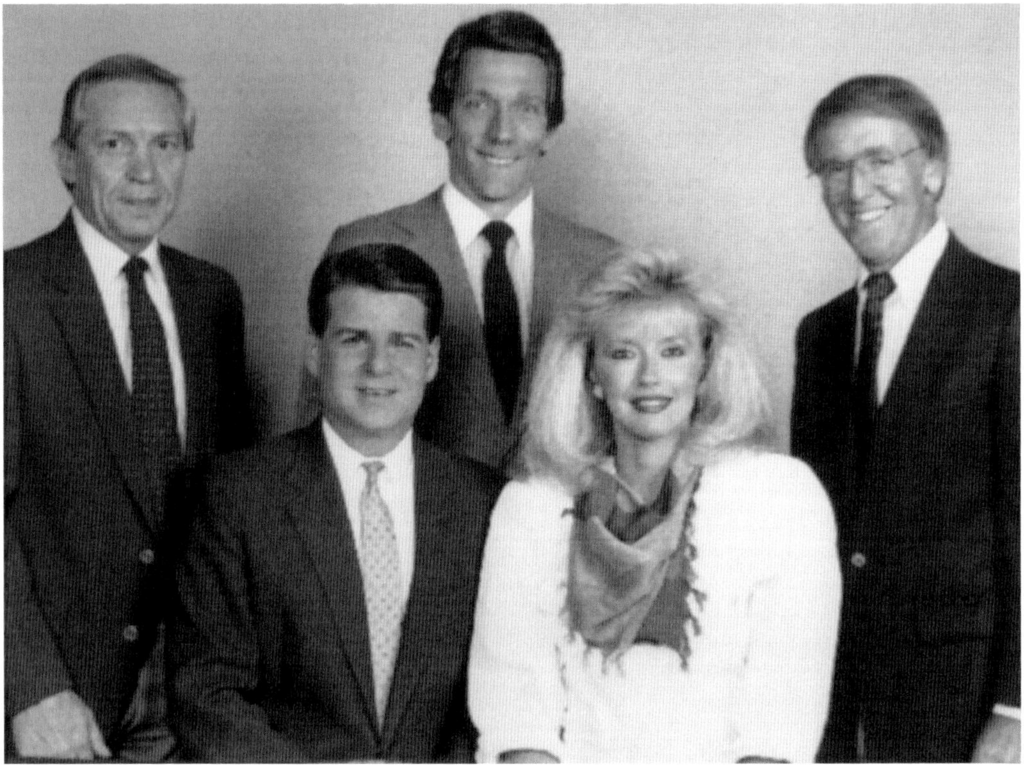

Judy Wagoner

Platinum locks, bombshell good looks, and a trusted, professional voice were all trademarks of news anchor Judy Wagoner, a Monroe broadcasting legend who graced area television screens for nearly three decades.

A Louisiana State University–Alexandria and University of Louisiana at Monroe (formerly Northeast Louisiana University) graduate, Wagoner joined Monroe's oldest television news program, KNOE-TV8, where she quickly worked her way up the ranks to assistant news director, and later, senior anchor, sharing the desk with other local news favorite John Denison.

Although she said goodbye to KNOE viewers in November 2009, Wagoner briefly reemerged as a co-anchor on NBC 10 News, KNOE's on-air rival. (Courtesy of Pete Battaglia.)

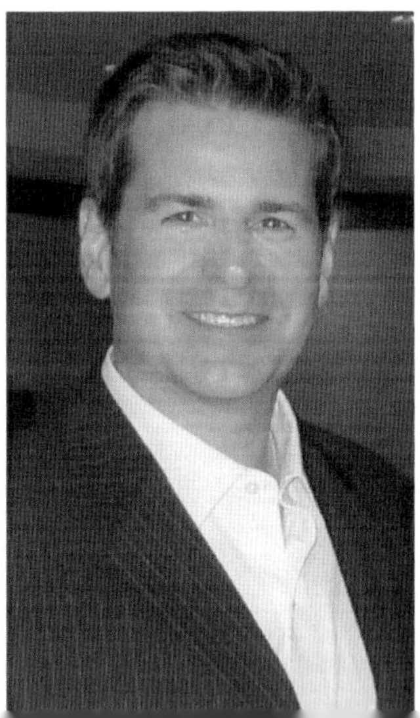

John Denison

For 31 years, Monroe television audiences could find trusted news anchor John Denison delivering their local news on KNOE, known by the locals simply as "channel eight." This award-winning journalist and Louisiana Tech University graduate was only 24 years old when he was named lead anchor of KNOE-TV8 News. Along with co-anchor Judy Wagoner, Denison became both a trusted face and the voice of news north of Alexandria.

In the 1990s, Denison briefly left KNOE to take the helm of a rival newscast, serving as both news director and lead anchor before returning to his home station, where he remained until he retired. He bid farewell to loyal viewers on his final newscast in February 2012. (Courtesy of John Denison.)

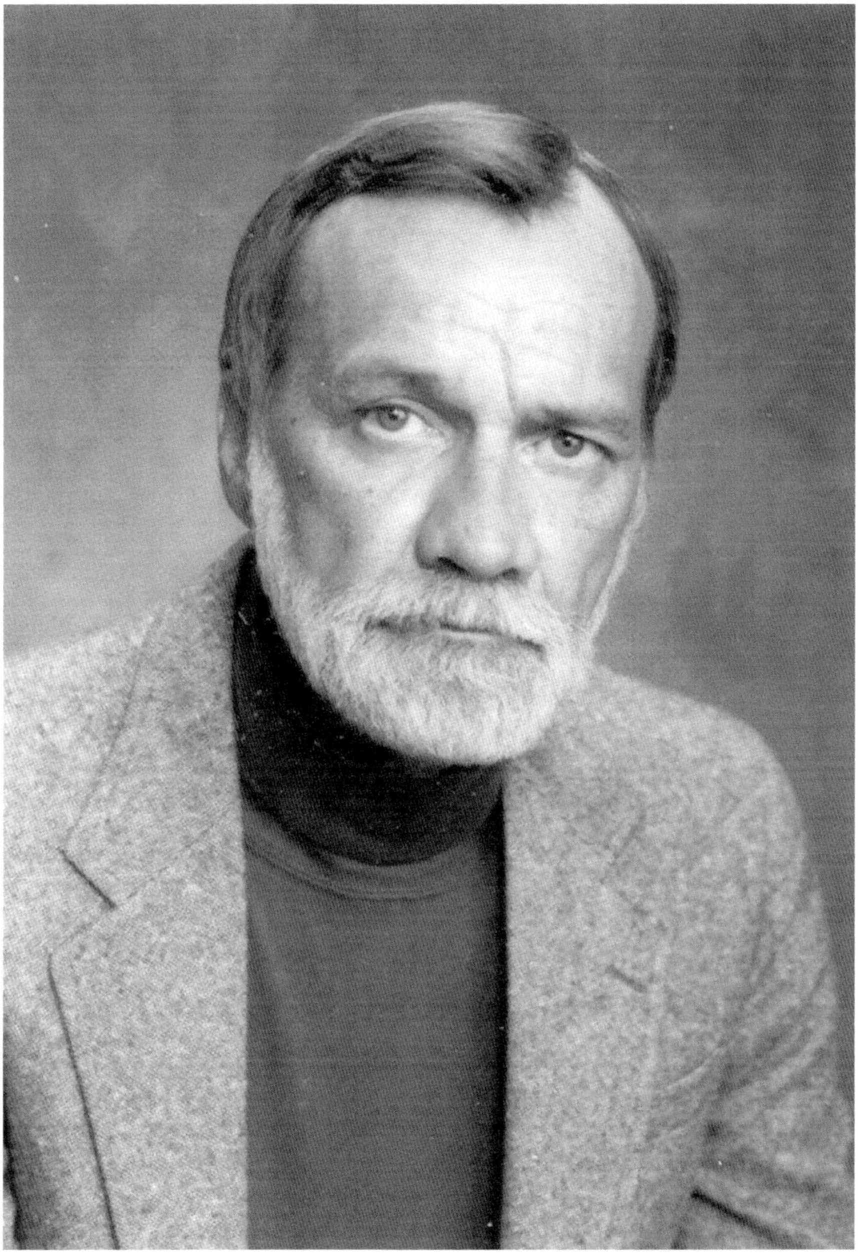

Ken Booth

As an award-winning television and radio journalist for almost 50 years, Ken Booth nipped the heels of corrupt politicians and public officials across northeast Louisiana.

Beyond his reports of local and state politics, Booth also traveled along with and reported on US state visits and world summits for five sitting US presidents: Nixon, Ford, Carter, Reagan, and George H.W. Bush, in over 40 different world capitals.

Before retiring from active reporting in 2006, Booth served as news director and special assignments reporter at KNOE, Monroe's CBS affiliate. He continues to write opinion pieces and is the author of the historical biography *Sheriffs of Ouachita Parish*. (Courtesy of Ken Booth.)

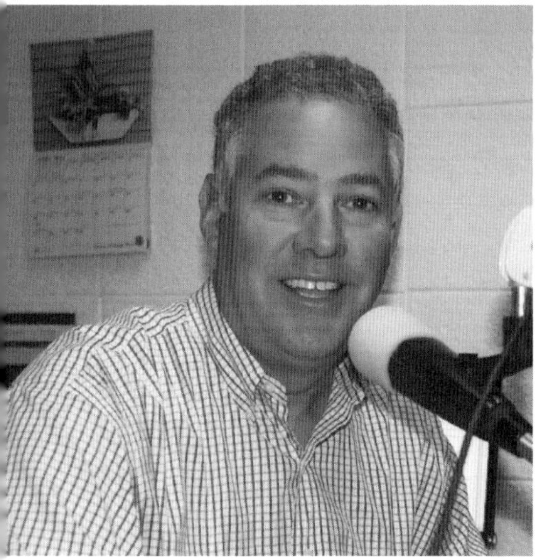

Moon Griffon

Not many political analysts come from the professional catering ranks, but Moon Griffon is not a typical anything. A colorful Cajun, Blaine Michael "Moon" Griffon was born and raised in south Louisiana but gained fame as a cook turned commentator on AM radio in and around northeast Louisiana. *The Moon Griffon Show* debuted in 1993, and soon thereafter, the unlikely talking head hung up his apron for good, taking to full-time political punditry.

Today, his popular program, a mix of fiery political conservatism and homespun charm, delivered with a south Louisiana drawl, can be heard on dials across Louisiana and in parts of neighboring Mississippi. Below, Pres. Ronald Reagan is seen leaving KMLB, where Griffon got his start in radio, during the president's visit to Monroe during flooding in 1982. (Left, photograph by Griffin Scott; below, courtesy of the Radio People.)

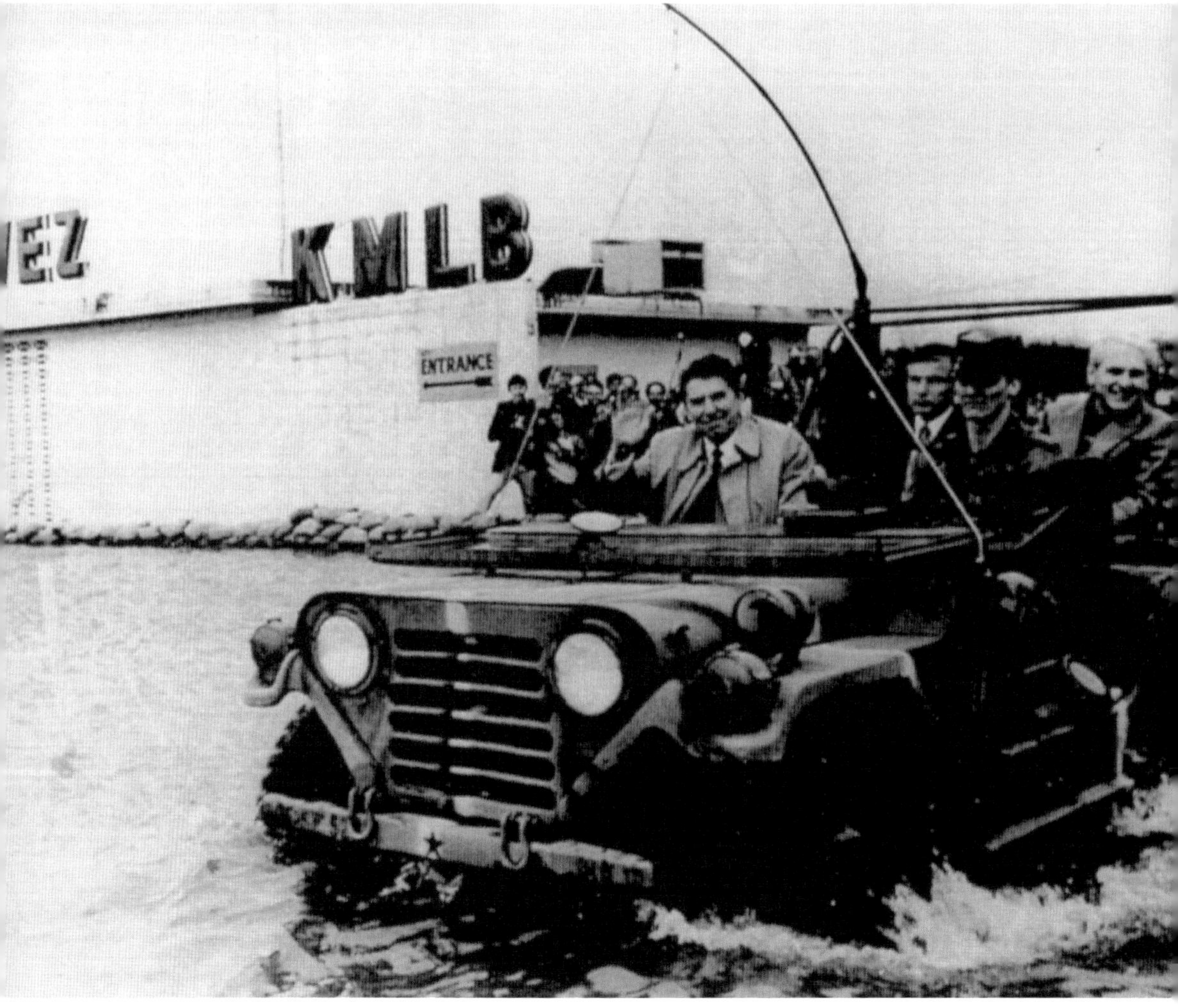

CHAPTER SIX

Literary, Culinary, and Visual Artists

This chapter is a real mixed bag, a gumbo of northeast Louisiana talent, including a group of writers, chefs, and illustrators who represent the area's most diverse blend of legends.

There is a young chef who shot to stardom after winning a reality television competition on the Food Network. Considered a "king' in culinary circles, his downtown Monroe restaurant, Cotton, is located in one of the city's oldest buildings.

A trio of siblings with a library of children's books and an internationally recognized T-shirt company are profiled, as well as an artist who produced beautiful outdoor sculptures that grace the downtowns of both Monroe and West Monroe, delighting area children for decades.

Meet an American Civil War veteran who became a photography studio and art gallery owner, and a World War II trooper who survived Iwo Jima and returned home to become a writer, chronicling his life growing up in Depression-era Monroe with a series of autobiographical books.

Another Southern writer, reporter, and sometime radio host, who often wrote about his upbringing in northeast Louisiana, is featured here too. A talented comic book illustrator who co-created the iconic Captain Marvel character is also profiled.

There is the story of the Monroe writer who enrolled at one of the world's most prestigious universities at only 16 years old. After rubbing elbows with Tennessee Williams and other famous scribes of the day, this writer penned a tome that many claimed was a scandalous expose of Monroe's high society thinly disguised as a work of fiction.

A look is also taken into the life of a teenage writer who later became one of the youngest editors at a major American daily newspaper. The young editor went on to teach reporting and newswriting at an area university, writing several books and a weekly column in his spare time.

Finally, a restaurateur and professional Southern gentleman rounds out this collection. Inheriting his kitchen skills from his mother, this beloved lifestyle guru entertained northeast Louisiana on television, in radio, and in print for decades.

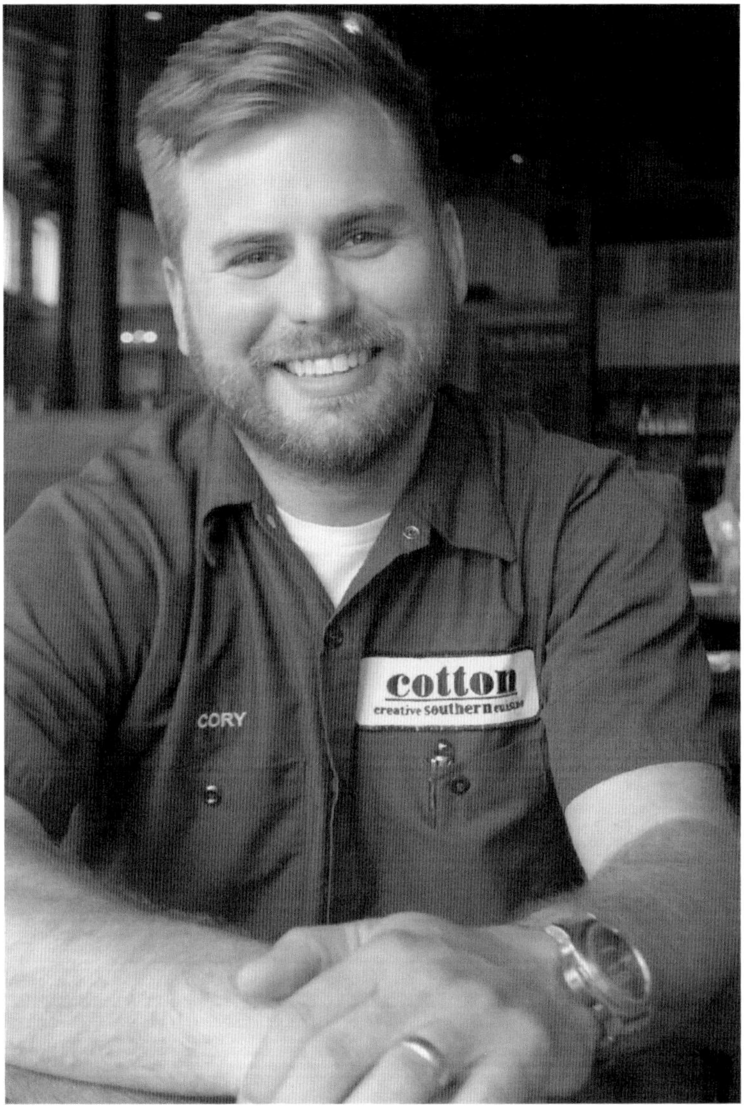

Cory Bahr

Cory Bahr, named People's Best New Chef, Gulf Coast by *Food & Wine* magazine, inherited his Southern-style culinary skills. In 2014 he told the *News-Star*, "My grandfather raised me on the Mississippi River, hunting and fishing. We always looked forward to Papa returning from a trip 'Down South.' This would bring Oysters, Blue Crab, Gulf shrimp, and lots of neighbors to help devour them. My grandmother to this day is the best cook I know."

Only in his mid-30s, the driven and talented Bahr has already racked up quite an impressive resume. In 2011, he was crowned "King of Louisiana Seafood" in the fourth annual Louisiana Seafood Cook-Off, presented by the Louisiana Seafood Promotion and Marketing Board. A year later, Bahr bested three other up-and-coming chefs from around the country on *Chopped*, a popular cooking competition show airing on the Food Network. To the delight of foodies near and far, he also owns and is executive chef at two local restaurants: Cotton, located in one of the city's oldest standing buildings, a former cotton warehouse overlooking the Ouachita River, and Nonna, an Italian eatery opened in 2014 in Monroe's historic Garden District. (Courtesy of Restaurant Cotton.)

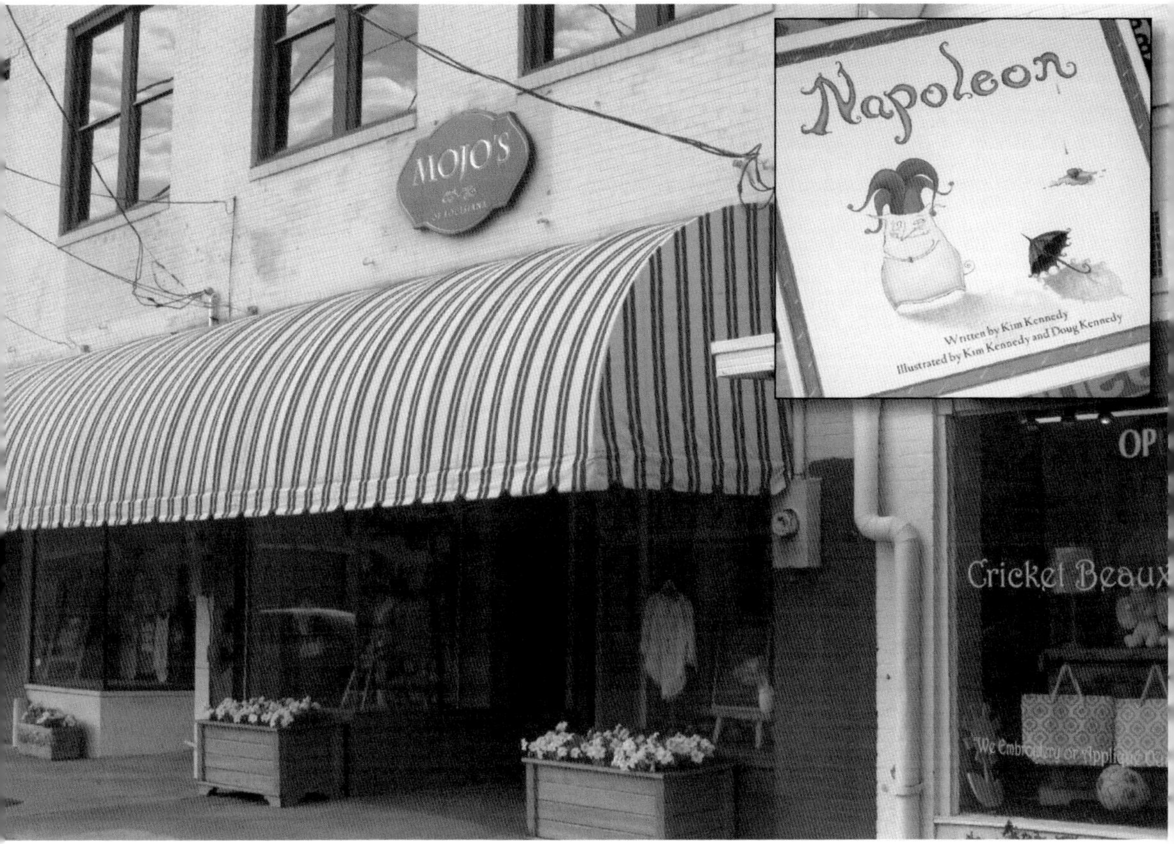

Kim Kennedy-Bryan and Doug and John Kennedy

Kim Kennedy-Bryan is the author, and her brother, Doug Kennedy, the illustrator, of several children's books, including the acclaimed *Pirate Pete* series. Along with their brother John, they also run a small but internationally renowned boutique in the historic Cottonport downtown district of Monroe's twin city West Monroe.

Family-owned Mojo Ware produces T-shirts featuring custom illustrations by Doug, a graphic artist and illustrator. His unique, signature designs are screen-printed by hand onto the shirts, a process almost unheard of in a time when almost all T-shirts are mass-produced on gigantic screen presses.

John Kennedy explained to *Country Roads* magazine, "It's all about the way you handle the squeegee; with different pressure and angle on the canvas you get different effects. Even if the print isn't perfect, there's beauty in that too. To me, nothing looks cheaper than a perfect t-shirt. There's no love involved, it's not a craft, nor an art. It's just a commodity." (Above, photograph by Griffin Scott; inset, photograph by Amy Sliger.)

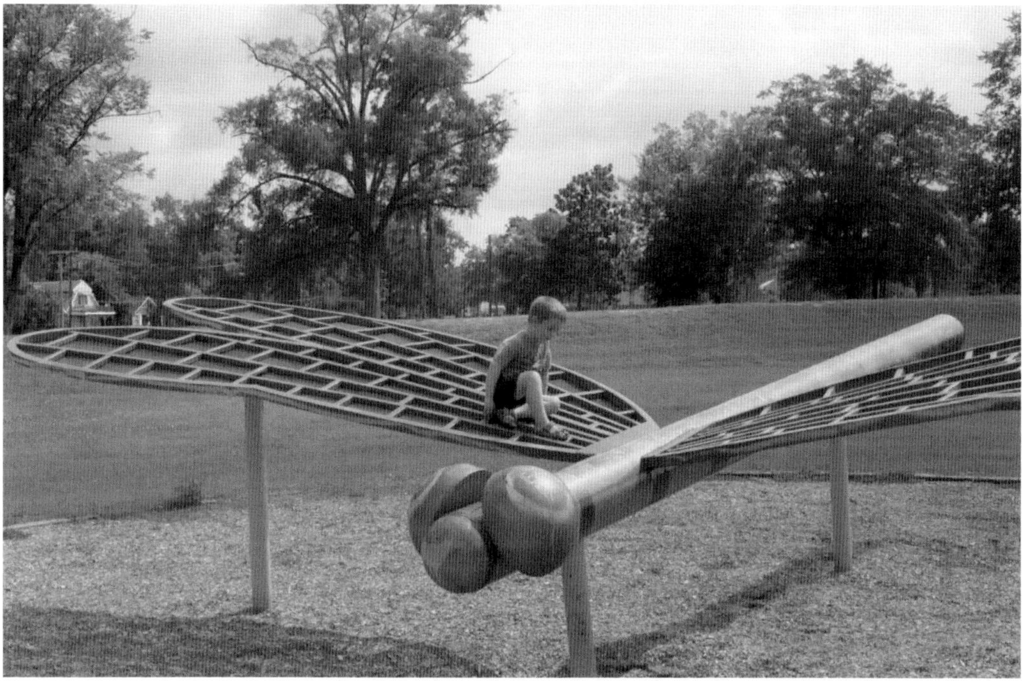

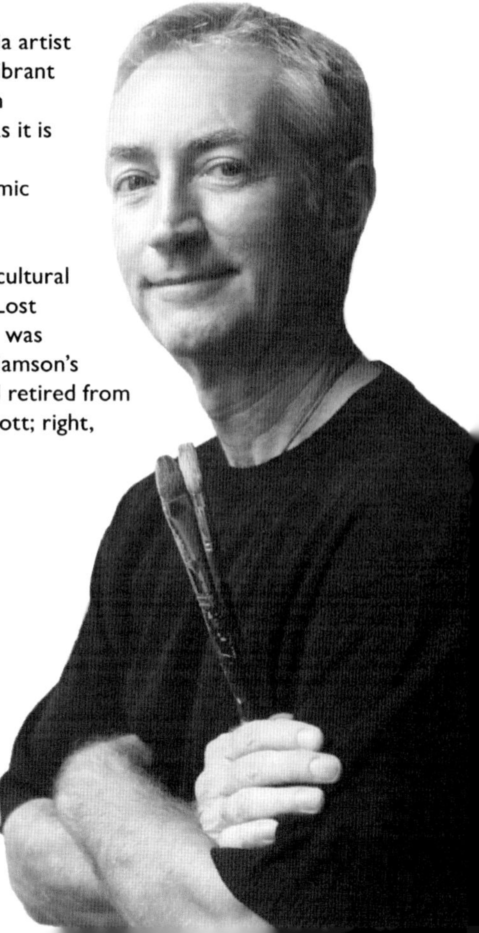

Edmund Williamson

Edmund Williamson was a distinguished regional multimedia artist who set out to bring art to the masses through his large, vibrant public sculptures and installations. When he passed away in 2009, he left behind a body of work as visually impressive as it is beloved by the community.

In addition to his daring community sculptures and dynamic installations, the multifaceted artist was also known for his paintings, portraits, graphic design, and murals.

He is also credited with kicking off the now burgeoning cultural revival of downtown Monroe when he opened his gallery, Lost Bazaar, on North Second Street, a closed-off alleyway that was officially renamed Art Alley in 2010. Pictured above is Williamson's sculpture *Dragon Fly*, formerly located in Forsythe Park and retired from public view in early 2014. (Above, photograph by Griffin Scott; right, photograph by Brad Arender, Arender Studio + Gallery.)

Elias W. "Eli" Mealy

Civil War veteran Elias W. "Eli" Mealy arrived in northeast Louisiana after that terrible conflict, and in 1867 set up an art gallery and photography studio on South Grand Street in downtown Monroe. Billing himself as a "photographer who was also an artist," Mealy's offerings included photographs in cameos, mattes, and other popular styles of the day.

Although a native of West Virginia, Eli Mealy's artistic success meant he was able to integrate into Monroe society quickly, and he married local Henrietta Vollman in 1868.

Mealy passed away in 1908. Henrietta followed in 1923. The two are buried in Old City Cemetery, one of Monroe's oldest cemeteries. This image shows two unidentified children photographed by Mealy in the late 1860s. (Courtesy of the Ouachita Parish Public Library.)

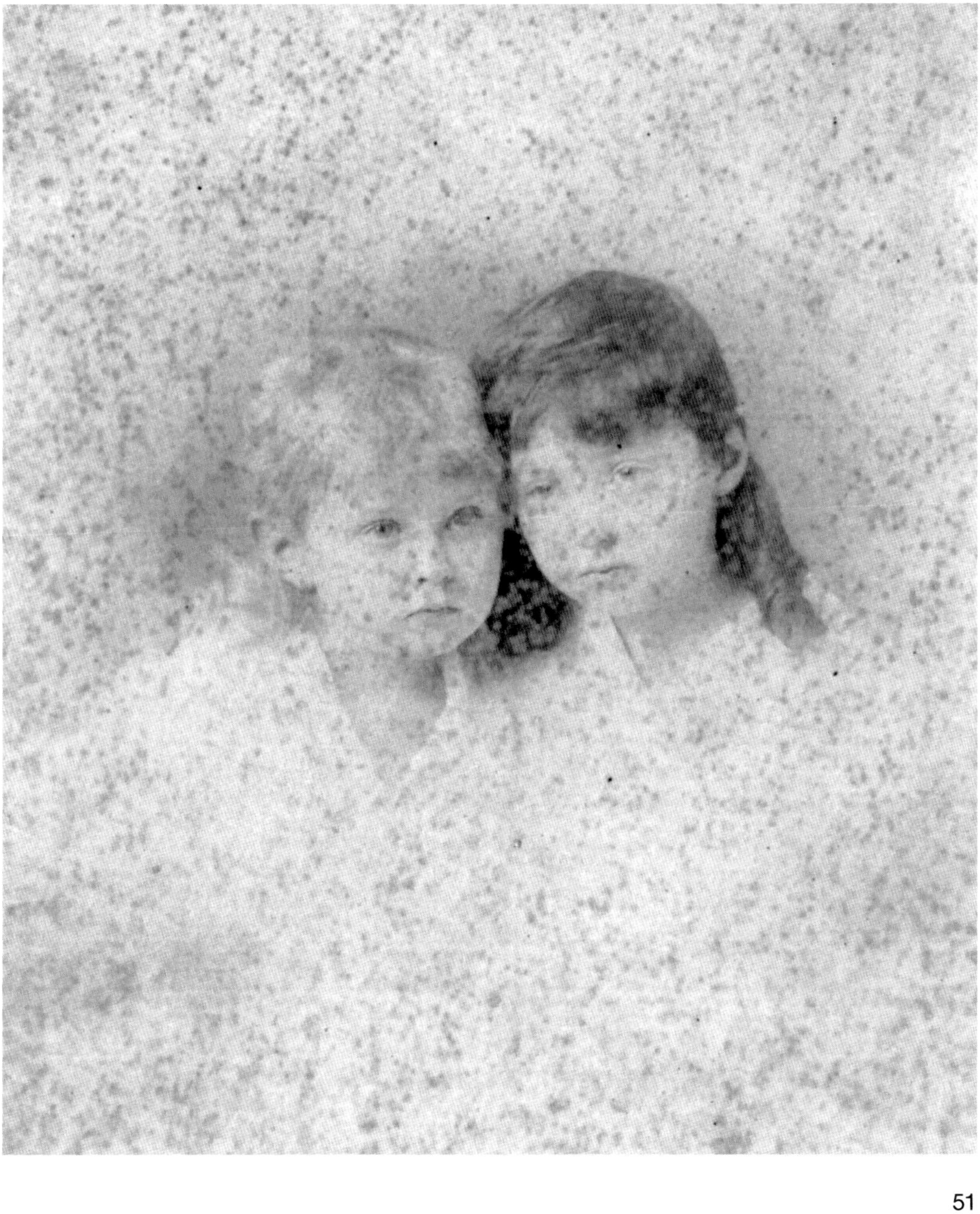

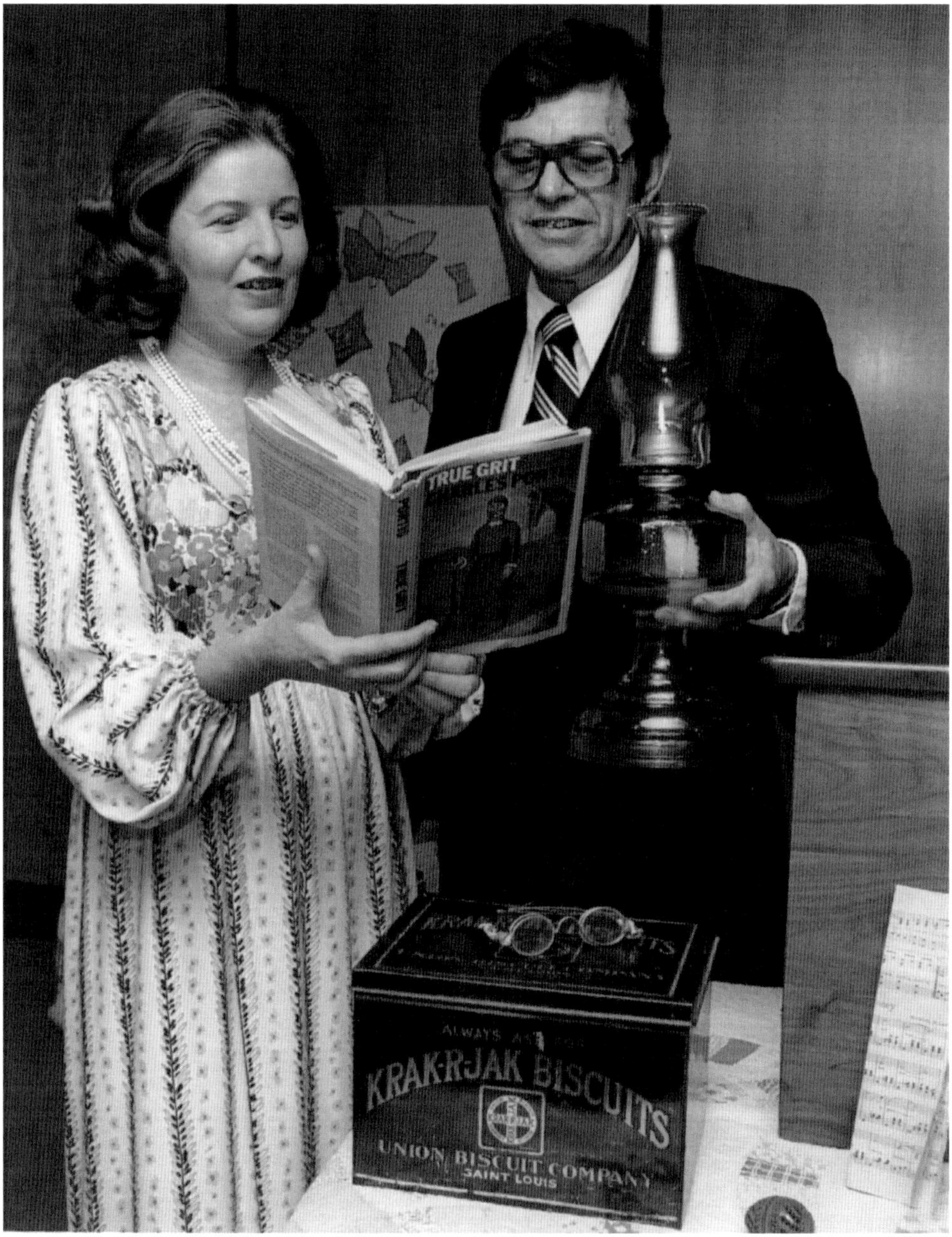

Harry W. Addison

A writer and humorist who entertained readers with tales of Depression-era America, Harry W. Addison, a World War II veteran awarded a Bronze Star for bravery in combat at Iwo Jima, published three books, all semi-autobiographical vignettes of his life growing up in northeast Louisiana.

His works include *Mama Was a Con Man, Papa Was a Christian*; *Write That Down For Me Daddy*; and *RFD #3*, the first chapter of which is entitled "Route 3, Monroe."

Addison's brand of Southern charm and homespun humor also translated into a full public speaking schedule at area civic groups, churches, and schools. He was a lifelong resident of Monroe until his passing in 2003 at the age of 83. (Courtesy of the Ouachita Parish Public Library.)

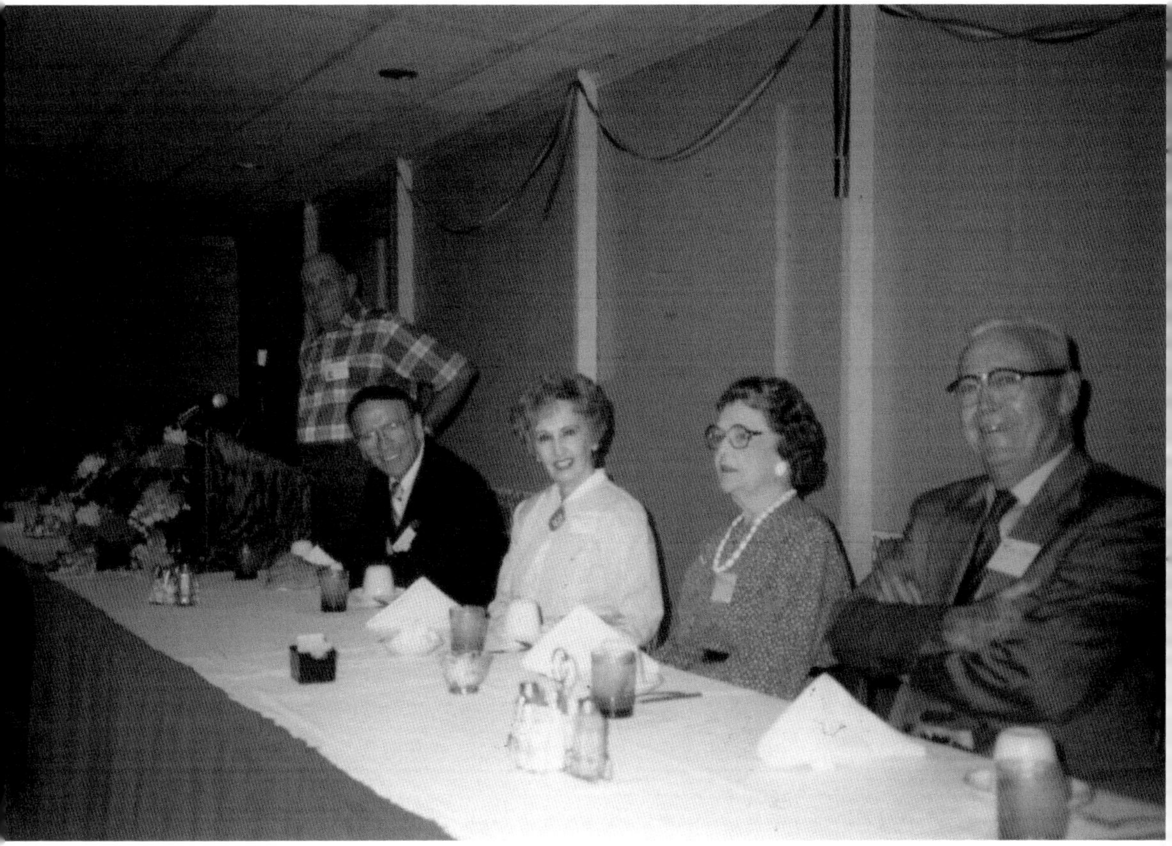

Lloyd E. Lenard

"So far out in the country from West Monroe they had to pipe sunshine to us," is how author Lloyd E. Lenard describes his upbringing in northeast Louisiana. In his 2005 book *Papa Left Us But Mama Pulled Us Through*, he details growing up on a tenant farm, part of a broken home, the second youngest of seven children.

In spite of those hardships, Lenard (second from left, seated) graduated high school and then went on to what is now the University of Louisiana at Monroe, and later Louisiana State University, where he graduated with a journalism degree.

Not solely a writer, the World War II veteran was also a reporter, radio host, politician, and successful businessman. After his service in the war, Lenard returned to north Louisiana, working first at the *Shreveport Times* before returning home to Monroe to become a television reporter for KNOE-TV8 News.

Lenard later left broadcasting to begin a successful career in the life insurance business. He served three terms on a parish commission and penned three additional books before his death in 2008 at the age of 85. (Courtesy of the Ouachita Parish Public Library.)

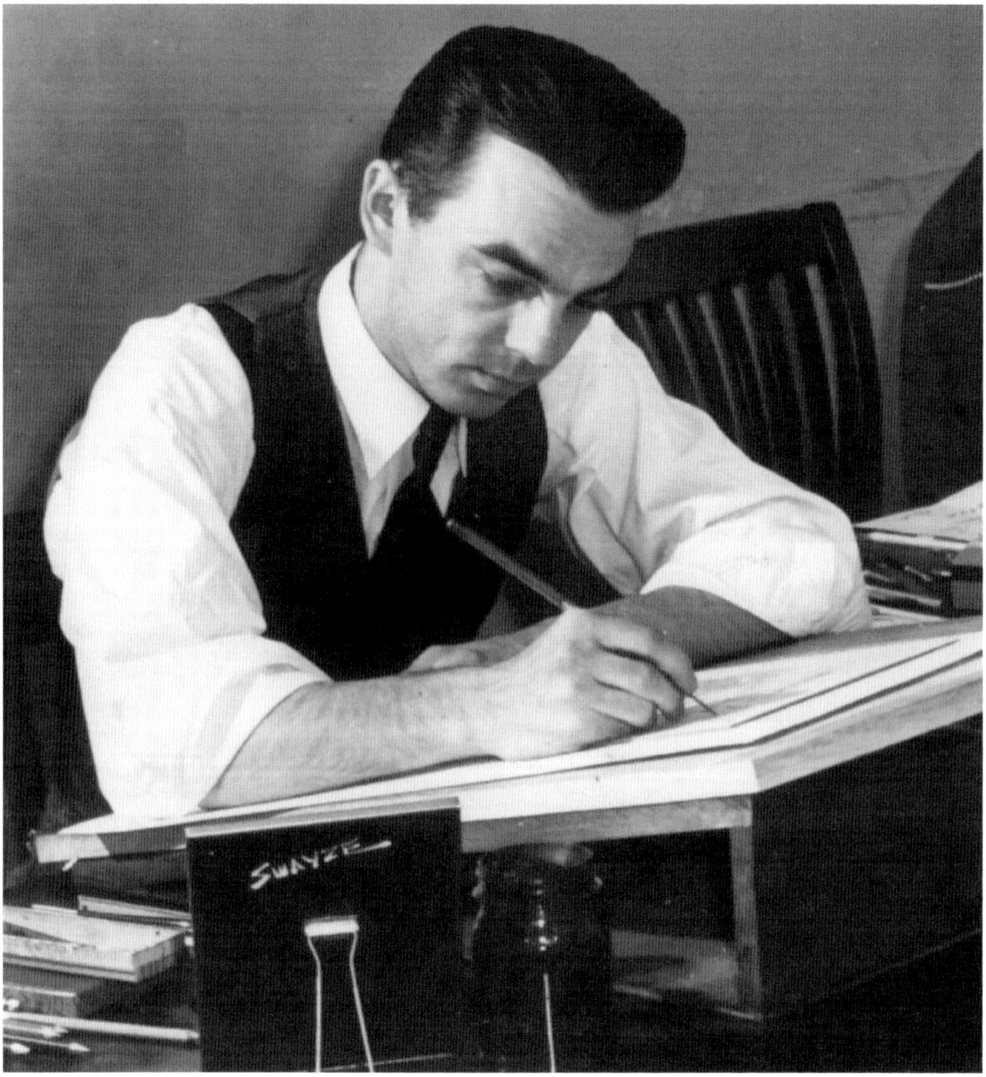

Marcus Desha "Marc" Swayze

In 2000, artist Marc Swayze told the *News-Star*, "My personal philosophy was to use the art in storytelling so that even a child who couldn't yet read could get a story out of it."

A career artist from the so-called "Golden Age of Comics," Swayze was part of a team of illustrators and writers who created Captain Marvel, the Marvel Family, and the character Mary Marvel, one of the first female superheroines to appear in ink.

Multi-talented, the Neville High School and Northeast Louisiana University graduate was also a gifted guitarist who performed with crooner Bing Crosby during his service in World War II.

In addition to creative endeavors, Swayze was also committed to community, serving on the Ouachita Parish School Board, as vice commander of the American Legion, and as a mentor to students of art and music. He stayed active in the comic book world too, with a regular column in *Alter Ego*, a bimonthly comic industry magazine focused on comics and comic creators from the 1930s through the late 1960s. Entitled *We Didn't Know It was the Golden Age*, his memoirs were published from 1996 until his death in 2012 at the age of 99. (Courtesy of P.C. Hamerlinck, Fawcett Collectors of America, editor, and Roy Thomas's *Alter Ego* magazine, twomorrows.com.)

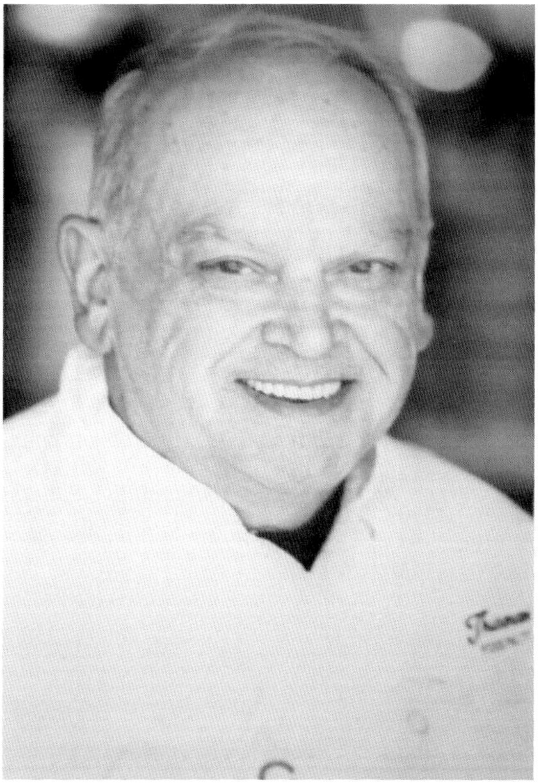

Thurman Dickey

Many consider Southern cuisine to be an art form, and Thurman Dickey is an undisputed master.

Dickey, a Winnsboro, Louisiana, native and the owner of Thurman's Food Factory in Monroe, has cooked for every Louisiana governor from Edwin Edwards to Bobby Jindal.

He has served Elvis and Sonny and Cher, and when Tim McGraw and Faith Hill got married in 1996, Thurman's Food Factory catered the event. (Left, courtesy of Thurman Dickey; below, photograph by Griffin Scott.)

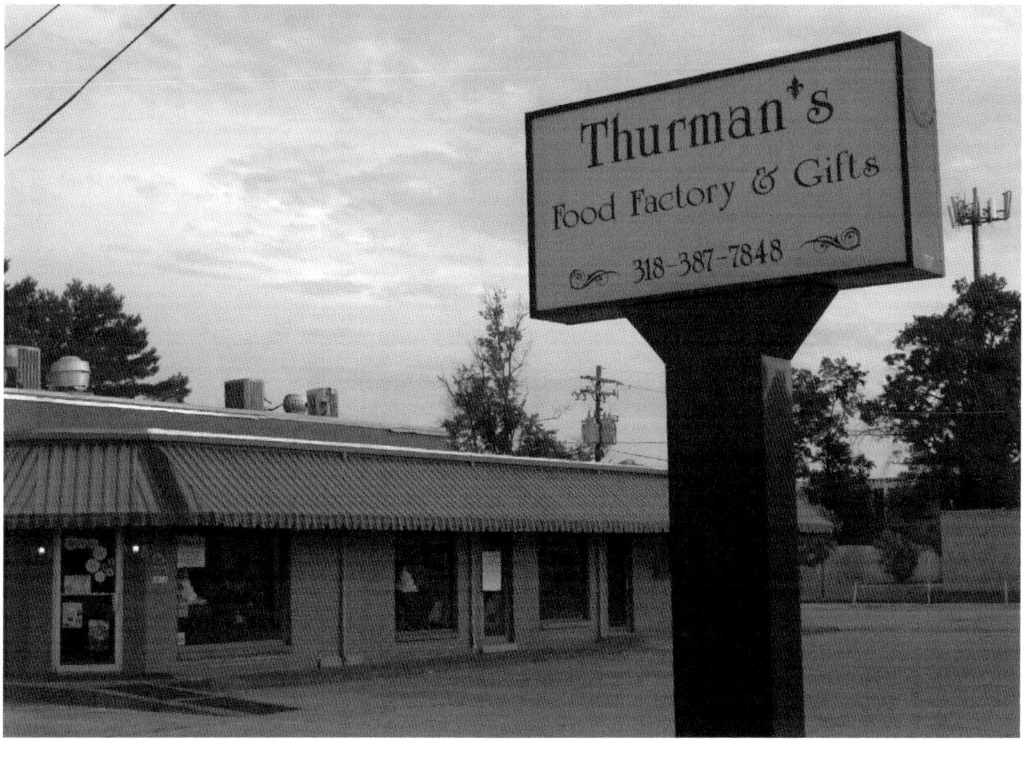

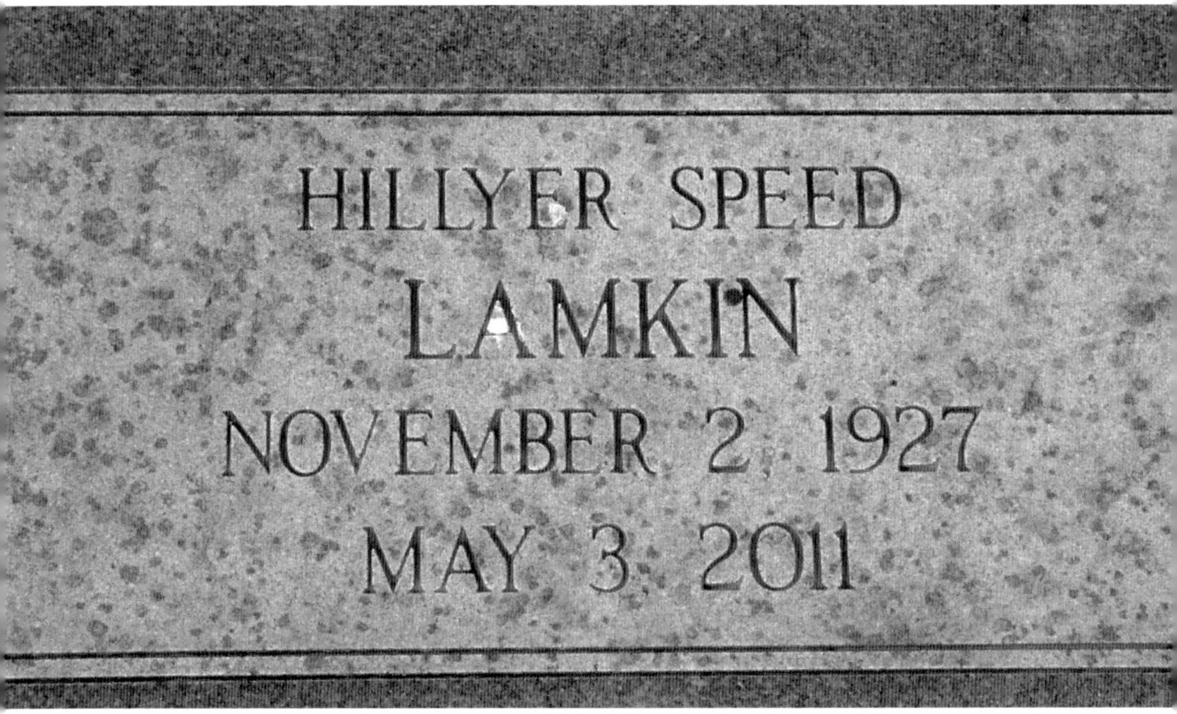

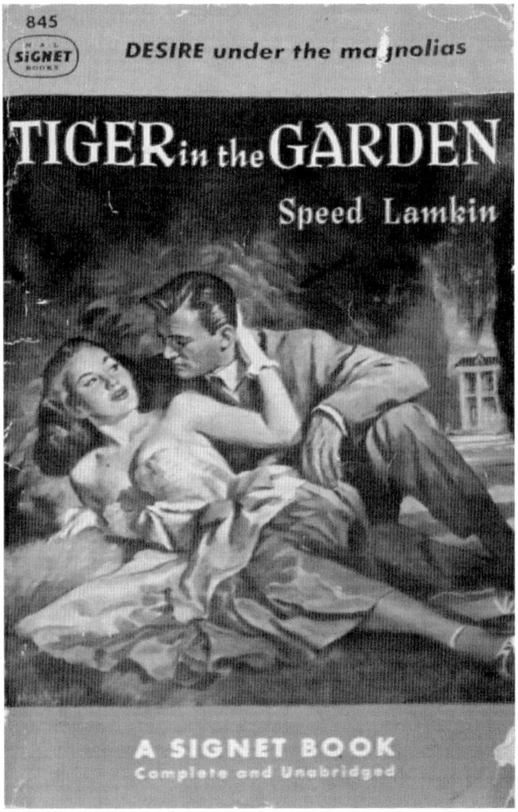

Speed Lamkin

In 1950, Hillyer Speed Lamkin was awarded the prestigious O. Henry Award for his short story "Comes a Day." Later that year, he published his debut novel, *Tiger in the Garden*, a controversial work of fiction rumored at the time to be inspired by some of Monroe's oldest, most influential families. Due to his success, Lamkin came to be known as a "poor man's Truman Capote." According to legend, upon hearing the label, Tennessee Williams noted of Lamkin, "He doesn't write as well but is more agreeable."

He remains one of Monroe's most celebrated creative visionaries. (Both photographs by Griffin Scott.)

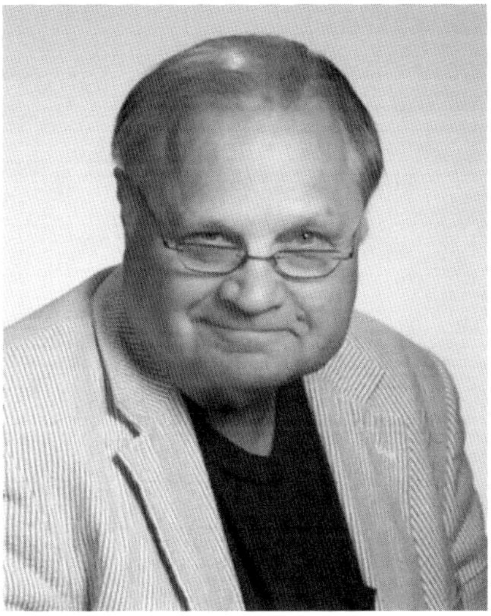

Wiley Hilburn Jr.

As an ambitious young man, Wiley Hilburn Jr. embarked on a journalism career, writing for his hometown paper, the *Ruston Daily Leader*, when he was only 16 years old. According to an interview he gave to the *Louisiana Anthology* podcast just a few months before his death in 2014, his early years covering the local scene were memorable.

One night in 1959, a young Hilburn was sent out to report on a car accident that had claimed the lives of seven college students. Just a few hours after leaving that horrible scene, he was covering a local baseball game; such is the life of a reporter.

He attended Louisiana Tech University (Tech), and later, Louisiana State University, earning a master's in journalism before returning to north Louisiana to serve as a reporter, editor, and columnist for the *Monroe Morning World*, the *News-Star*, and the *Shreveport Times*.

At the age of 18, Hilburn interviewed Louisiana's 45th governor, Earl K. Long, and subsequently sat down with every remaining Louisiana governor of his lifetime, including Bobby Jindal.

In 1968, Hilburn returned to Tech to lead the journalism department, a post he held for 41 years before retiring in 2009.

Several generations of students have called Hilburn a mentor. Reggie Owens was one such student. Entering college during a turbulent time in the late 1960s, Owens met his future advisor by chance. In the same interview where Hilburn recalled the tragic wreck of 1959, he also tells of rescuing Owens from an art professor who was, in Hilburn's recollection, doing the young man a disservice. "[The professor was] chewing Reggie out 'cause he was wearing a dashiki. I said 'this kid can wear anything he wants to.' He, the professor, walked off in a huff, and I said [to Owens], 'what is your major,' and he said 'art,' so I said 'why don't you take journalism?' "

Several decades later, Owens succeeded Hilburn as chairman of the Tech journalism department. Owens recalls, "I was the first black journalism major and the first black columnist for the paper. [Hilburn] was very insistent that everybody's voice be heard even to the detriment of making some people not like him. He believed in the truth and he didn't back down from it."

In addition to his teaching duties, Hilburn continued to write. His weekly columns were published in the same Monroe and Shreveport daily newspapers where he had begun his career decades before. They were always different; one week, a tale of his youth, a sweet reminiscence of porch swings, sweet tea, and cornbread, and the next week, a thorough skewering of a Louisiana politician. Regardless of the topic, he always wrote with humor and grace.

Hilburn is also the author of three books: *New Seasons*, *Fragments*, and *Reflections of North Louisiana*. A giant in Bayou State journalism, he was inducted into the Louisiana Political Museum and Hall of Fame in 2001. (Courtesy of Greg Hilburn.)

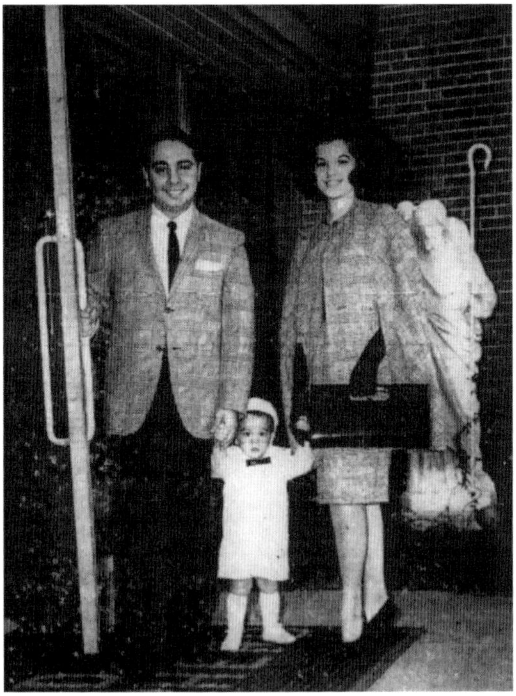

Victor Cascio

A beloved and well-known restaurateur, lifestyle guru, columnist, and television host, Victor Cascio was a Monroe notable from an early age.

As a child in the 1950s, he danced and charmed his way into local hearts on *Happiness Exchange*, an original television program originating from KNOE studios in Monroe. Until his death in 2012, the popular decorating segment *Holidays with Victor*, starring the vivacious Cascio, was a fixture on KNOE News.

Born into a prominent local restaurant family, his parents opened the Spaghetti Garden in 1943, a time when Monroe was home to Selman Field, where thousands of young American GIs trained to fight against Nazi Germany and Imperial Japan.

According to family legend, baby Victor played in a cardboard playpen while his mother, Josephine, and father, Joseph, sowed the seeds for a succession of eateries that followed, including the legendary Chateau. There, Victor and the Cascio family served everyone from Elvis to Danny Thomas to every single Louisiana governor since 1960, including Big John McKeithen and Bobby Jindal.

Cascio was not content delighting diners, however. He wanted everyone, even people who would never visit one of his restaurants, to enjoy the experience of dining, particularly for holiday feasts. As the host of *Holidays*, he advised generations of locals on just about every table-setting imaginable, including Sunday dinners, casual birthdays, St. Patrick's Day bashes, formal Christmas parties, and every seasonal celebration in between.

As Monroe's most gracious host, he was also a much-loved figure and, by all accounts, a true gentleman.

Only a few months before his death, the *Hawkeye*, a University of Louisiana at Monroe campus newspaper, asked him for his fondest memory. He recalled, "When Liberace was here. My mother tried on all of his jewels and his mink coat."

After his passing, former Louisiana fifth district congressman Rodney Alexander stood up on the floor of the US Capitol and said on record of the late Cascio, "To say that he left his fingerprint on the world would be an understatement. Victor Cascio brought joy to so many, and he will live in our hearts forever." (Courtesy of the Ouachita Parish Public Library.)

CHAPTER SEVEN

Musicians, Actors, and Perfoming Artists

Keeping up with Louisiana's theatrical, musical culture, Monroe's legendary performing artists have produced a rich tapestry of work that has made a lasting mark in the realm of entertainment.

A slew of notable musicians from an impressive cross-section of genres, including country, rock, jazz, classical, and blues, pepper our list. Meet a country singer who perfected his craft in front of local crowds before taking Nashville, and the world, by storm.

Also hailing from this tiny river city is one of the greatest jazz trombonists in music history, a master who played on over 70 albums and shared stages with Duke Ellington, Benny Goodman, Sammy Davis Jr., and Frank Sinatra, just to name a few.

Monroe can also claim a multitalented rock-n-roller who not only fronts his own chart-topping band but also finds time to write and produce hits for groups such as crossover sensation Sugarland and pop smash Train. After a humble start playing area skating rinks, yet another local notable has jammed alongside such top-shelf musicians as Keith Richards and Herbie Hancock.

The daughter of one of Louisiana's most prominent historical figures and celebrated businessmen was herself a gifted, successful opera singer whose talents took her far from the banks of the Ouachita River to the delight of audiences around the globe, much like a world-renowned classical composer who has also appeared with orchestras all over America, as well as in London, Hong Kong, Sydney, and Rome.

Also making the list is an intellectual who established the University of Louisiana at Monroe's theater and speech department, an immeasurable contribution that continues to enrich the community to this day. Named professor emeritus during his teaching tenure, this local legend also has the distinction of being a member of the very first cast to perform onstage at Monroe's Strauss Theatre.

A category-five hurricane drove one New Orleans–based star of the classic television drama *Peyton Place* to the northeast corner of the state, where he still resides nearly 10 years later. Three more who count Monroe as their hometown are a very successful Broadway producer of such iconic shows as *Bye Bye Birdie*, an "Indie Queen" of film who remembers her Monroe-area upbringing less than fondly, and a groundbreaking African American actor who played a very famous sidekick to Charlie Chan in several movies.

The creative talent pool is deep in northeast Louisiana, and while many of the biggest and brightest have moved away to larger cities to pursue their dreams of music, movie, and stage stardom, this collection of artists and performers will all be remembered for cultural contributions, locally and beyond.

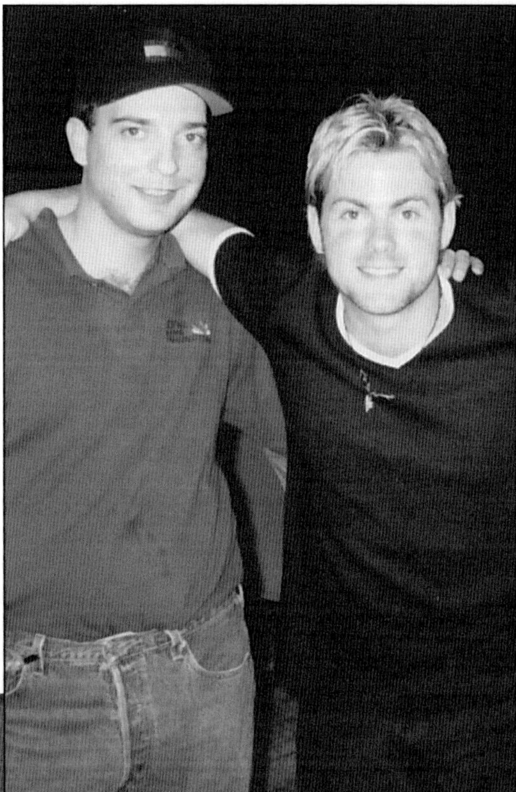

Andy Griggs

Raised on what he calls a "gumbo of rock-a-billy, country, gospel, and hard rock," Andy Griggs shot to the top of music charts in 1999 with the hit *You Won't Ever Be Lonely*, a single that reached country music gold, propelling the Monroe-bred musician to bonafide stardom.

Like fellow northeast Louisiana native Tim McGraw, Griggs (pictured at right in the image at left) attended Northeast Louisiana University and got his start playing to tiny crowds in small venues in and around the area. (Both courtesy of Joey Cruse.)

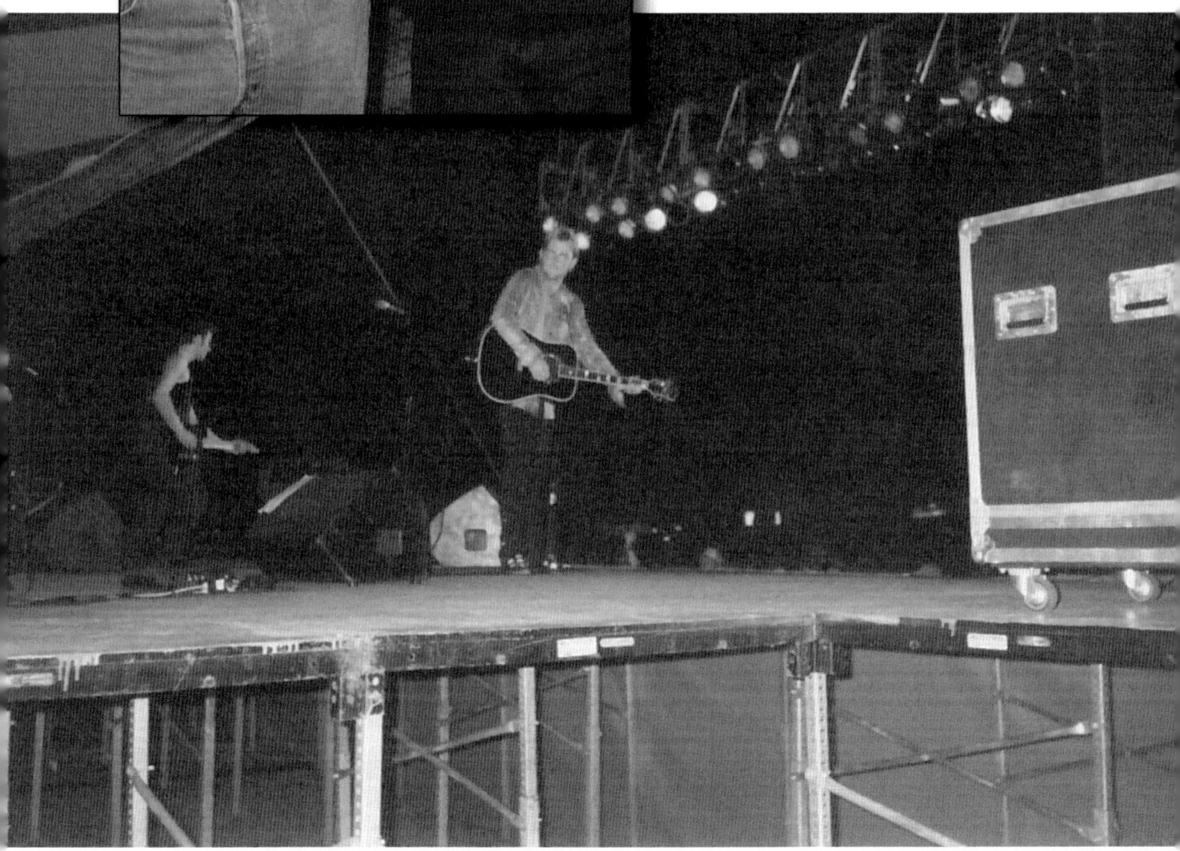

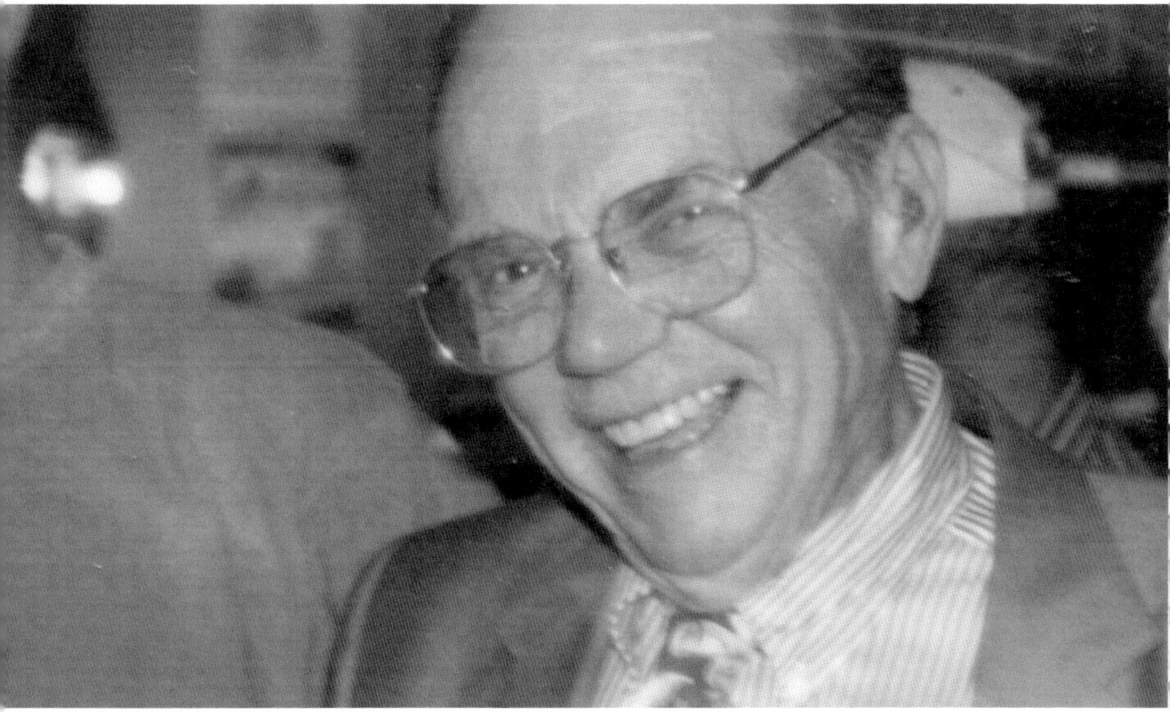

Christopher Ringham

Christopher Ringham delighted generations of Monroe and northeast Louisiana residents during his 34-year tenure as director of the Strauss Theatre Center. After earning a master's from the University of Minnesota, Ringham served as the director of theaters across the country before landing in Monroe, where he lived until his death in 2003.

Ringham did not just entertain, he also inspired a love of theater and arts in area youth. In 1984, his lifelong dream was realized when the Younge Troupe, a children's theater offshoot of the Strauss Theatre Center, was formed.

His legacy will always be a part of the Strauss Theatre Center. The theater's annual awards ceremony is named in his honor, where winners are rewarded for excellence in performing and directing with a Christopher Award.

Following his death, instead of a traditional funeral, a memorial was held at his beloved Strauss Theatre, where Ringham's ashes were permanently placed in the courtyard. (Courtesy of the Strauss Theatre Center.)

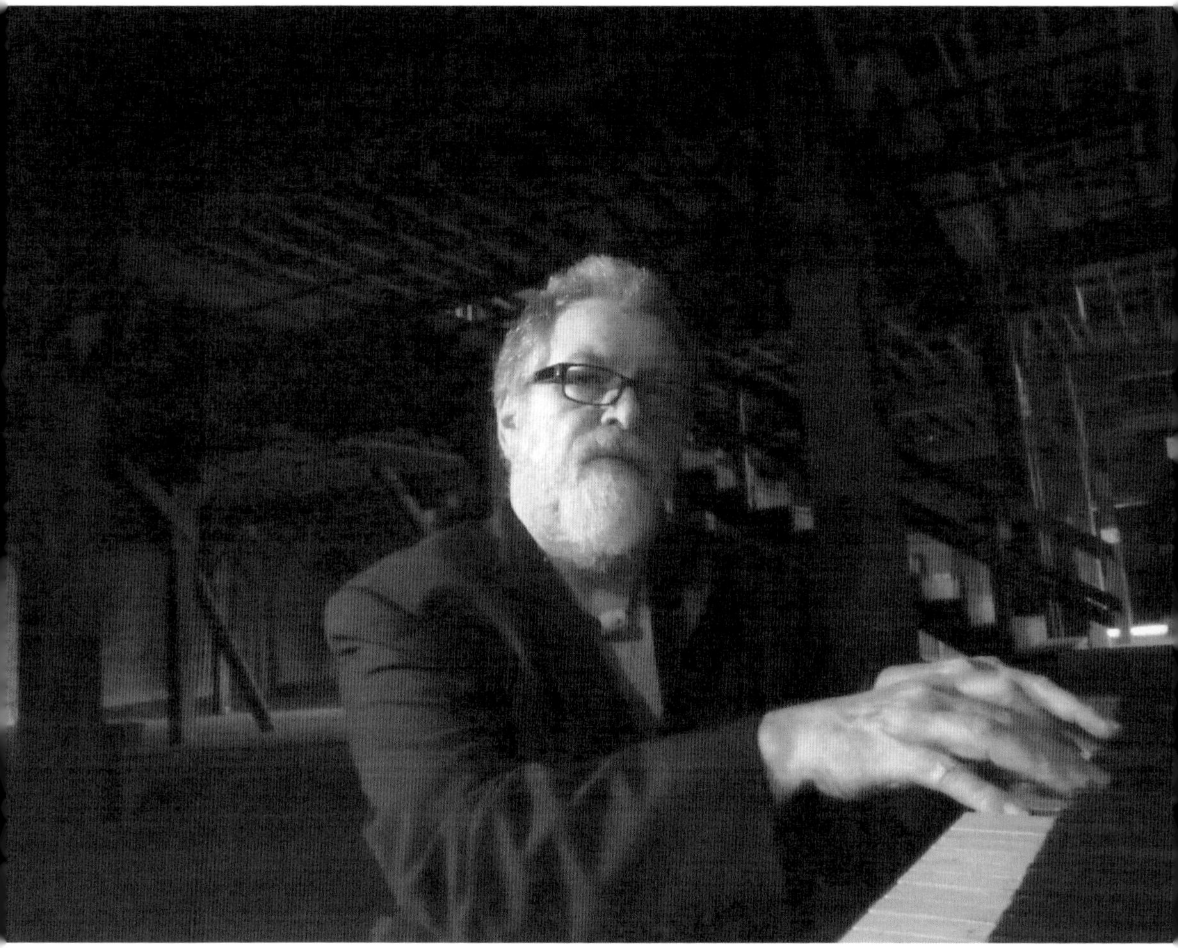

Doug Duffey

Multitalented performing artist Doug Duffey began his professional music career at the tender age of 14. After paying his dues at school dances and skating rinks, Duffey left Monroe and toured the nation, playing with celebrated artists like jazz legend Herbie Hancock and Rolling Stones guitarist Keith Richards.

A musician, vocalist, and composer, Duffey is a regular performer at the New Orleans Jazz & Heritage Festival, the Montreal Jazz Festival, and the Louisiana Folk Life Festival. He has been a member of the Louisiana Hall of Fame since 2001 and was inducted into the National Blues Hall of Fame in 2009.

When not touring the globe with the Doug Duffey International Soul Band, he resides in the Monroe home built by his grandfather in the 1920s. (Courtesy of Doug Duffey.)

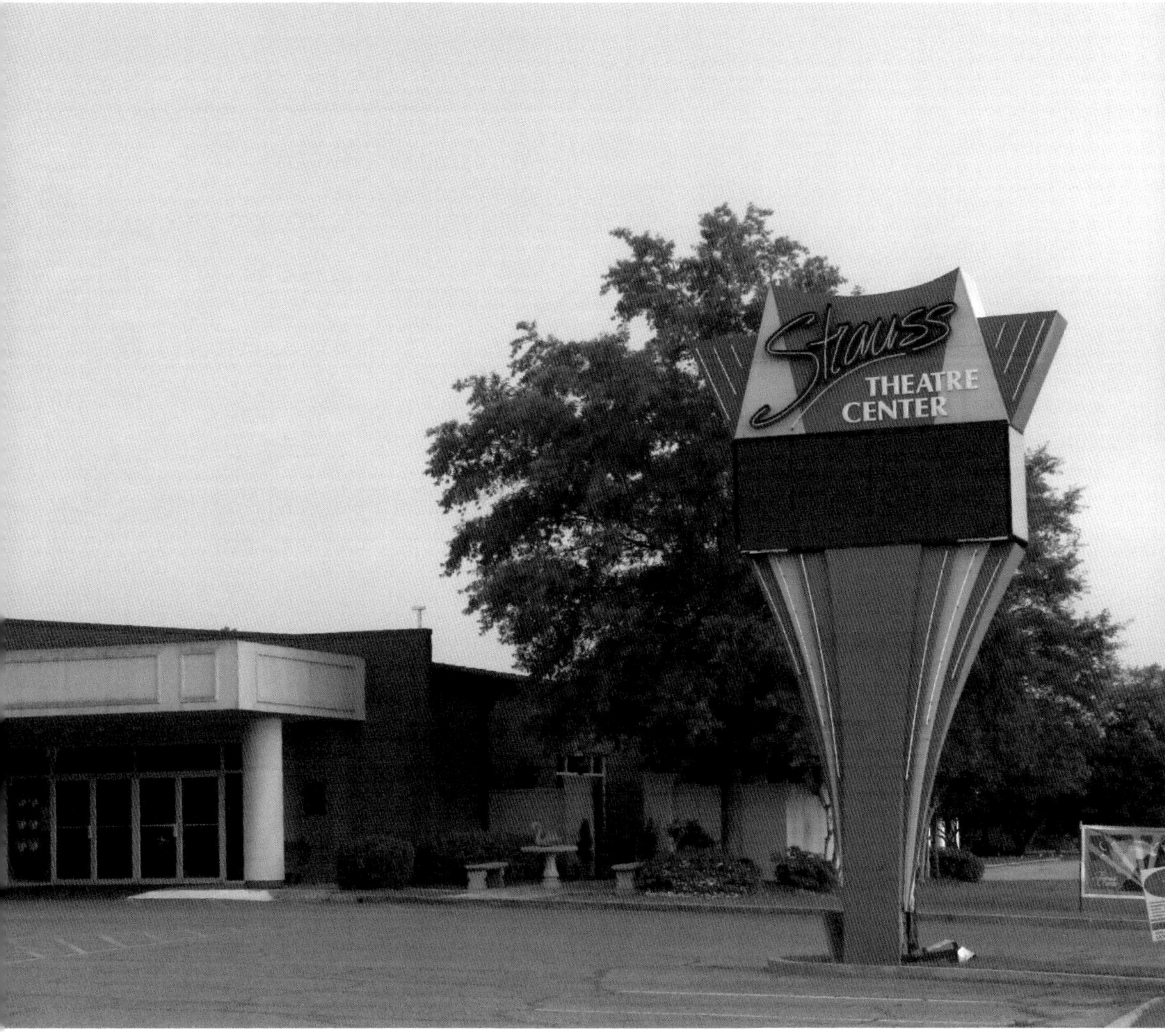

Dr. George Brian

During his lifetime, George C. Brian, PhD, had a massive cultural impact on Monroe. He established the theater and speech department at Northeast Louisiana University in 1953, inspired and mentored young performers as the director of Monroe's Youth Theatre, produced films and documentaries about northeast Louisiana, and delighted tens of thousands of patrons of the Twin City Ballet for over 30 years as a popular actor, singer, and dancer.

When Monroe's historic Strauss Theatre opened in 1961, Brian was featured in a role as the devil in *Damn Yankees*, the newly opened theater's debut production.

In 2007, the multitalented Brian, a professor emeritus of speech and theater at the University of Louisiana at Monroe, died at his home in Monroe. (Photograph by Griffin Scott.)

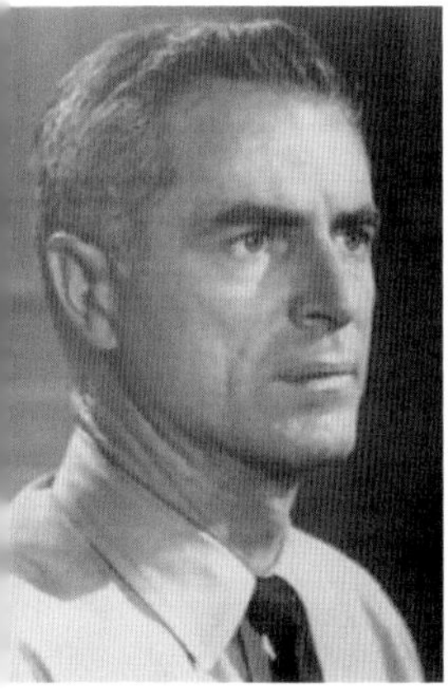

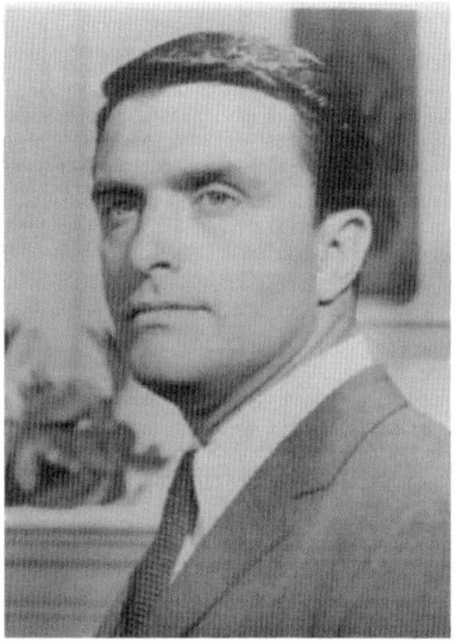

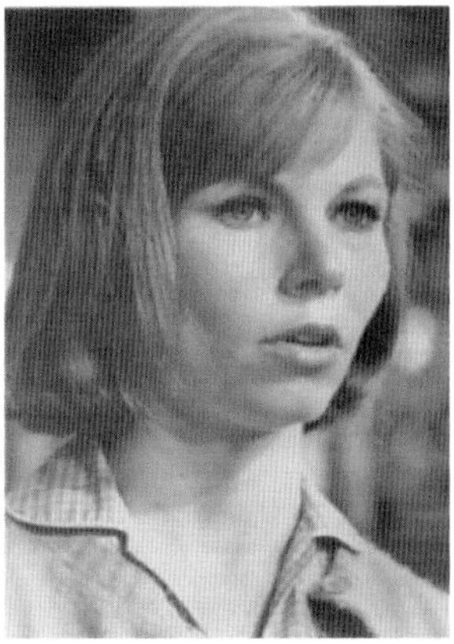

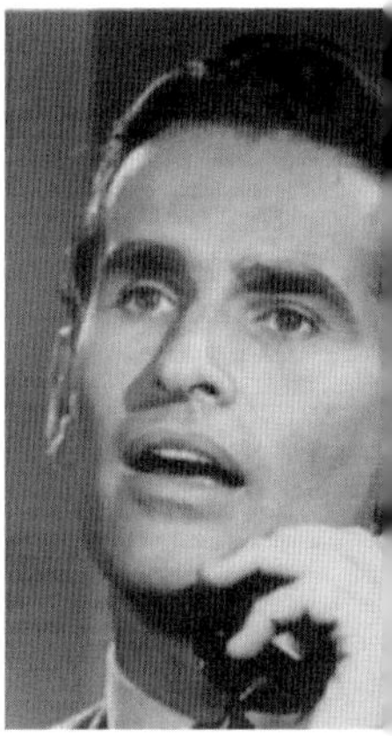

Ed Nelson

New Orleans native and *Peyton Place* star Ed Nelson was driven to the northeast corner of Louisiana in August 2005, when the category-five Hurricane Katrina devastated the Big Easy, sending hundreds of thousands of evacuees clamoring for drier lands in the midst of a violent, destructive storm.

Nelson (above, second from left and at right, center) secured his place in Hollywood history when he won the role of Dr. Michael Rossi in the first primetime television soap opera, *Peyton Place*.

As of 2014, Nelson still resides in his adopted hometown. (Both photographs by ABC Television.)

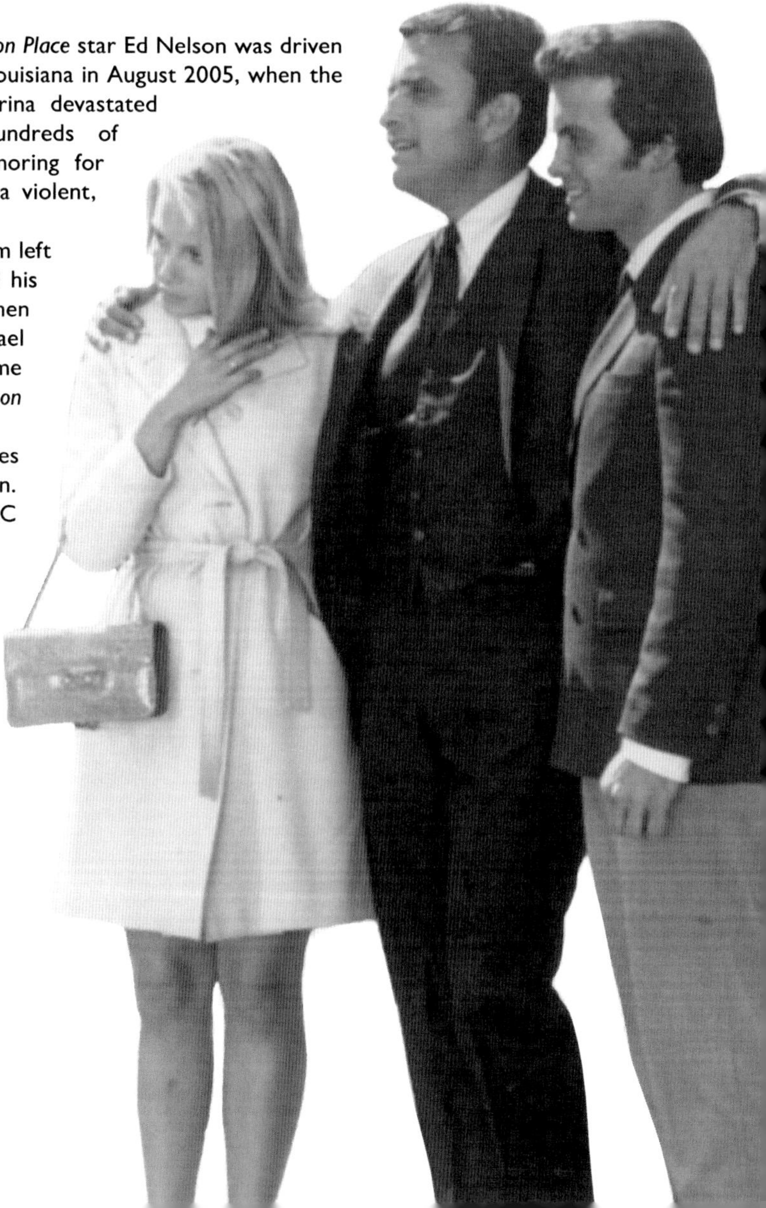

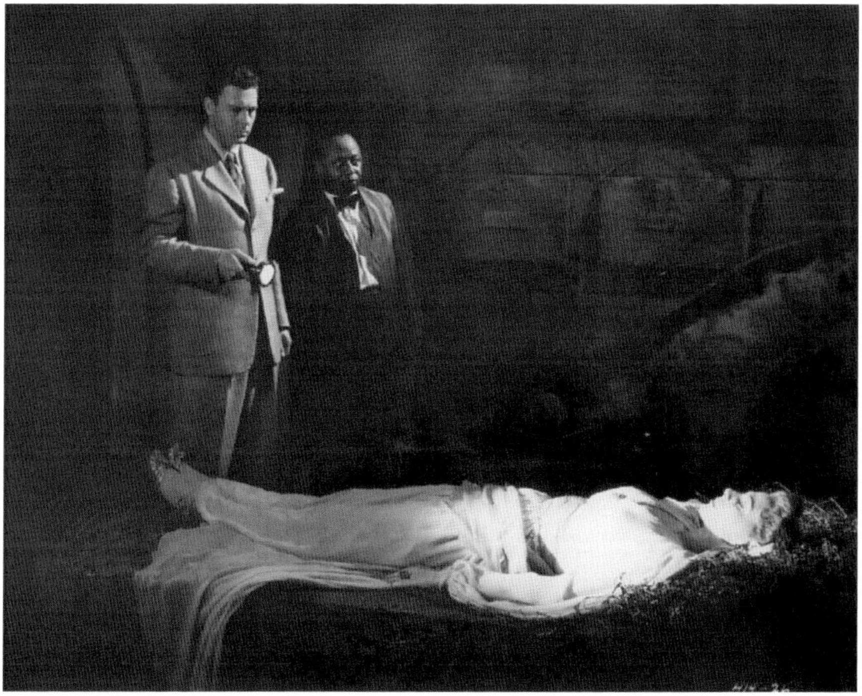

Mantan Moreland

Just after the dawning of the 20th century, African American actor Mantan Moreland was born in Monroe. A natural performer, Moreland ran away from home and joined the circus at the age of 12. He eventually returned home, but his urge to perform did not die.

Moreland went on to appear in hundreds of films. His most notable role was as Birmingham Brown, the sidekick and chauffeur of Charlie Chan. (Both photographs by Monogram Pictures.)

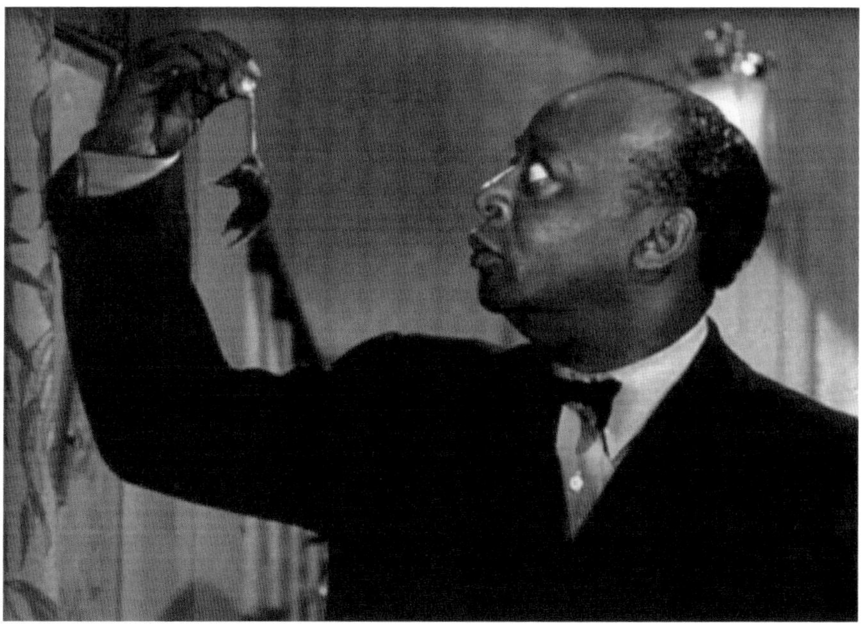

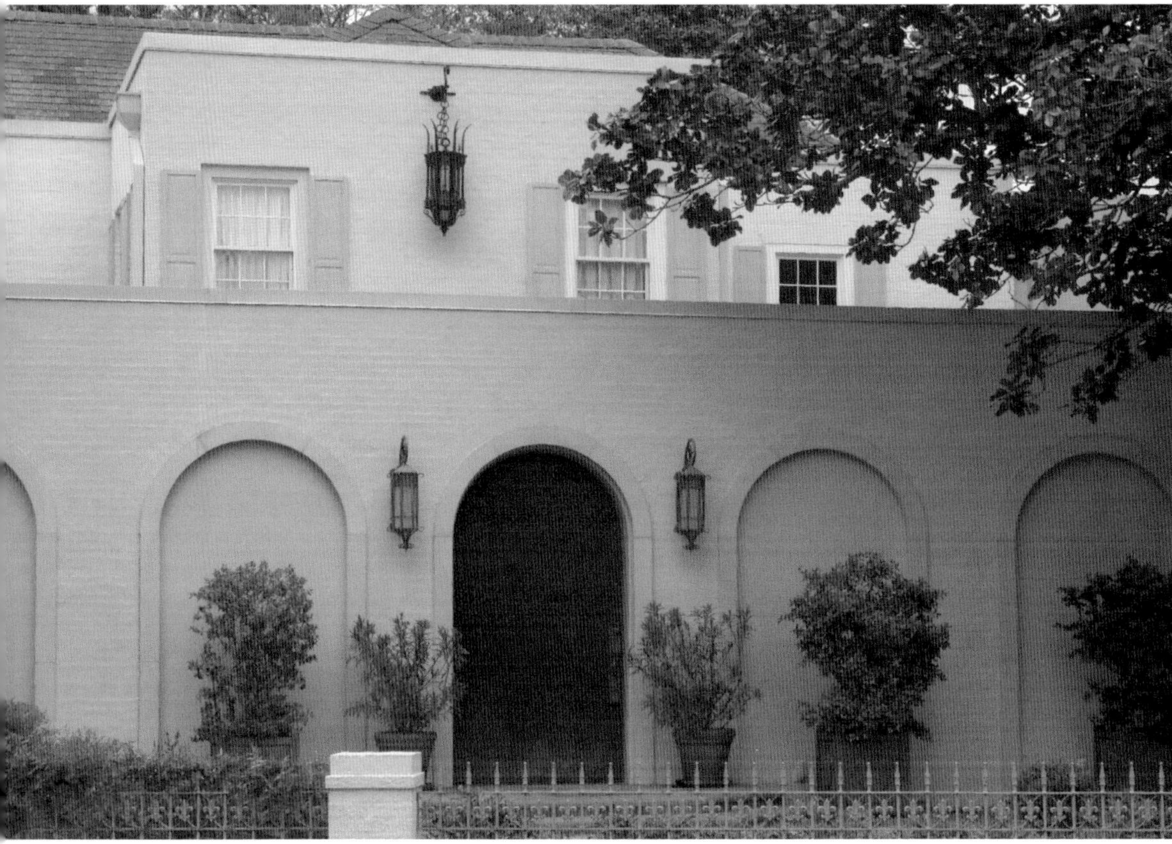

Emy Lou Biedenharn (ABOVE AND OPPOSITE PAGE)
Emy Lou Biedenharn was the daughter of Joseph Biedenharn, the first bottler of Coca-Cola and the cofounder of Delta Airlines, but, as an opera singer with remarkable abilities, the younger Biedenharn made an imprint all her own.

Successful and critically acclaimed, Biedenharn spent many years in Europe, but Adolph Hitler's relentless march across the continent ended all that. In 1939, Biedenharn retired from active performing, returning to Monroe, where she spent the rest of her days living in the Biedenharn family home, transforming the grounds into a magnificent series of gardens. (Above, photograph by Griffin Scott; opposite page, courtesy of the Biedenharn Museum & Gardens.)

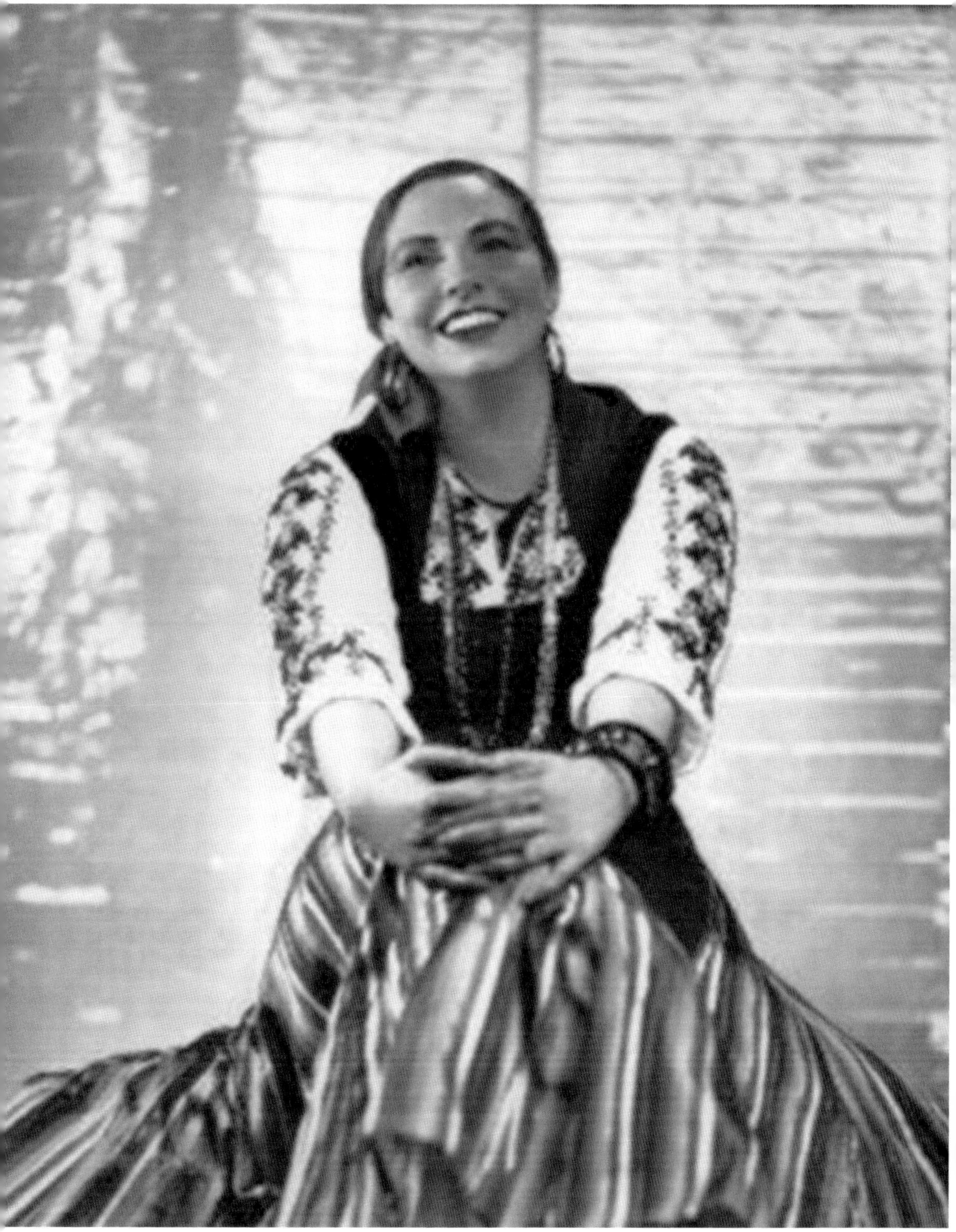

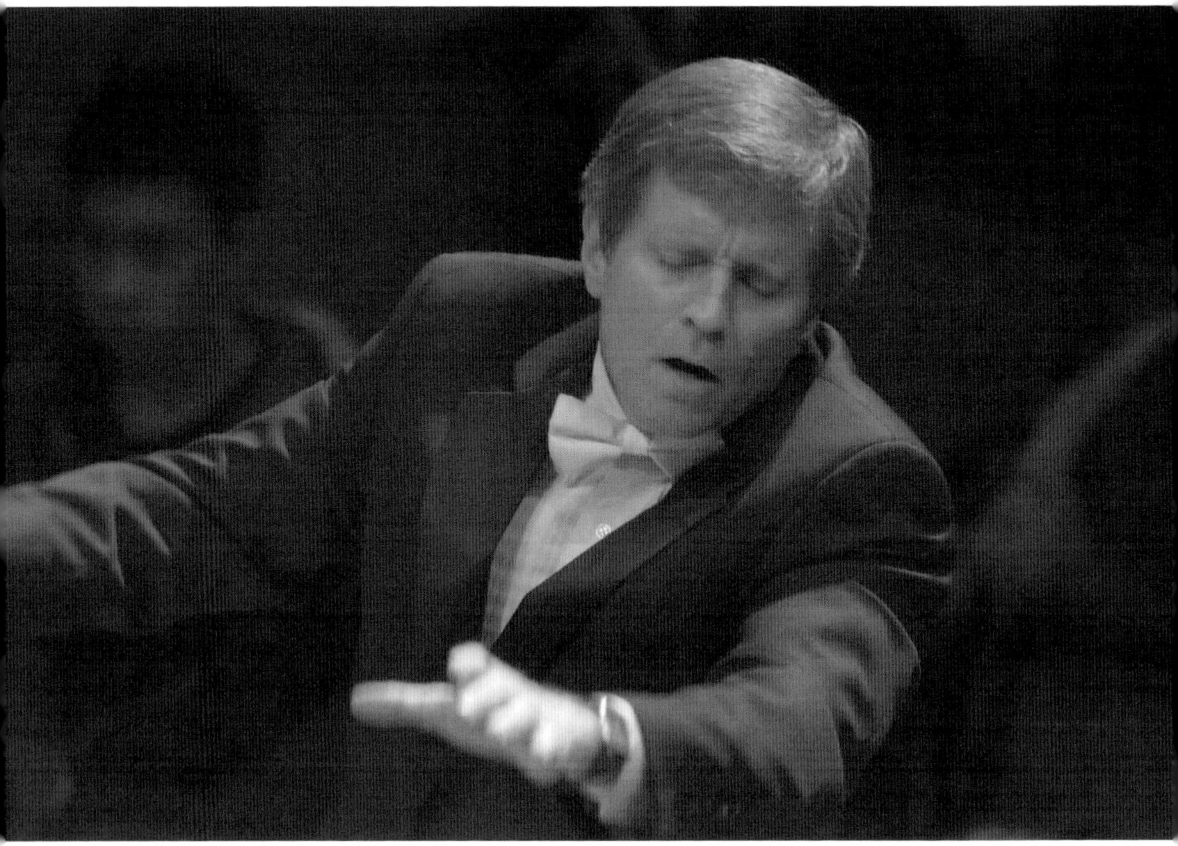

Frank Ticheli

Although acclaimed composer Frank Ticheli was born in Monroe, orchestras the world over have performed his exquisite works.

After earning doctoral and master's degrees in music composition from the University of Michigan, Ticheli has appeared with orchestras from around the globe, in global cultural capitals like London, Hong Kong, Sydney, and Rome. He has also served as a guest conductor of his own compositions at the prestigious Carnegie Hall.

A professor of composition at the University of Southern California, Ticheli continues to compose music and inspire new artists, overseeing an international music composition contest launched in 2005 that bears his name. (Above, photograph by Graham Lindsey/Wavelength Media, courtesy of Frank Ticheli; right, photograph by Charlie Grosso, courtesy of Frank Ticheli.)

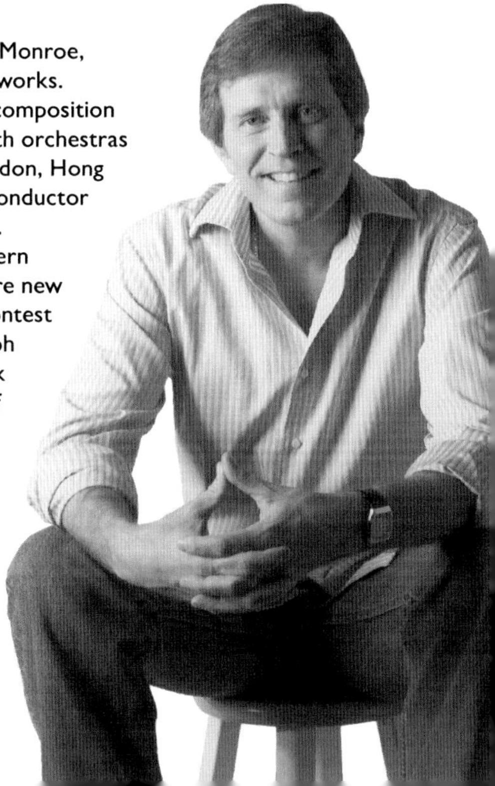

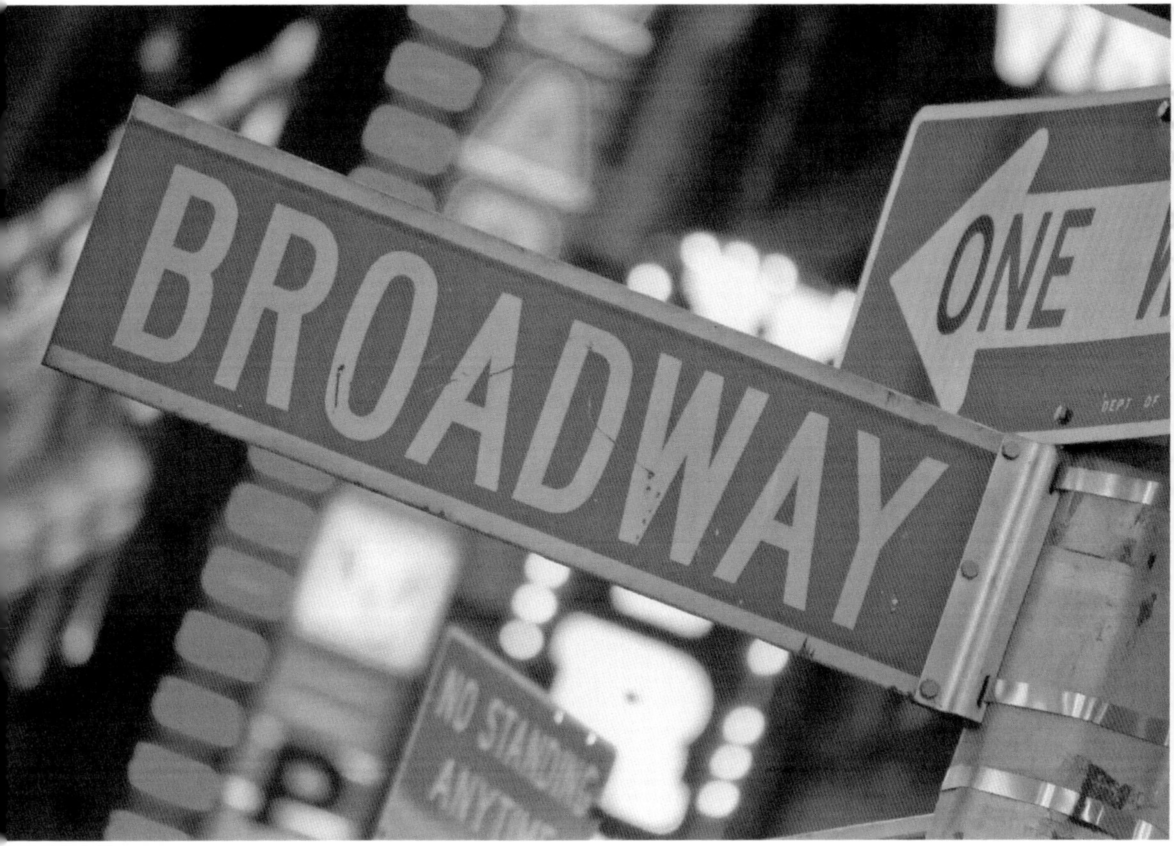

Luther "L." Slade Brown

A man of diverse interests, Lutcher "L." Slade Brown was the president of the company that founded a West Monroe paper mill still in existence today, as well as an enormously successful Broadway producer.

Brown financed the Tony Award–winning *Bye Bye Birdie* in 1961. The show, which featured a young Dick Van Dyke, as well as Chita Rivera and Richard Gautier, was a tremendous hit. He later produced several other knockouts, including *All American* and *A Joyful Noise*. (Photograph by Darren Johnson.)

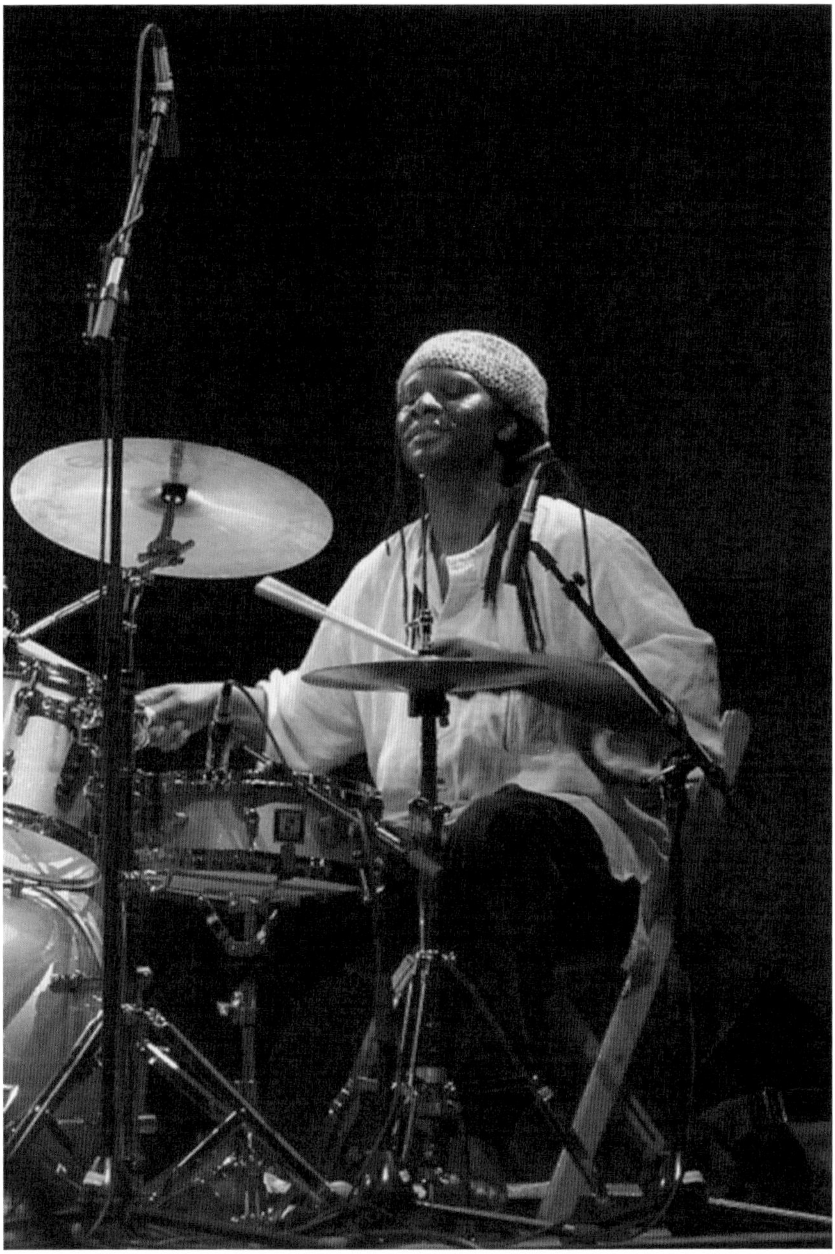

Hamid Drake

Born in 1955, jazz and avant garde drummer Hamid Drake used hometown connections to become an international star. After moving to Chicago in the 1960s, Drake met a kindred spirit who was, coincidentally, a fellow Monroe native, saxophonist Fred Anderson, a man Drake cites as his greatest musical influence.

After mastering the traditional drum set, Drake branched out, temporarily tossing his drum sticks to explore hand percussion, which he incorporated into his unique style of freestyle jazz.

Today, Drake conducts jazz workshops when he is not touring the world, performing and recording with fellow jazz legends like Archie Shepp and Herbie Hancock. (Photograph by Michael Hoefner.)

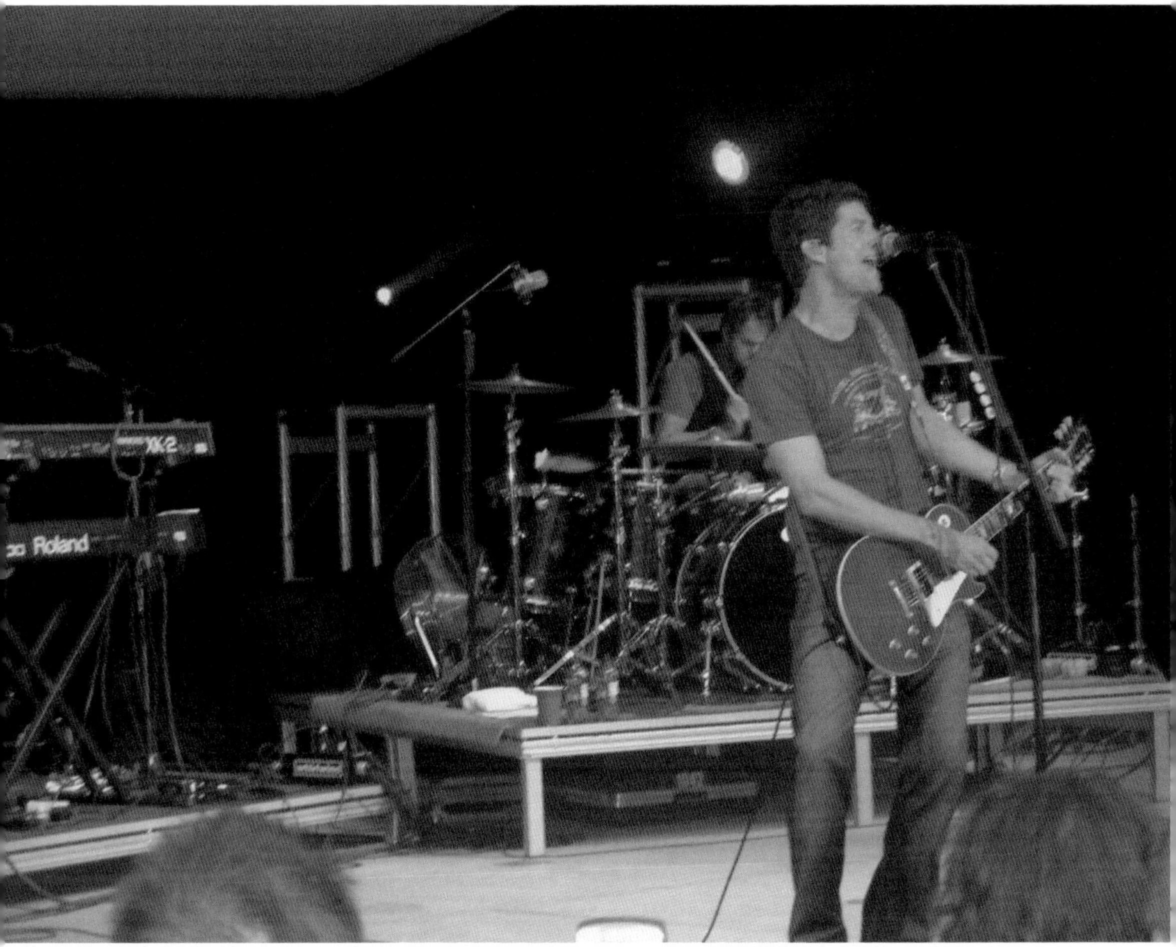

Kevin Griffin

After graduating high school in Monroe, musician Kevin Griffin set off for college at Louisiana State University, where he met fellow students and musicians Joel Rundell, Tom Drummond, and Cary Bonnacaze. The foursome formed a band in 1988, becoming known as alternative rockers Better than Ezra.

Paying their dues on the New Orleans music scene, the group perfected their sound and found commercial success with the hit single "Good." A follow-up album later produced two top-10 hits, establishing Better than Ezra as a major rock act.

Griffin has stretched himself creatively in recent years. In addition to his work with the band that made him famous, he has also written and produced hits for pop groups like Sugarland and Train. (Photograph by Jessica Fiess-Hill.)

Parker Posey (OPPOSITE PAGE)
Restlessness has always motivated actress Parker Posey, who originally embraced acting as a means of escaping her upbringing in Monroe.

Posey left the bayous and pine forests of northeast Louisiana behind, finding her big break in 1991 on the CBS soap opera *As the World Turns*. Two years later, Posey made her major motion picture debut in the cult coming-of-age classic *Dazed and Confused*.

Following a string of lead roles in independent films, earning her the Indie Queen moniker, Posey recently returned to her small-screen roots with memorable guest-starring roles on *Louie* and *The Good Wife*. (Courtesy of the Ouachita Parish Public Library.)

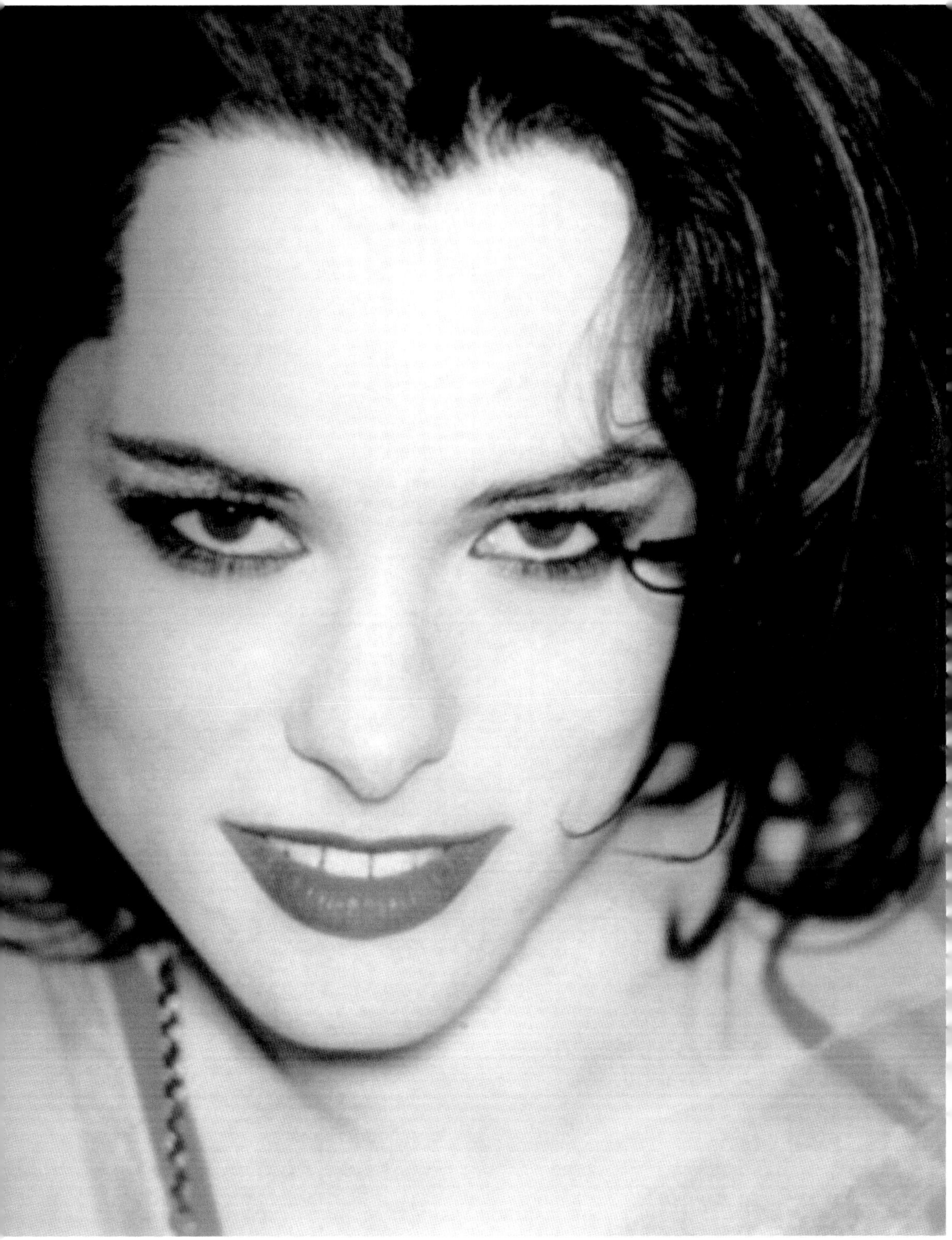

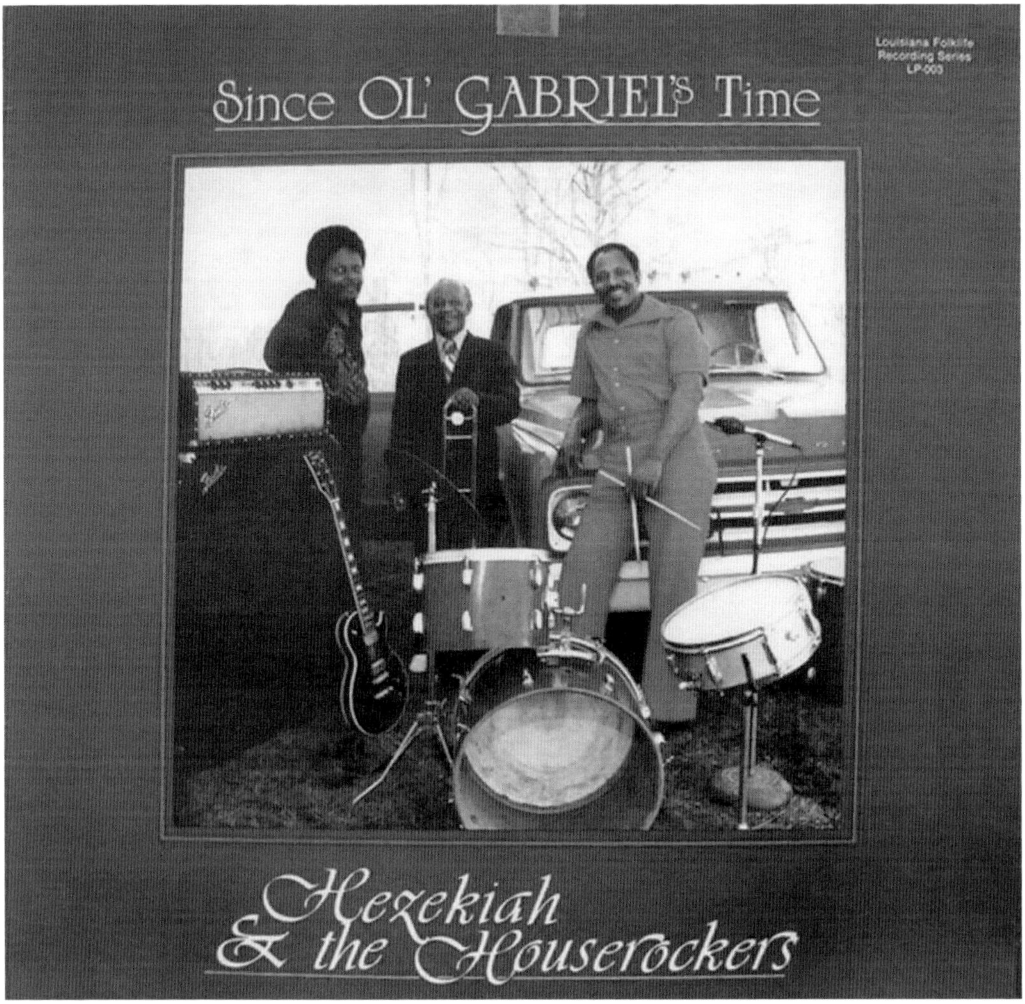

Leon "Pee Wee" Whittaker

The product of a broken home, some of Leon "Pee Wee" Whittaker's earliest memories were of touring with his mother, Kizzie, an accomplished musician. The elder Whittaker took young Leon along when she toured until he was old enough to attend school, after which he lived with his maternal grandfather, himself an avid violinist.

Whittaker was living in Monroe when he joined the famed Rabbit's Foot Company, a variety troupe that toured the region, producing shows for audiences across the South.

Although he became well known as a proficient trombonist, Whitaker was also a skilled mandolin, guitar, and clarinet player.

Whittaker died in 1993. He was inducted into the Delta Music Museum in 2002. Pictured here from left to right are James Baker, Whittaker, and Hezekiah Early. (Courtesy of the Louisiana Folklife Center.)

CHAPTER EIGHT

Politicians and Public Servants

What does one think of when they hear the words "Louisiana politics?" Historically, the Bayou State is famous, or perhaps infamous, for its unique blend of Southern fried politics.

But behind the smoke and mirrors of political rhetoric, campaign slogans, bumper stickers, and yard signs are the men and women who dedicate their lives to public service. This chapter is an effort to examine the people behind the politicians.

There are several long-term incumbents among the mayors profiled in this chapter, including Monroe's current chief executive, a former Northeast Louisiana University (now University of Louisiana at Monroe) basketball star who has held the office since 2001.

Another mayor was remembered decades after his death when a major bridge connecting the Twin Cities was renamed in his honor. It was a fitting tribute, as this gentleman, a German immigrant and six-term incumbent known as Monroe's "Reconstruction Mayor," was the first person to walk across the structure, then a footbridge, when it opened for traffic on July 4, 1899.

There is a profile of the first African American mayor of Monroe, as well as the story of a lieutenant colonel in the Army who served briefly as the city's leader after the incumbent abruptly resigned mid-term.

Several current and former members of the Louisiana legislature are featured here, including one of Louisiana's few female state representatives.

If old-school Louisiana political opulence and good old-fashioned charm is what the reader seeks, the story of a representative named Shady, a colorful character with a penchant for carrying a pistol underneath the layers of his flamboyant suits who splits his free time between a West Monroe mansion and a bright pink downtown Monroe penthouse, more than delivers.

Meet a state senator who went on to become president of the University of Louisiana at Monroe, a few judges, including one justice of the Louisiana Supreme Court, and a Louisiana broadcaster turned governor who only spent a few months in office.

There is a Monroe city councilman who was part of a family that ran a downtown business for 123 years, an oilman who served one of the shortest terms in US Senate history, and a US congressman who represented Monroe and the surrounding region during the height of the Great Depression.

The players in the Louisiana political landscape are themselves as diverse and interesting as the scene itself.

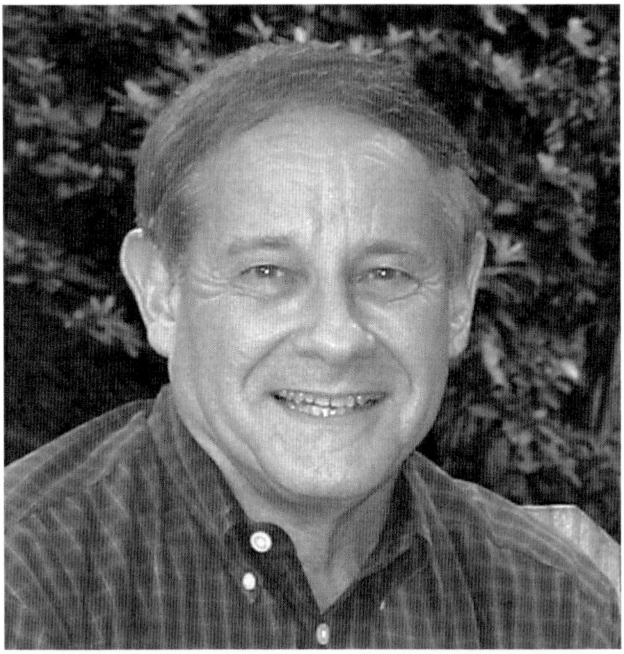

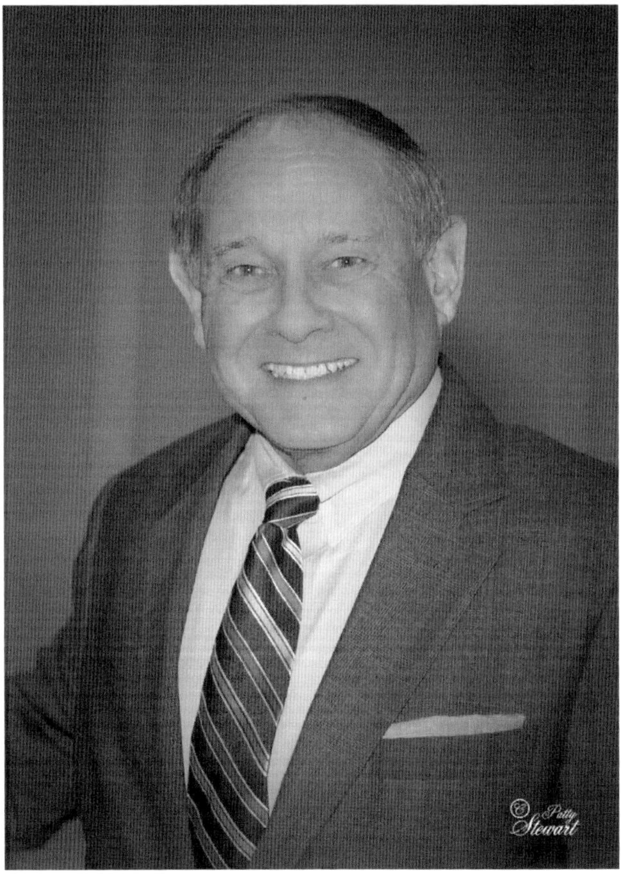

Robert Kostelka

A native of Shreveport, Robert W. "Bob" Kostelka left northwest Louisiana for this part of the boot several decades ago.

After Kostelka graduated from historic Byrd High School, he first attended Centenary College before going on to law school at Louisiana State University.

He worked in private practice, as a district attorney, and as a judge before winning election to the Louisiana state senate in 2003. (Both courtesy of Robert Kostelka.)

Abe Pierce

Abe Edward Pierce III made history in 1996 when he was elected the first African American mayor in the history of Monroe.

Pierce, the son of Dr. Abe Pierce II, one of Monroe's first African American dentists, came from pioneering stock. This legacy of success, combined with a community spirit and 24 years of public service experience as a Ouachita Parish police juror, were major catalysts in his mayoral victory.

In 2000, he was defeated by local businessman Melvin Rambin in a bid for reelection. Rambin died unexpectedly only two months into his term, paving the way for Monroe's second African American mayor, James E. "Jamie" Mayo, profiled on page 83. (Courtesy of the City of Monroe.)

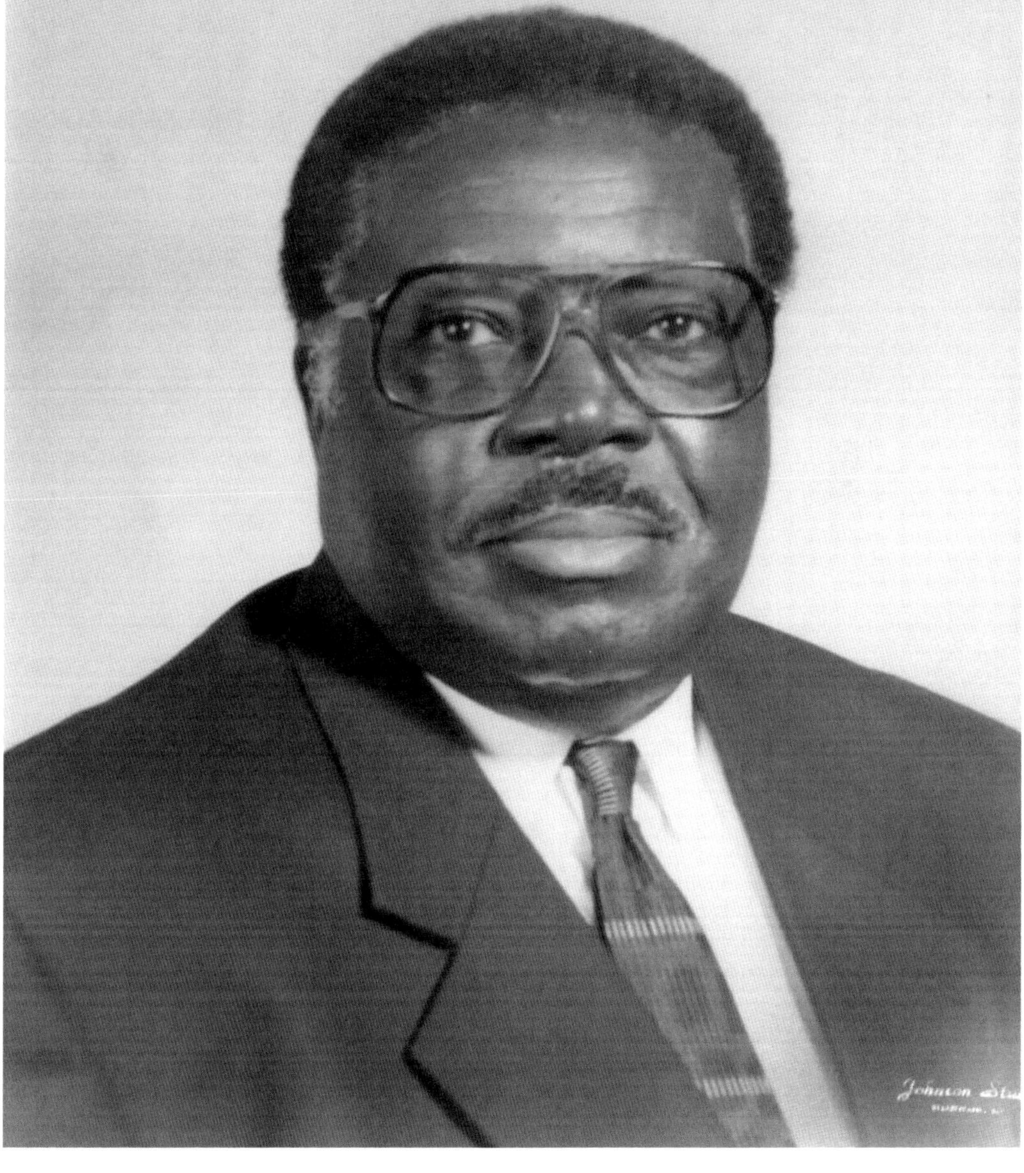

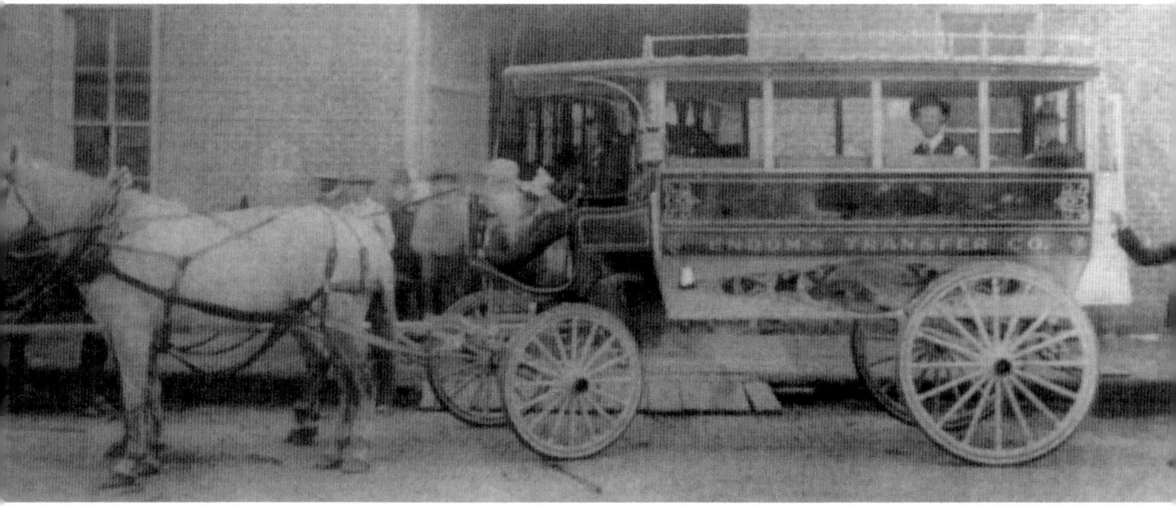

Fred Endom

One of the most notable immigrants in city history, Fred Endom was born in Germany and arrived in Monroe in 1857 to open Endom's Livery & Transfer Company downtown, only a few blocks from the Ouachita River.

Known as the "Reconstruction mayor," Endom served two terms as the city's leader. Following retirement, Endom was honored by the city in 1898 when he was the first person to walk the newly completed footbridge that spanned the river, leading a parade from Monroe into West Monroe.

About 90 years later, the Desiard Street Bridge was officially renamed the Endom Bridge. (Above, courtesy of Mike Takewell; below, photograph by Griffin Scott.)

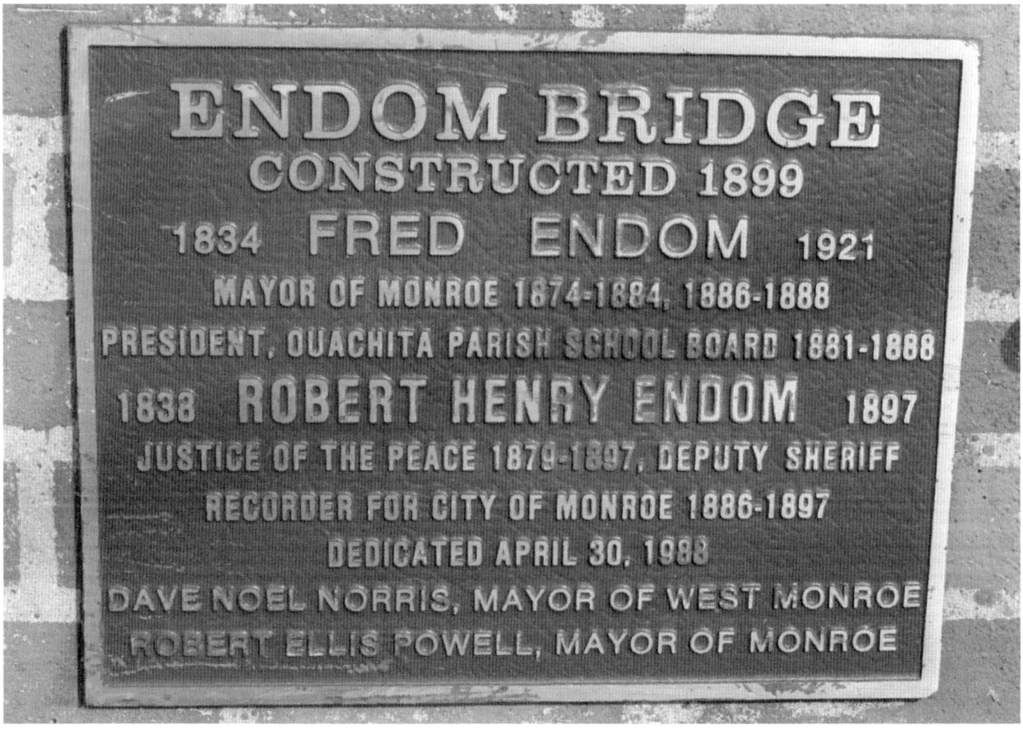

Robert J. Barham

As a young man, Robert J. Barham undoubtedly learned to love the land while hunting and fishing near his family's northeast Louisiana farm.

With a natural-born sense of civic duty, the military veteran served as both a town councilman and mayor of his native Oak Ridge.

Barham went on to represent the region in the state senate from 1994 to 2007. He was appointed secretary of the Louisiana Department of Wildlife and Fisheries shortly after leaving office. (Courtesy of Louisiana Department of Wildlife and Fisheries.)

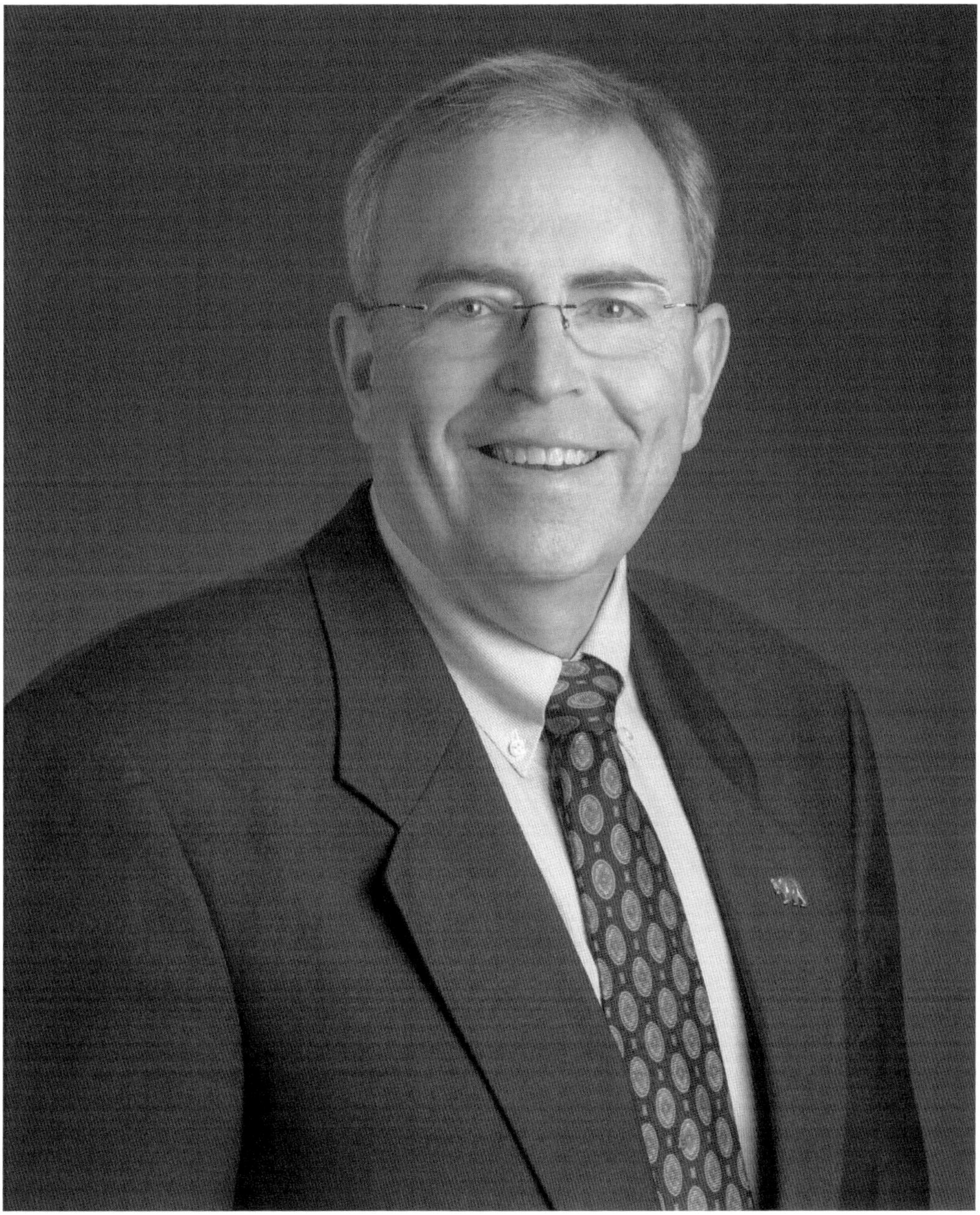

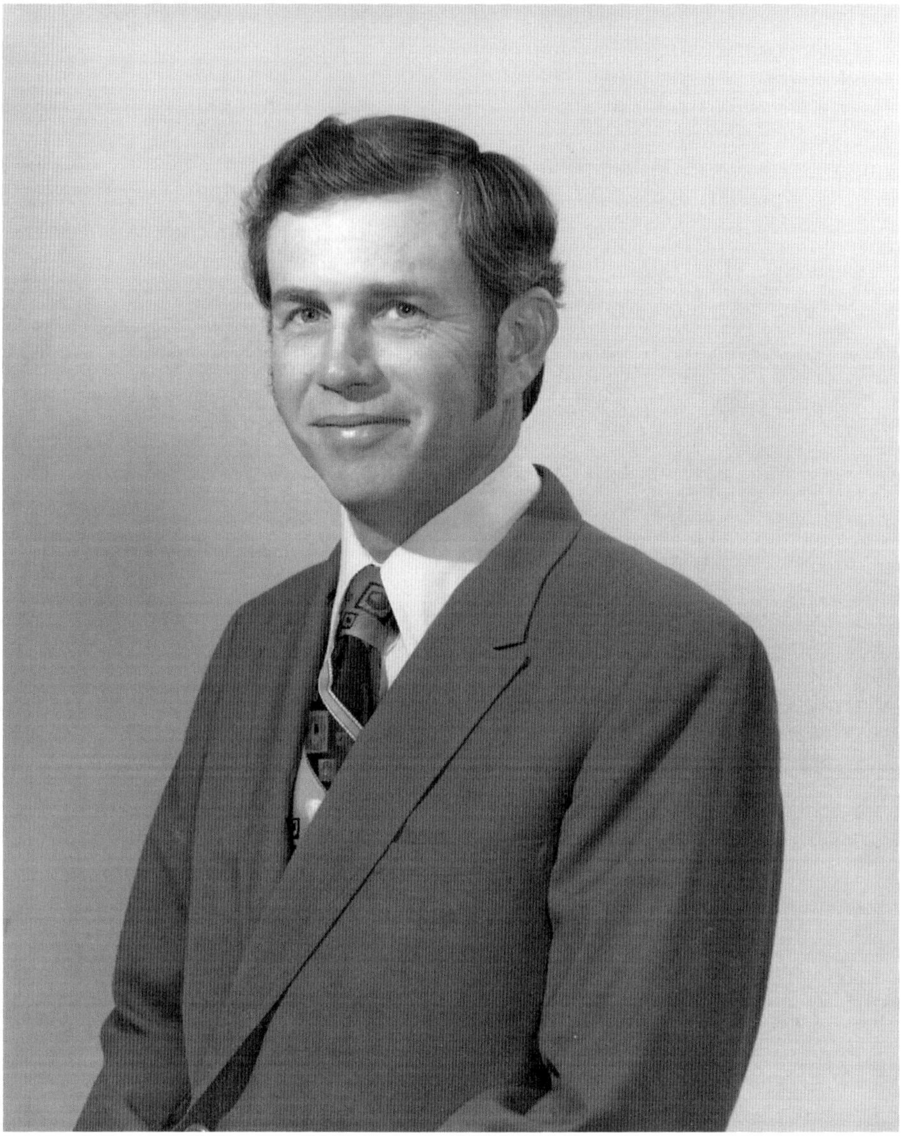

Edwards Barham

Service and soil are in the veins of the Barham family. Edwards Barham, a Morehouse Parish native and the brother of Robert J. Barham, represented northeast Louisiana in the state senate from 1976 to 1980 and is a former chairman of both the Louisiana Board of Trustees and the Louisiana Board of Regents. He also serves on the board of supervisors for the Louisiana technical and community college system.

A third-generation farmer, Barham's father, Erle M. "Ninety" Barham, was a driving force behind the Tensas Wildlife Refuge. Young Barham attended both Louisiana State University and the University of Louisiana at Monroe.

An ornithologist, Barham was named to the White House conservation initiative by Pres. Richard Nixon in the early 1970s and is sometimes called the "quail man" because of his preservation efforts for the bobtail quail.

The owner of Flying Tiger Aviation School in Oak Ridge, he is also a successful businessman and pilot. (Courtesy of Edwards Barham.)

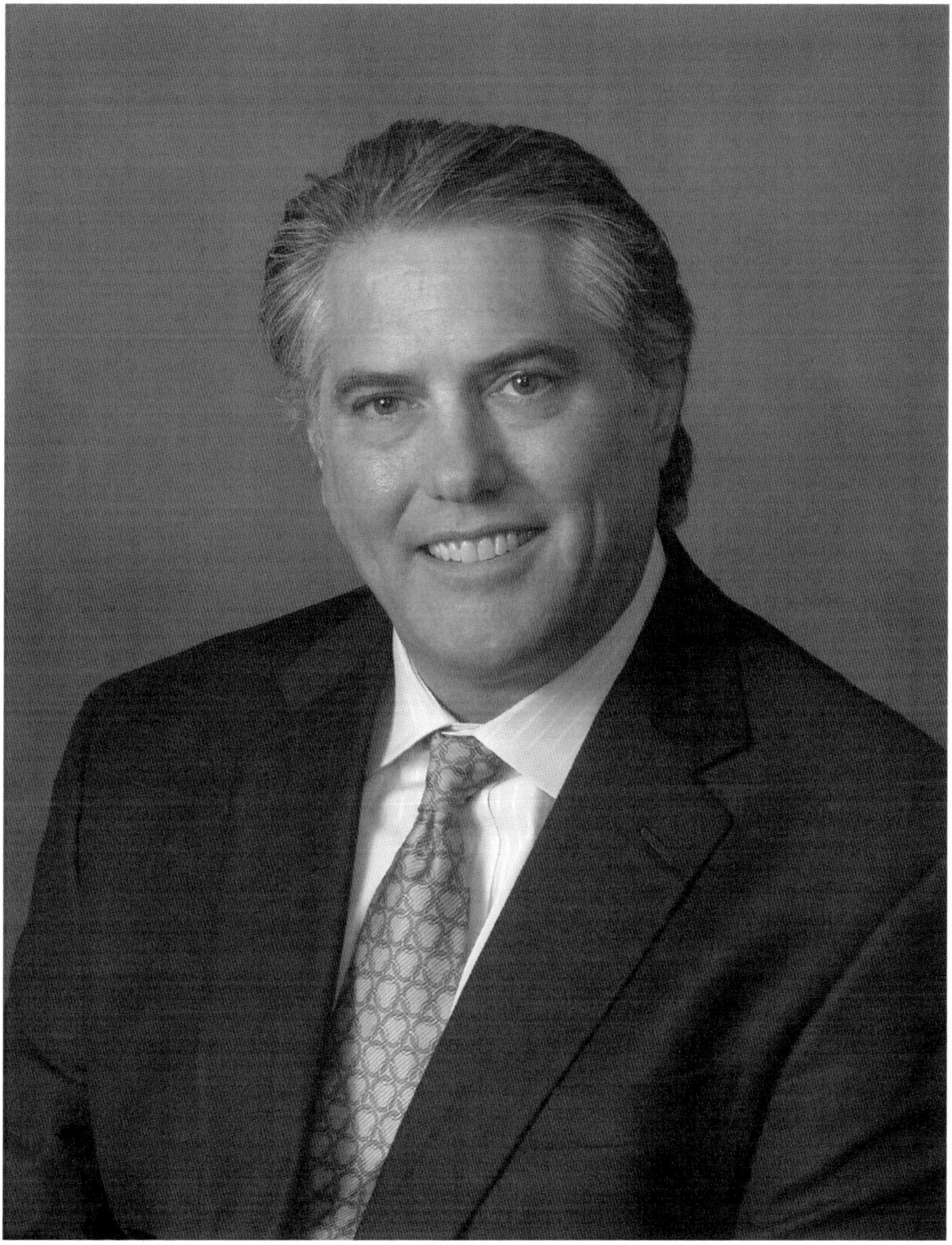

J. Robert Wooley

J. Robert Wooley served as Louisiana's insurance commissioner in the mid-2000s, post– Hurricane Katrina. As the son of an educator, academics were always a priority for Wooley. After graduating from Ouachita Parish High School in 1971, he attended Northeast Louisiana University.

Wooley obtained a law degree from Louisiana State University, and after serving as insurance commissioner until 2006, returned to private practice in Baton Rouge. (Courtesy of J. Robert Wooley.)

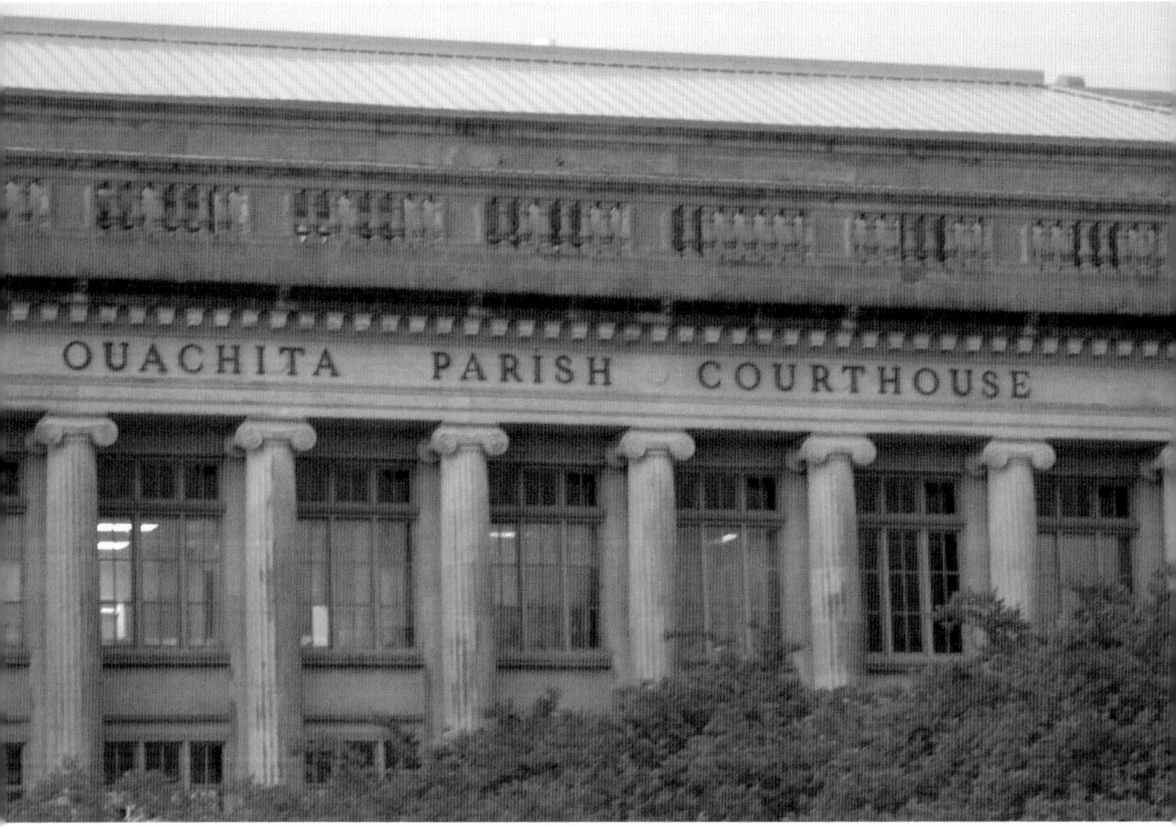

James L. Dennis

In 1936, James Leon Dennis was born in Monroe. Following high school, he graduated from Louisiana Tech University before attending law school at Louisiana State University.

Dennis spent some time in private practice, later serving four years in the Louisiana House of Representatives. Following his stint in the legislature, he was a judge for the Fourth District Court in Monroe and later became an associate judge of the Supreme Court of Louisiana. In 1995, Dennis was named a federal judge by presidential appointment. (Photograph by Griffin Scott.)

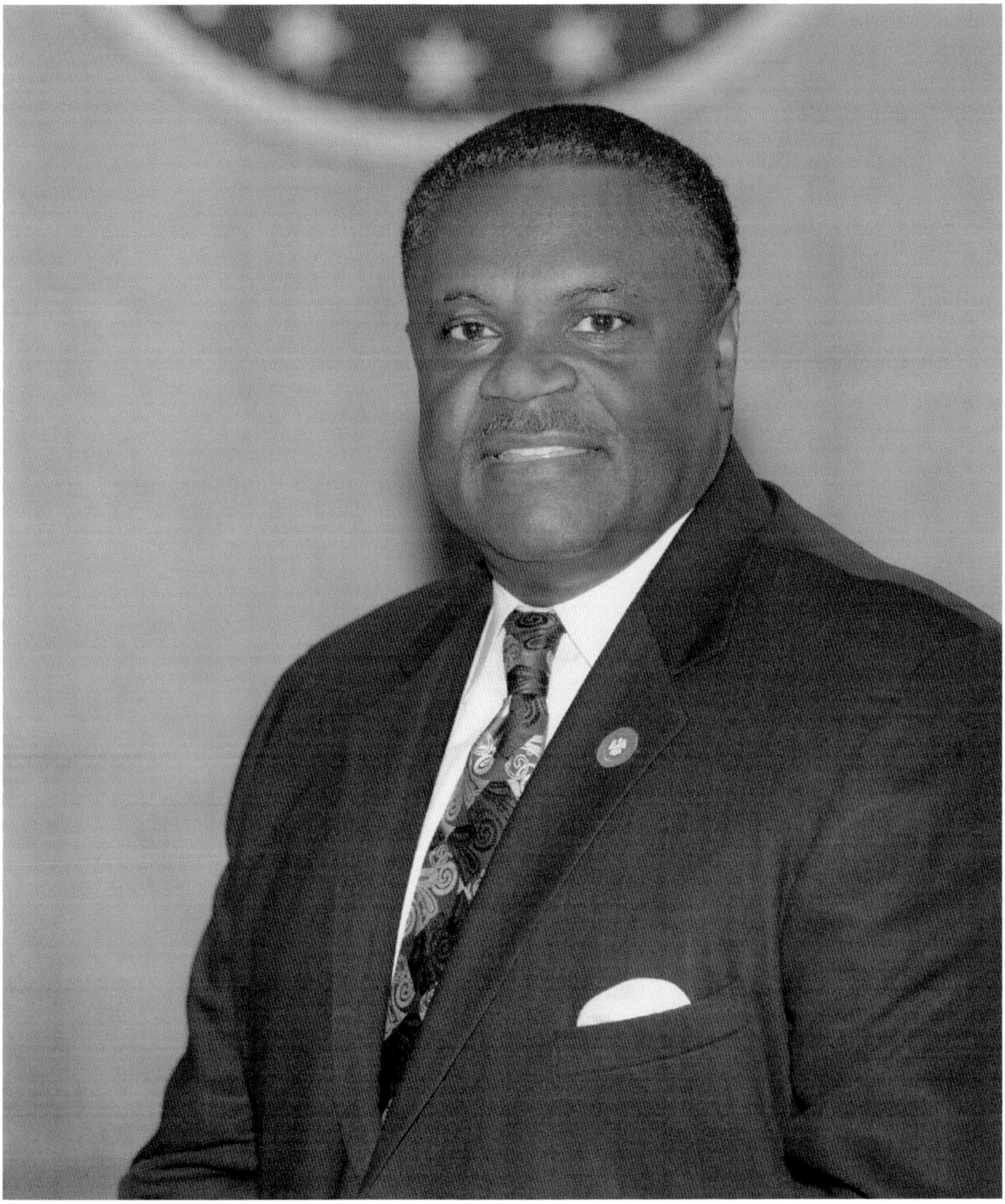

James E. "Jamie" Mayo

Born in Morehouse Parish in 1957, Jamie Mayo first caught Monroe's collective eye as a basketball star for Northeast Louisiana University in the 1970s.

A Bastrop High School standout, Mayo hung up his high-tops after four years on the NLU team and left college armed with a degree in business administration. After spending several years in the insurance industry, Mayo jumped into politics, serving on the Monroe City Council.

In 2001, when Monroe mayor Melvin Rambin unexpectedly passed away, Jamie Mayo was appointed interim mayor. A few months later, he won a special election to officially take the city's helm, becoming the city's second African American leader. In 2012, he was sworn in for his fourth consecutive mayoral term. (Courtesy of the City of Monroe.)

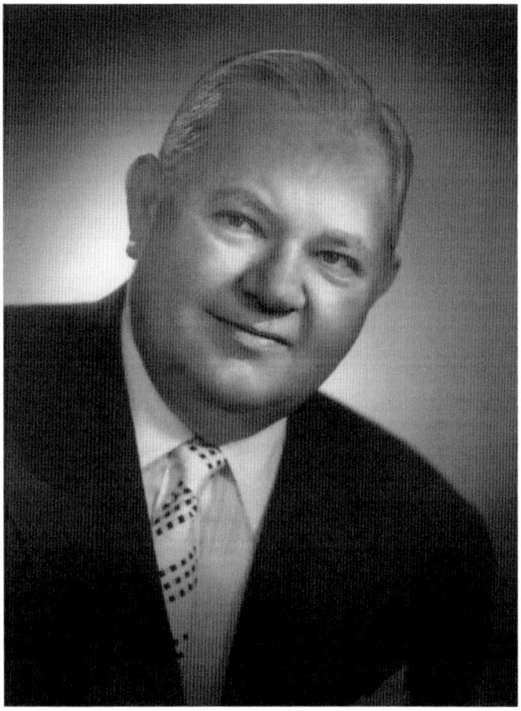

James A. Noe

A World War I veteran, James A. Noe was elected to the Louisiana state senate in 1932 after a successful career as an independent oilman. He was appointed lieutenant governor when the man elected to the office resigned, and in 1936, following the unexpected death of Gov. O.K. Allen, Noe became the 43rd governor of Louisiana. He is pictured at left and below, at left, with Gov. Huey P. Long.

His tenure was brief, lasting only a few months. After an unsuccessful bid for a permanent position as governor, Noe turned to broadcasting, founding radio and television group KNOE TV/AM/FM in Monroe, as well as WNOE, a New Orleans television station.

Noe died at age 86 in 1976. (Left, courtesy of the Ouachita Parish Public Library; below, courtesy of Louise Khoury and the family of Mary Savana.)

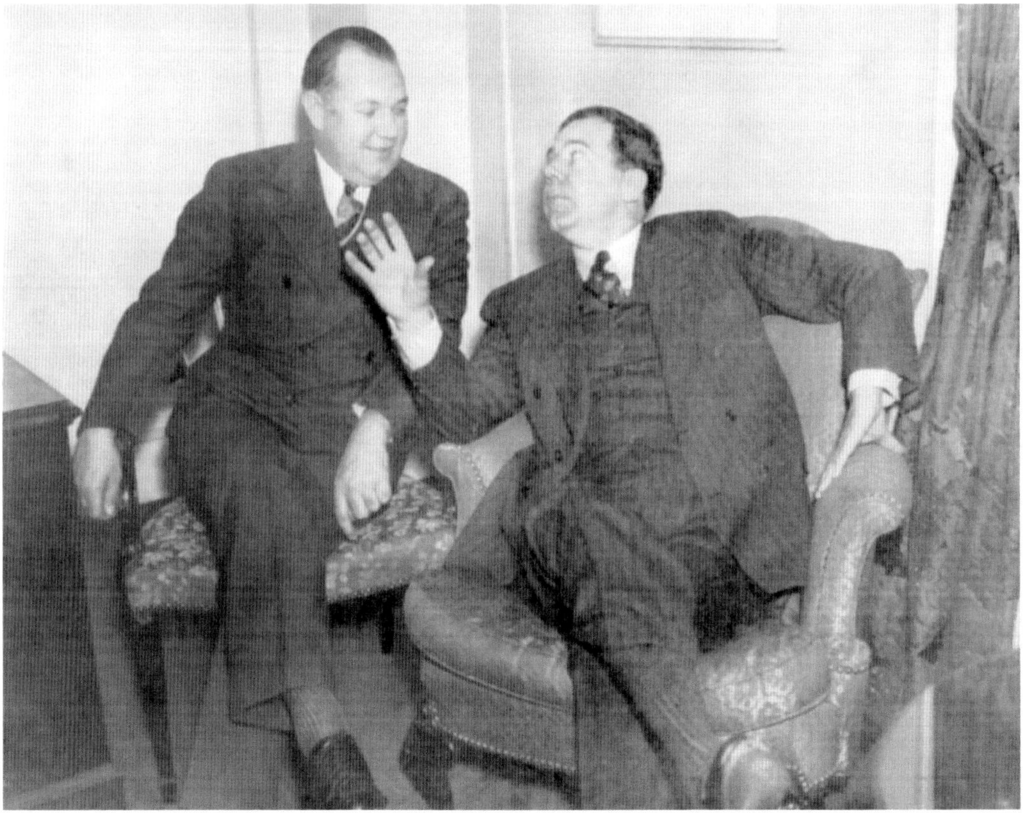

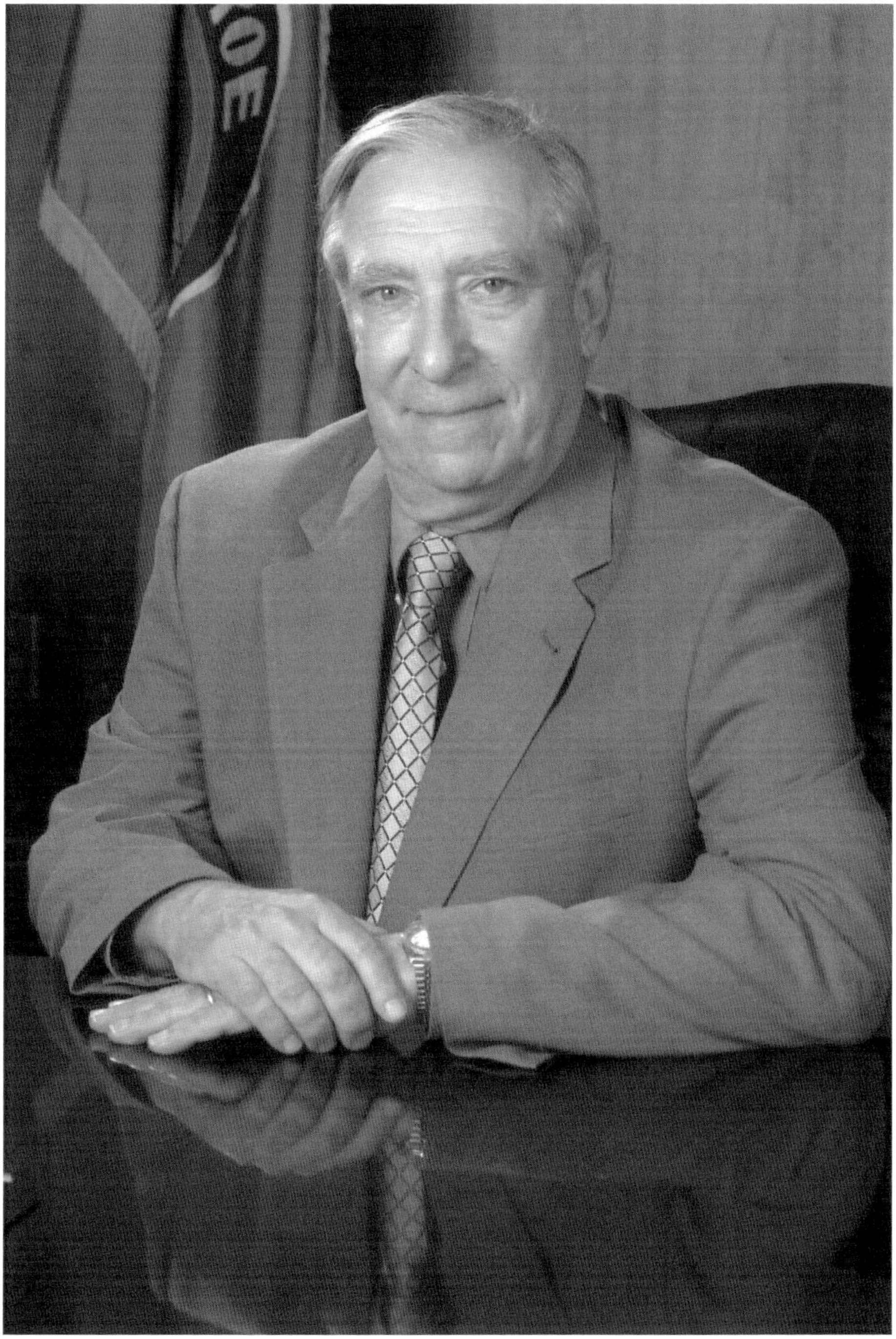

Jay Marx

Jay Marx learned about service long before his days on the Monroe City Council. For 123 years, Marx's family operated Southern Hardware, one of Monroe's oldest family-owned retailers, which closed in 2013. He was the fourth generation of family members to run the business. Marx served eight years on the Monroe City Council. (Courtesy of the City of Monroe.)

John C. Ensminger

Born in 1934, state representative John Clifford Ensminger spent two decades serving in the Louisiana legislature. After graduating from Neville High School, he went to work for State Farm Insurance and built a successful practice before running for office. Ensminger won his first election in 1972. He left public service 20 years later and returned to private business. (Courtesy of John C. Ensminger.)

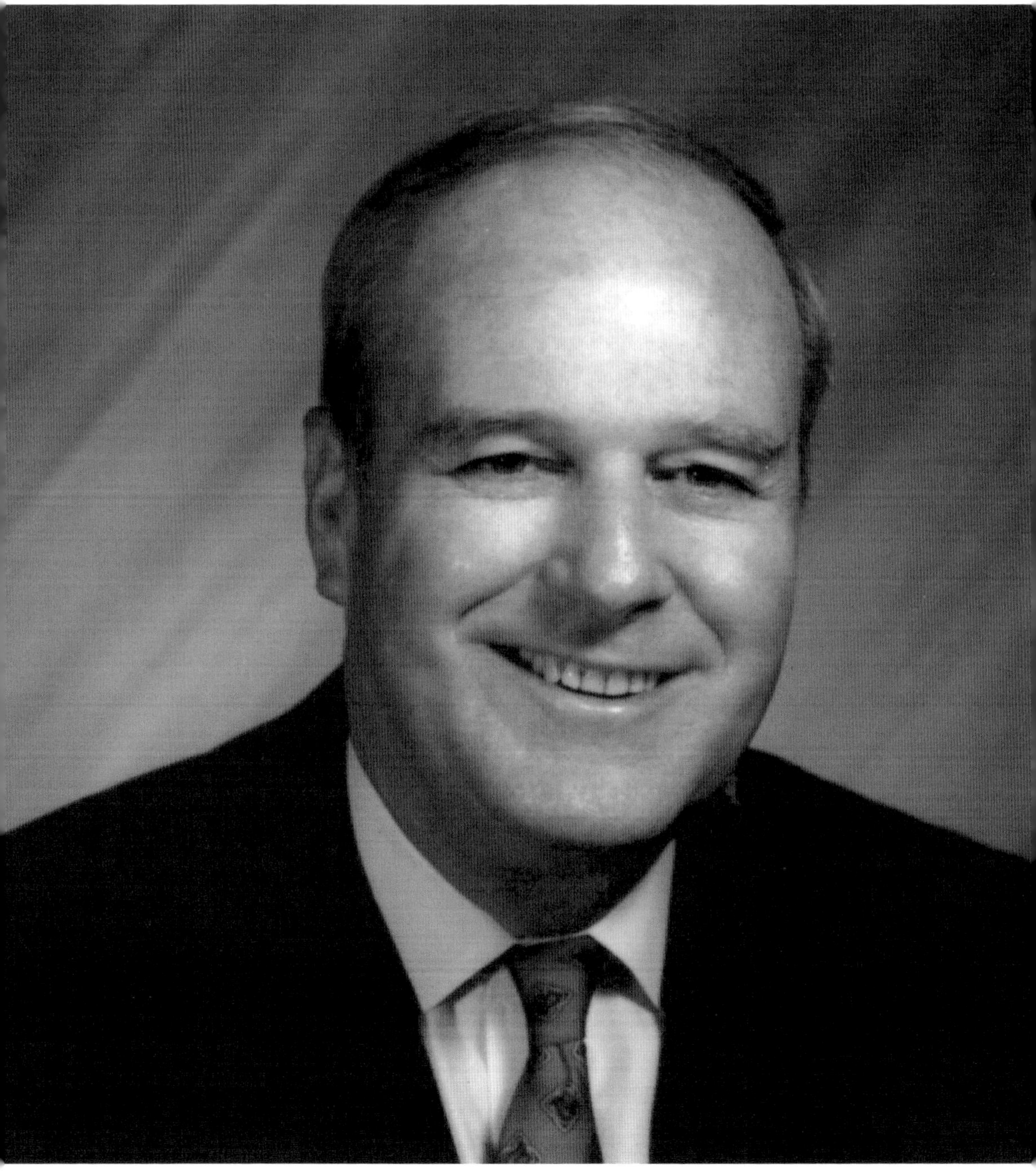

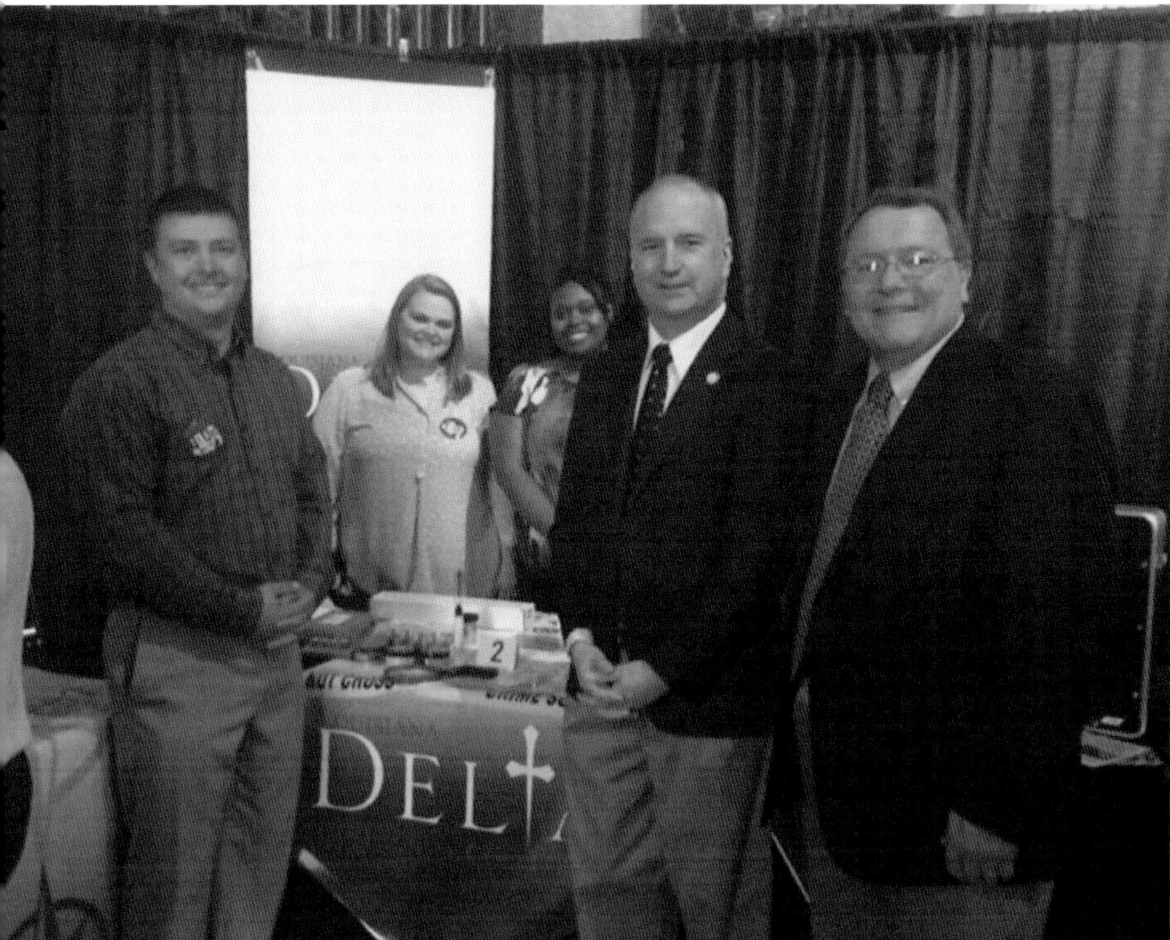

Marcus R. Clark

As a teenage Eagle Scout in Sulfur, Louisiana, Marcus Clark took a ride with a local police officer, and along the way developed a lifelong love for law enforcement and public service.

Clark (pictured at right) came to Monroe in the 1970s to attend Northeast Louisiana University, earning a degree in criminal justice. Upon graduation, he immediately accepted a position with the parish sheriff, working as a narcotics detective in Monroe. After a few years, Clark returned to school, attending law school at Louisiana State University.

After earning his legal license, he returned to Monroe to work as an assistant district attorney before winning a district judgeship in 1996. In 2009, Clark won an election to become a Louisiana Supreme Court justice. (Photograph by Mark Sanders.)

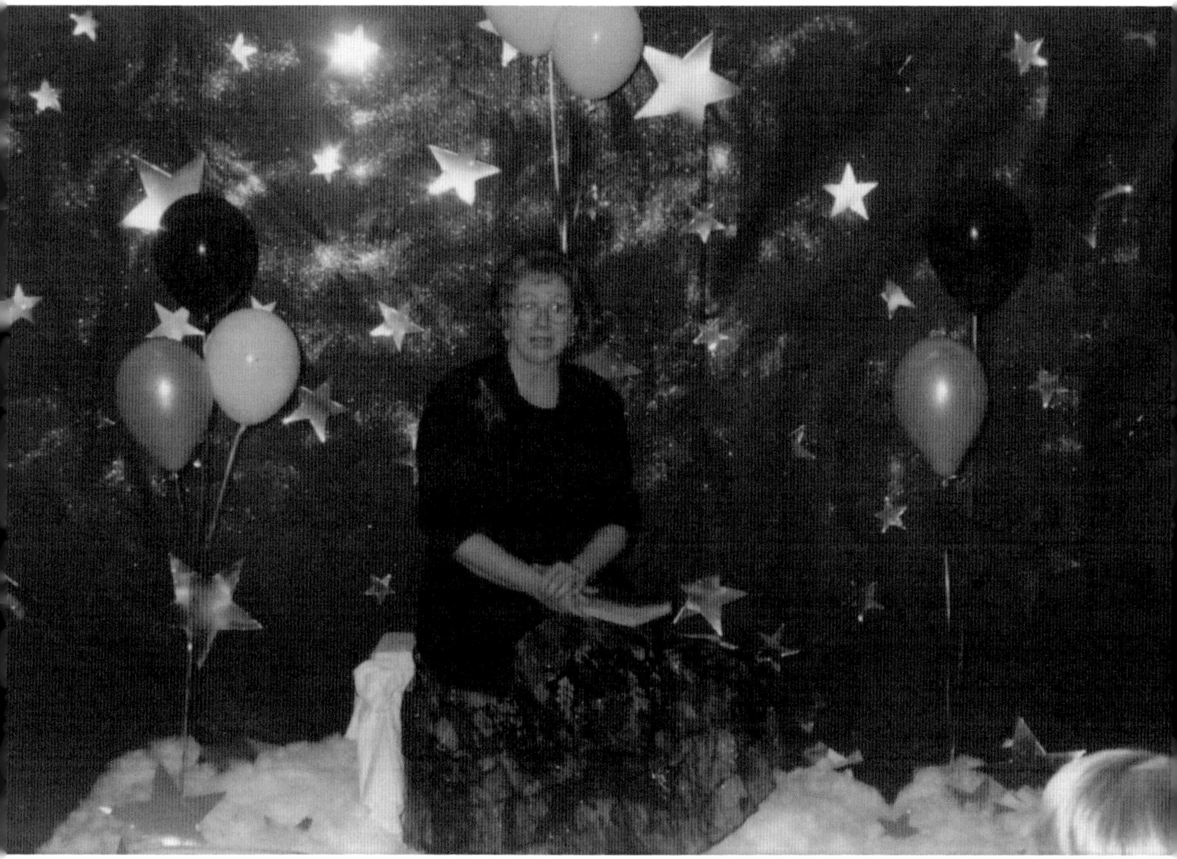

Kay Katz

A Neville High School graduate, Kay Katz attended Mississippi State University, earning an English degree before returning to Monroe to work as a teacher.

In 2000, Monroe City Council member Katz won an election to represent the area in the Louisiana House of Representatives, a distinction very few women share. She went on to represent Monroe citizens for 13 successful years, leaving office in 2012. (Courtesy of the Ouachita Parish Public Library.)

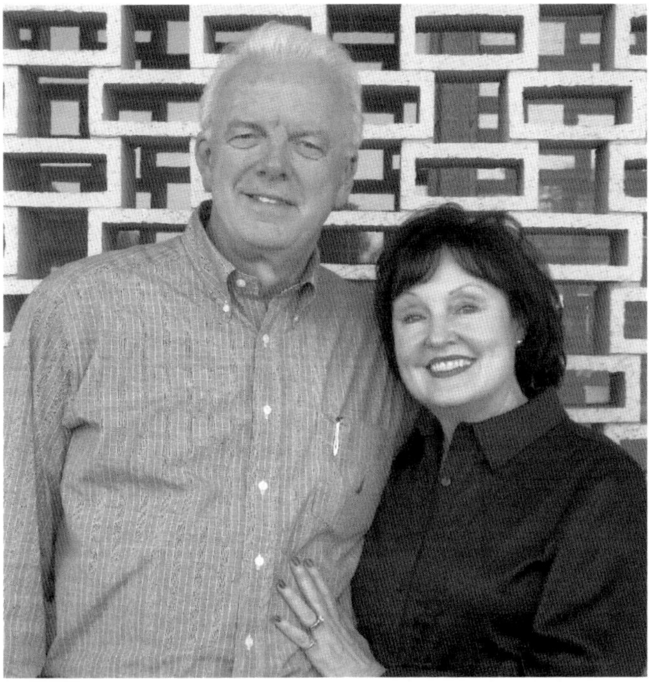

Lawson Swearingen
Before he served as a Louisiana state senator from 1980 to 1991, Lawson Swearingen starred on the basketball courts for the same university he would eventually become president of decades later.

Following his political career, he returned to his undergraduate alma mater, Northeast Louisiana University, serving as president and overseeing the college's controversial name change to the University of Louisiana at Monroe in 1999. Swearingen retired as president in 2002. (Left, photograph by Richard David Ramsey; below, photograph by Griffin Scott.)

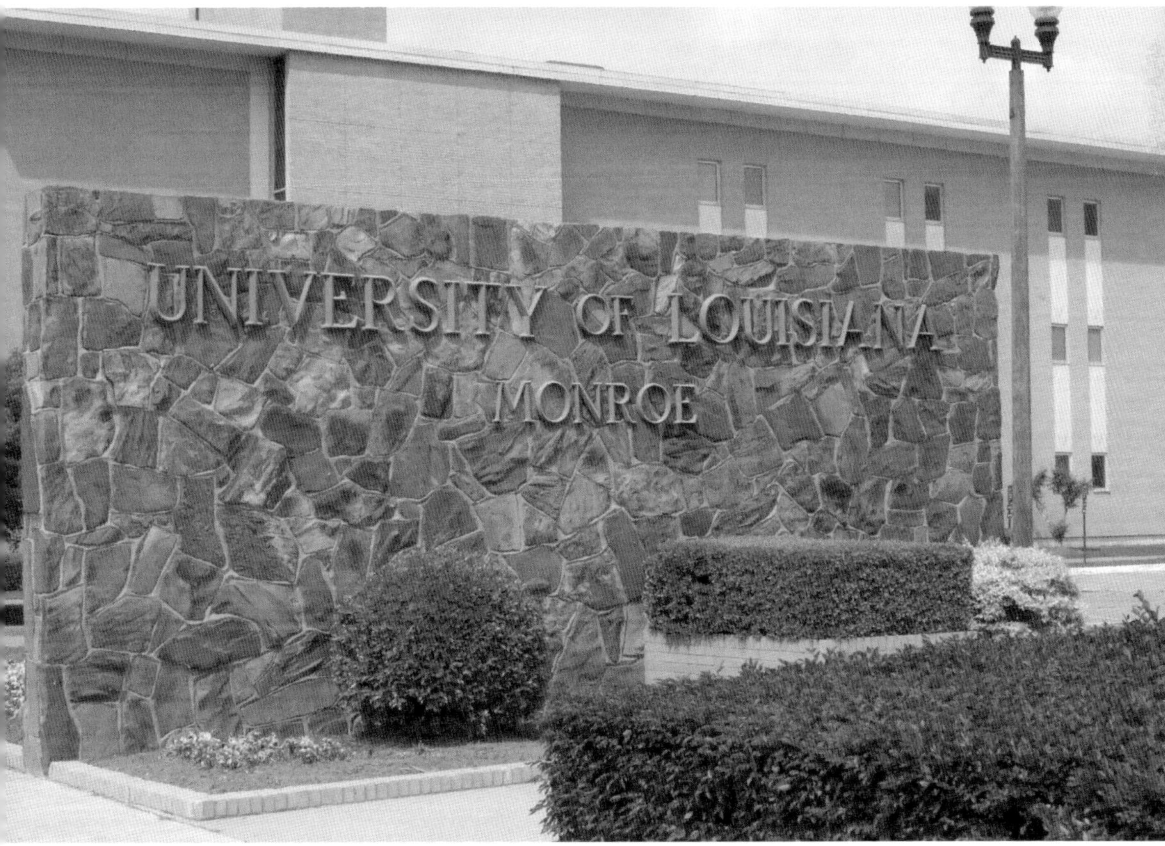

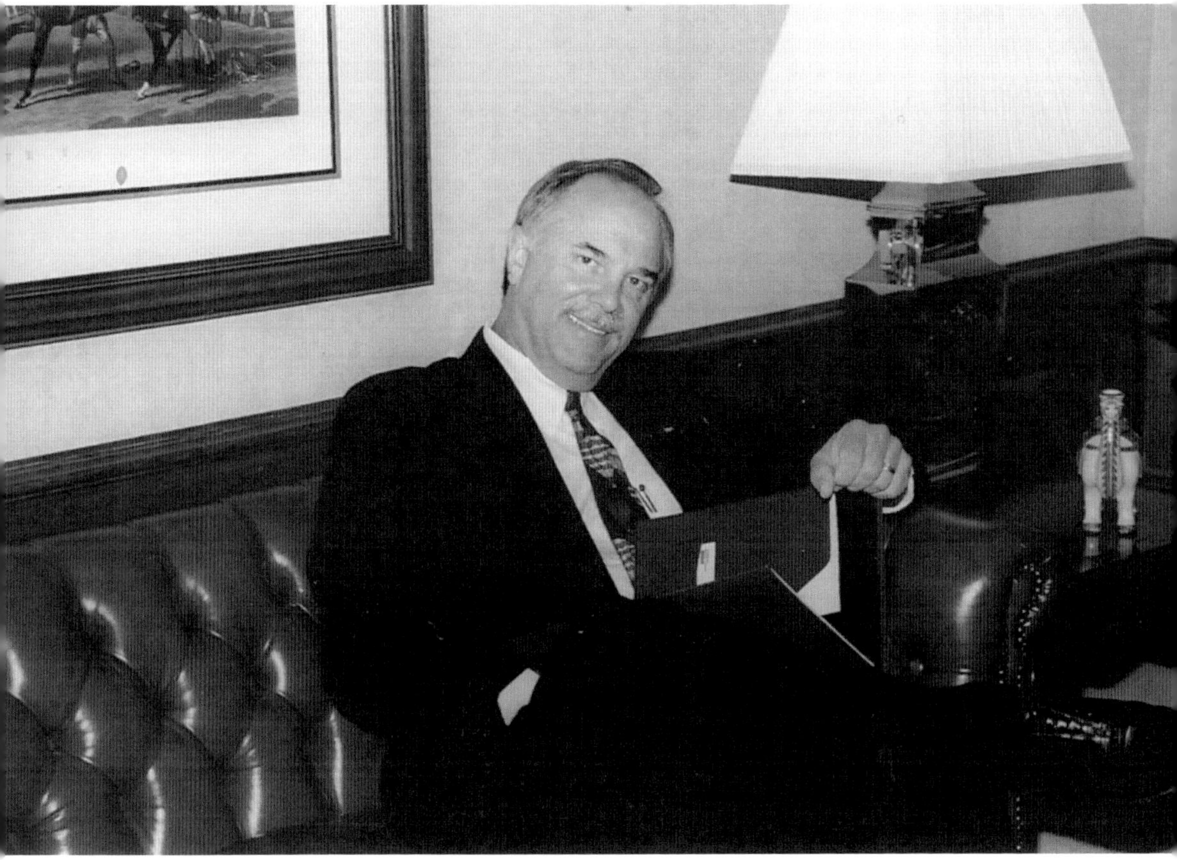

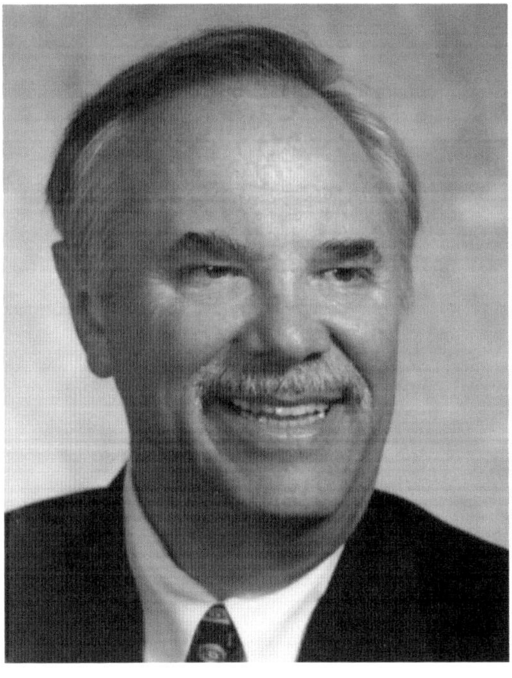

Melvin Rambin

The brief political career of Monroe mayor Melvin Rambin is historical for three reasons. Rambin was the first Republican to win a mayoral seat in Monroe since Reconstruction, after narrowly defeating the city's first African American mayor, Abe Pierce III, only to unexpectedly pass away after just under a year in office. He was only 59 years old.

Born in 1941, Rambin graduated from Neville High School before attending Northeast Louisiana State College.

He earned his master's from Louisiana State University, embarking on a successful career in banking before running for office in 2000. (Above, courtesy of the United Way of Northeast Louisiana; left, courtesy of the City of Monroe.)

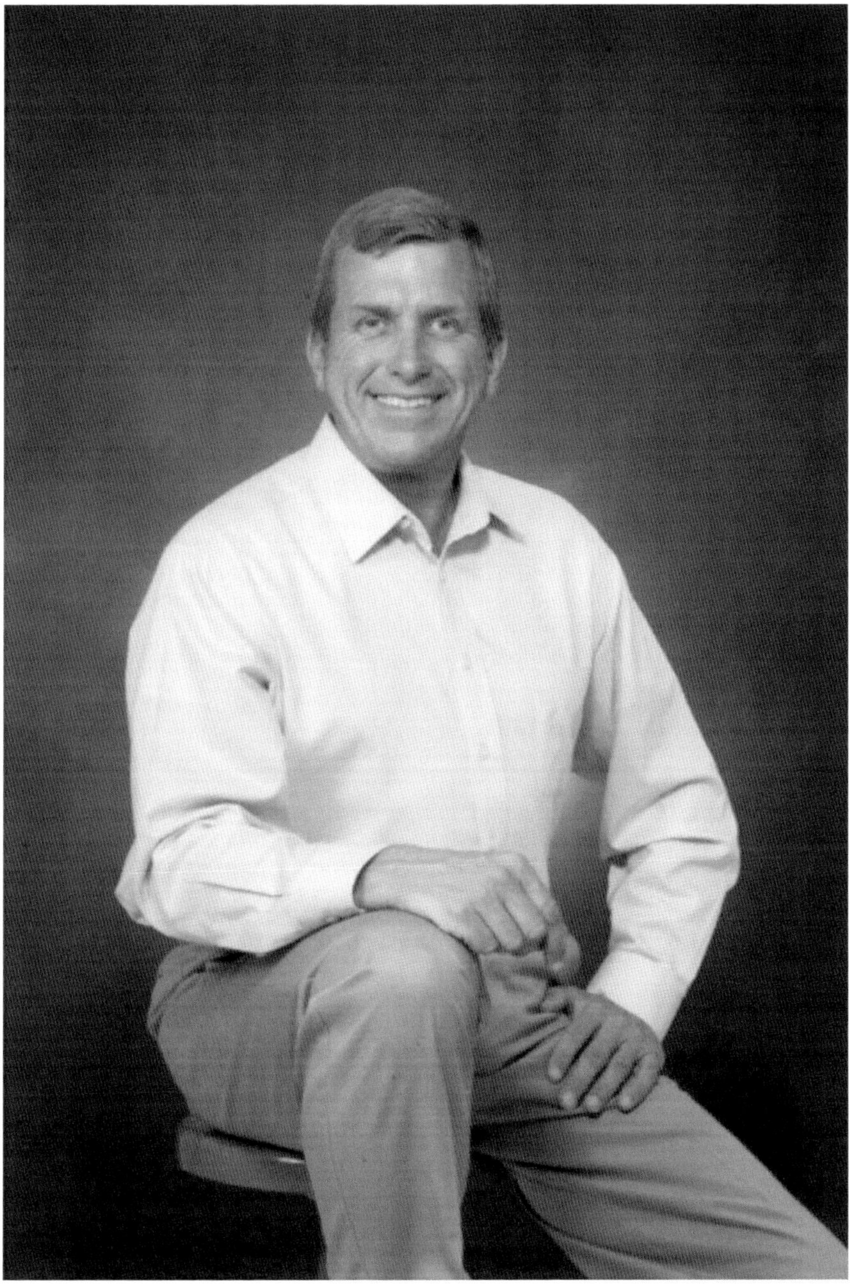

Mike Walsworth

The grandson of local grocers, state senator Michael Arthur "Mike" Walsworth has spent his entire life in northeast Louisiana.

A graduate of West Monroe High School and the University of Louisiana at Monroe, Walsworth won his first election in 1995, following a successful career at the regional Coca-Cola plant.

Having served in the state senate since 2007, Senator Walsworth represents the people of Claiborne, Lincoln, Morehouse, Union, West Carroll, and Ouachita Parishes in 2014. (Courtesy of Mike Walsworth.)

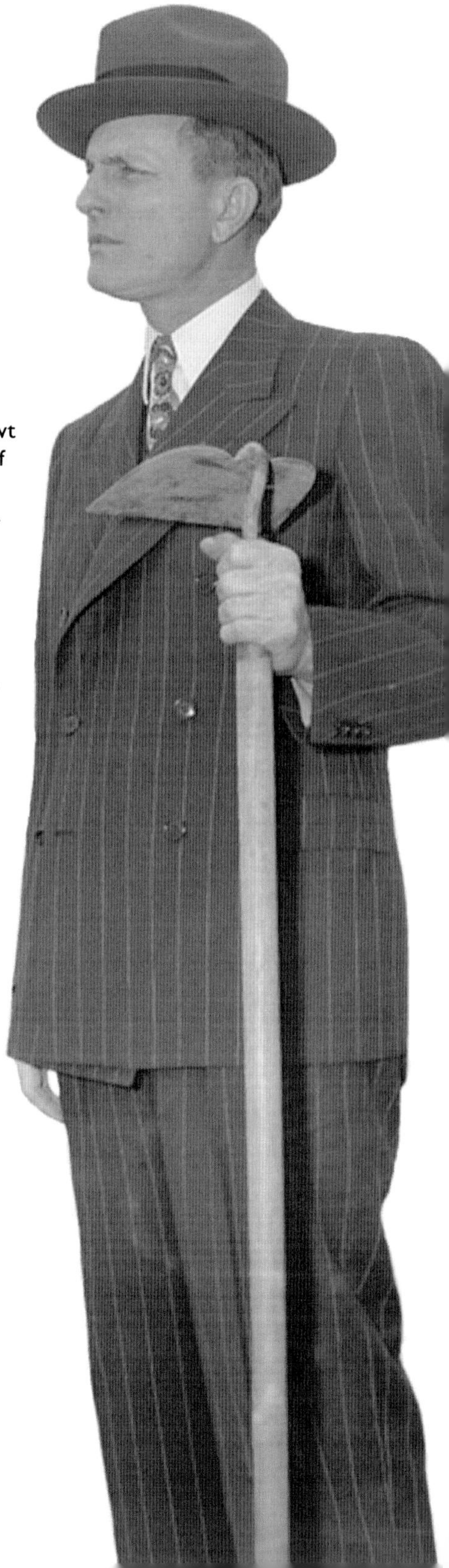

Newt V. Mills

His political career spanned only a few short years, but Newt Virgus Mills represented northeast Louisiana during some of America's toughest times. Elected in 1936 during the Great Depression, he served as the area's congressman until 1943.

Mills was born in 1899 in Calhoun, a rural Ouachita Parish community a few miles west of Monroe. After graduating high school, he attended both Louisiana Tech University and Louisiana State University. Post-college, Mills worked for a time as a schoolteacher, and later in the cattle and farming business, before winning his first election to public office as the US representative of Louisiana's Fifth Congressional District.

After losing his seat, he resumed his agribusiness and expanded his interests into oil and gas. Mills lived the rest of his life in Monroe, where he died in 1996. (Courtesy of the Harris & Ewing Collection.)

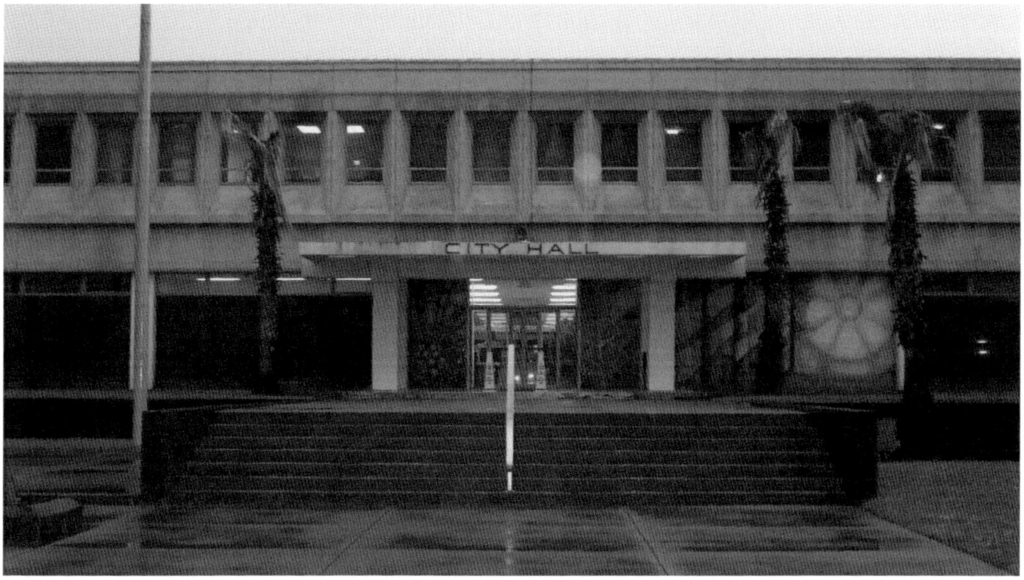

Ralph T. Troy

Though his stretch as Monroe mayor was brief, Ralph Talbot Troy is credited with critical flood-prevention efforts and modernization of the city's police and fire departments.

Born in Monroe in 1935, Troy left northeast Louisiana to attend college in Tennessee, where he obtained a degree in political science. He returned to the southern half of the Louisiana boot, where he attended Tulane University, earning a law degree before returning to Monroe to work at his father's insurance and mortgage business.

Troy was only 37 years old when he was elected mayor in 1972. Declining to seek reelection in 1976, he later moved to North Carolina, where he lived until his death in 2014. (Both photographs by Griffin Scott.)

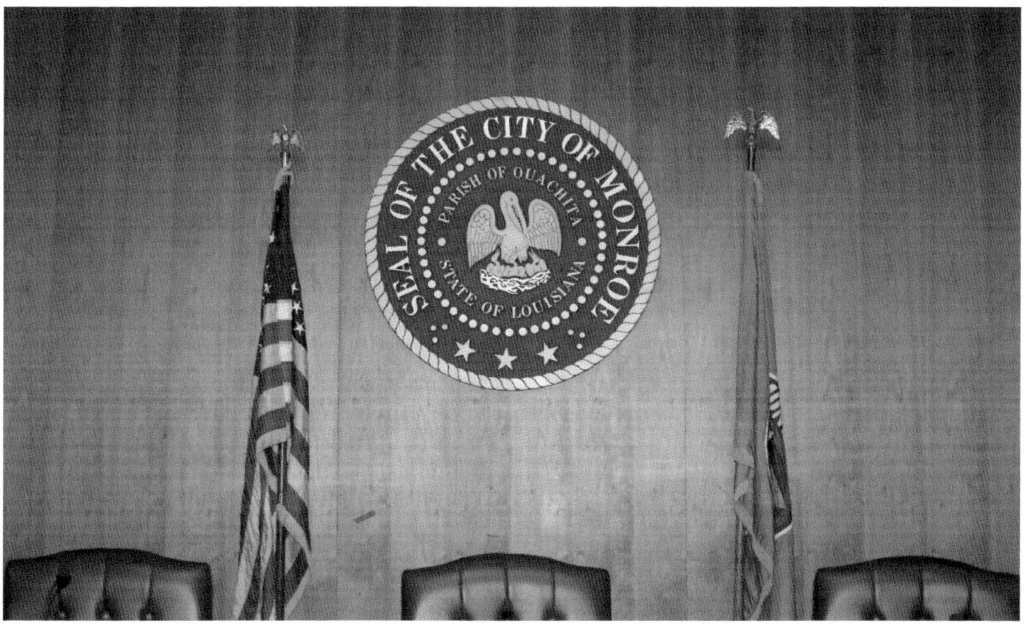

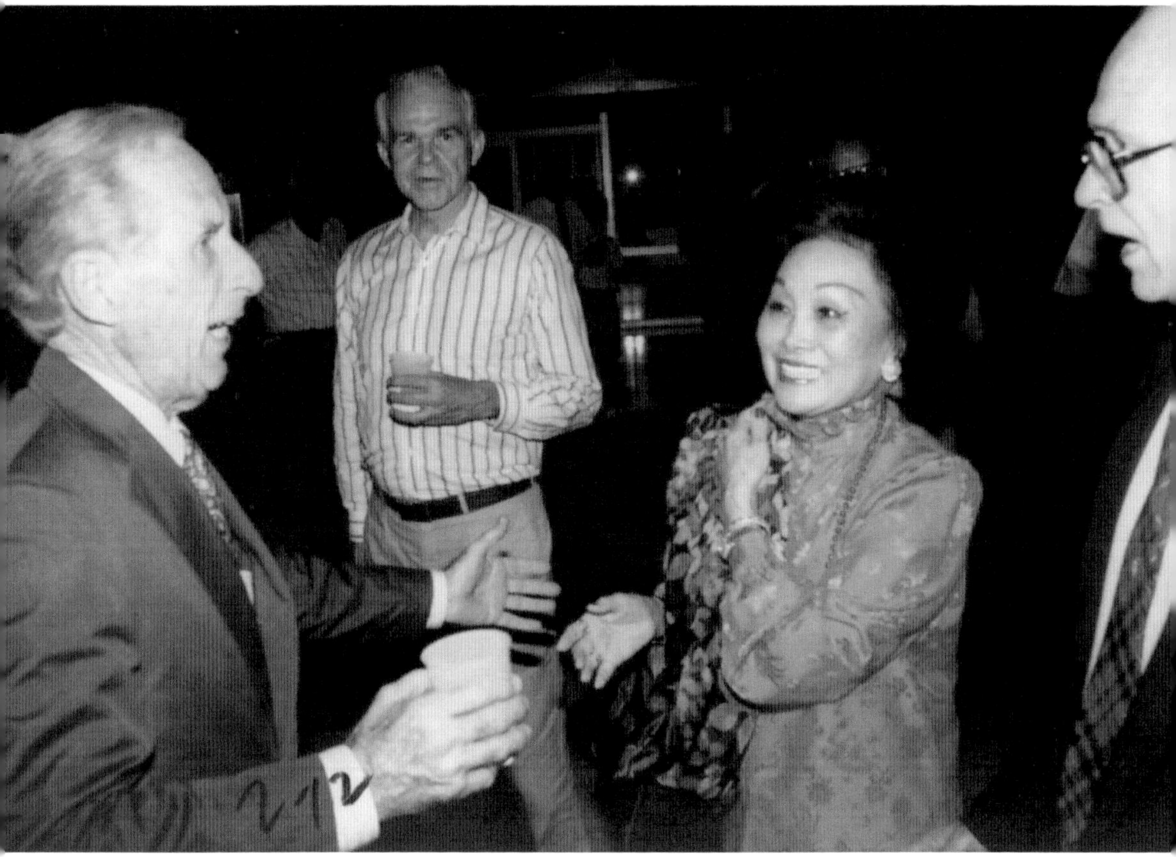

Robert E. "Bob" Powell

A longtime broadcaster, Bob Powell gave up the airwaves in 1979 to serve 17 years as mayor of Monroe. Powell was victorious in a special election against interim mayor William D. Cann (profiled on page 100), who briefly held the city's top office after W.L. "Jack" Howard resigned mid-term. Powell then enjoyed a long, successful run at the helm. Among many other accomplishments, he is praised for his efforts at racial reconciliation, as Powell was the first Monroe mayor to appoint African Americans to fill important positions in city government.

Powell worked with local African American clergy and politicians, including Ouachita Parish police jury president Abe Pierce III (see page 77), who went on to defeat Powell to become Monroe's first African American mayor in the 1996 mayoral race. (Courtesy of the Ouachita Parish Public Library.)

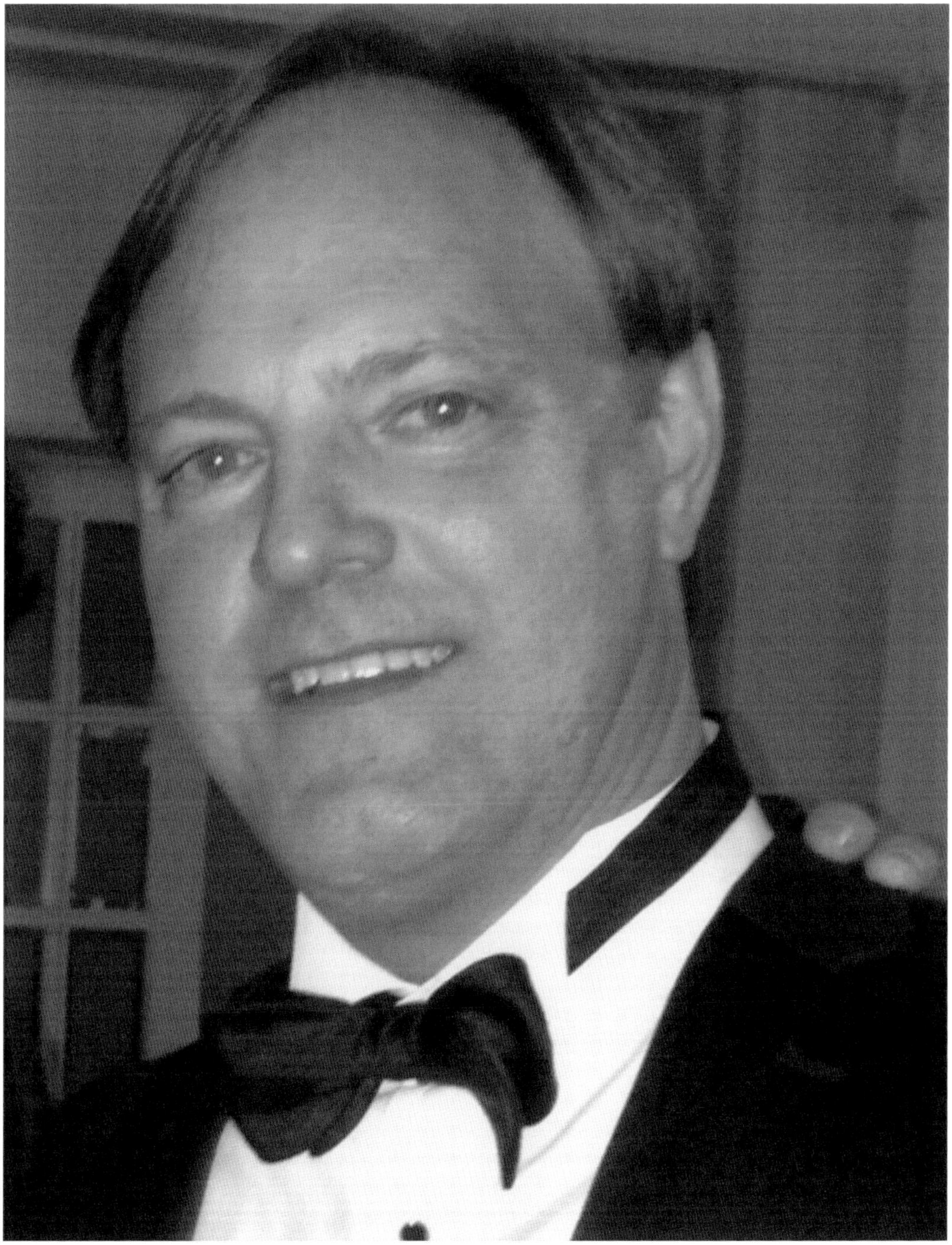

Scott Leehy
After graduating from West Monroe High School, Scott Leehy attended Northeast Louisiana University before heading off to law school in Mississippi.

Following graduation Leehy returned home, and after passing the bar, set up shop as an attorney in Monroe. In 2006, he ran for and won a district judgeship in the state's Fourth District Court. (Courtesy of Charlynn Cicero Leehy.)

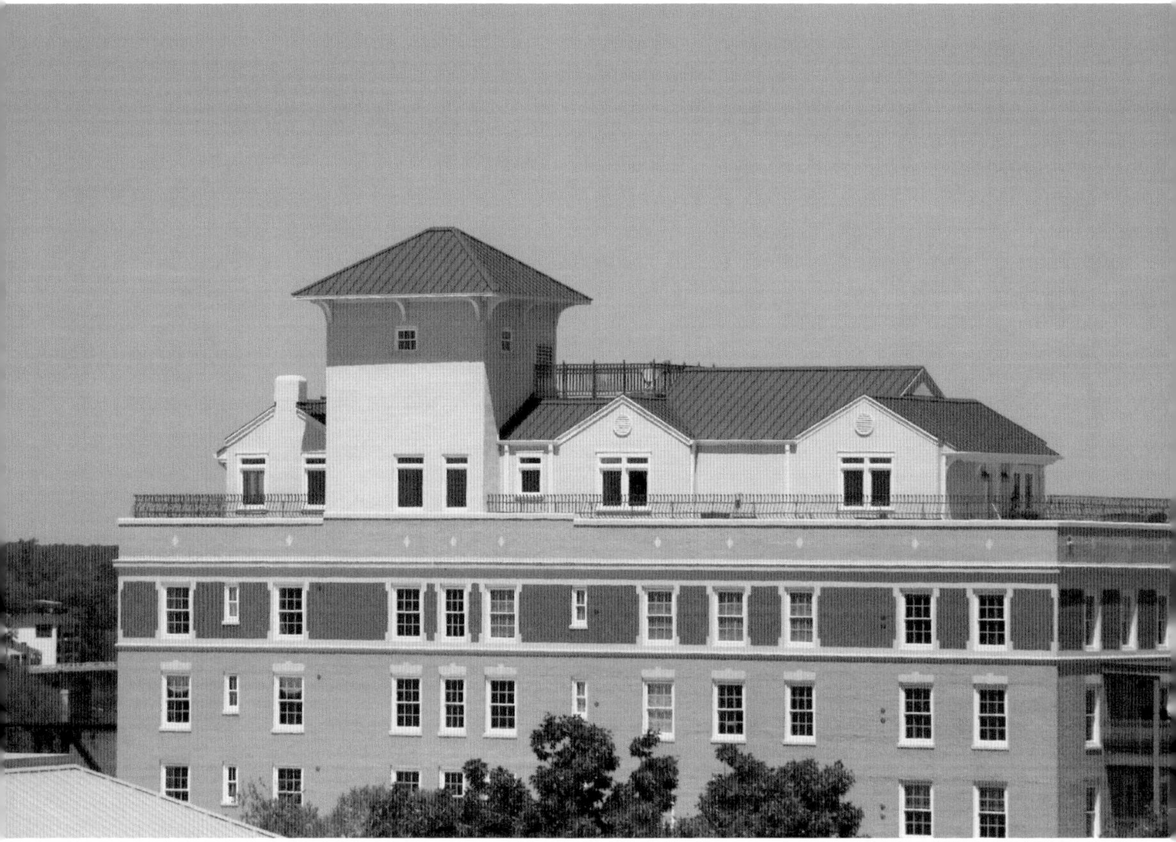

Shady Wall (ABOVE AND OPPOSITE PAGE)
In 1948, Shady Robert Wall began his long, colorful political career.

An ironfisted lawmaker, Wall (pictured at center on opposite page) was also known as a flamboyant dresser with a penchant for white linen suits and luminous ties. His extravagant tastes also spilled over into his two homes. Wall's downtown penthouse, which sat atop one of Monroe's tallest buildings, was famously painted bright pink so that it could be seen for miles. His second, plantation-style home was located just a mile away in neighboring West Monroe, separated from Monroe by the Ouachita River.

Wall was just 63 years old when he died in 1985. (Above, photograph by Griffin Scott; opposite page, courtesy of John C. Ensminger.)

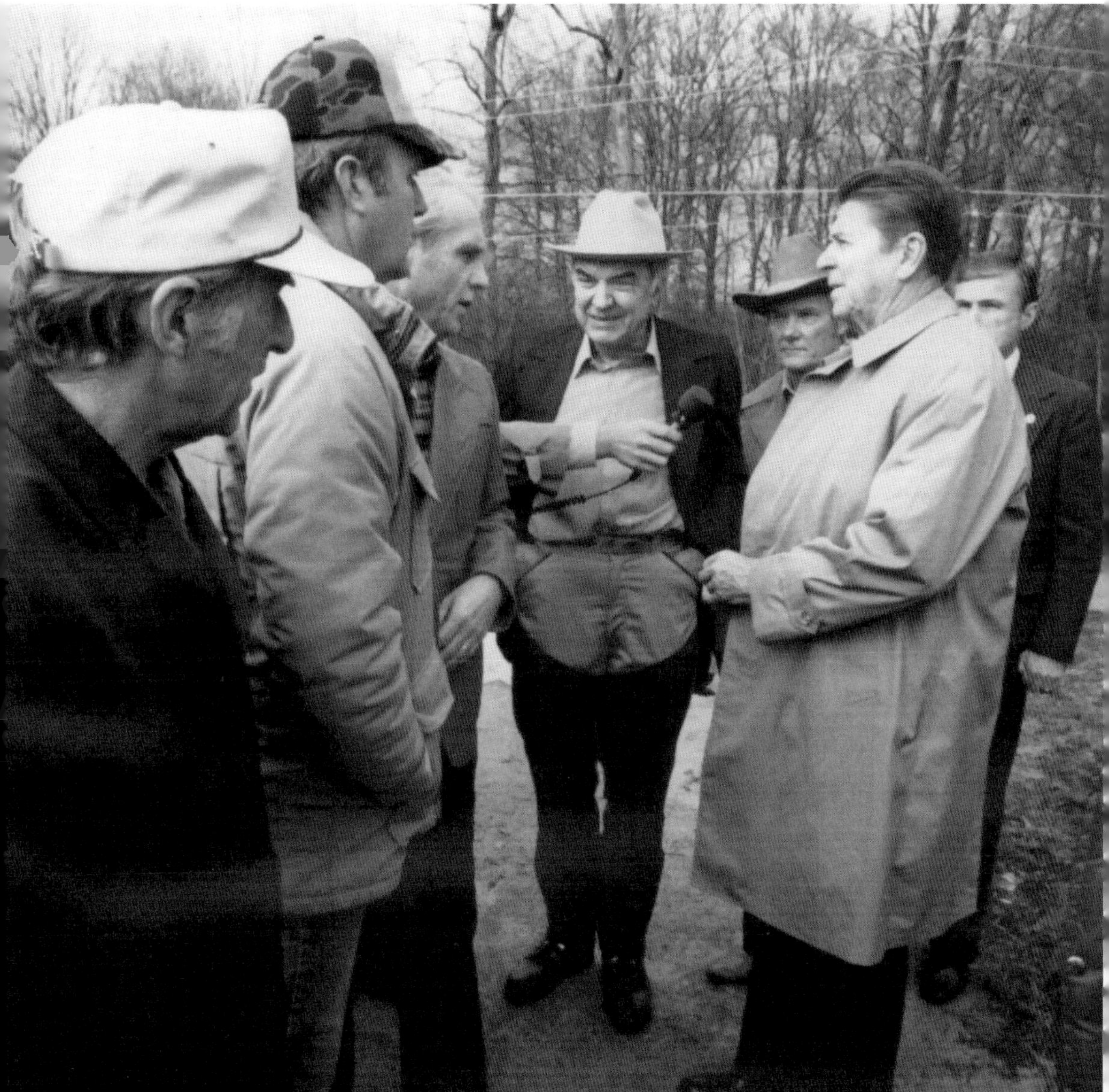

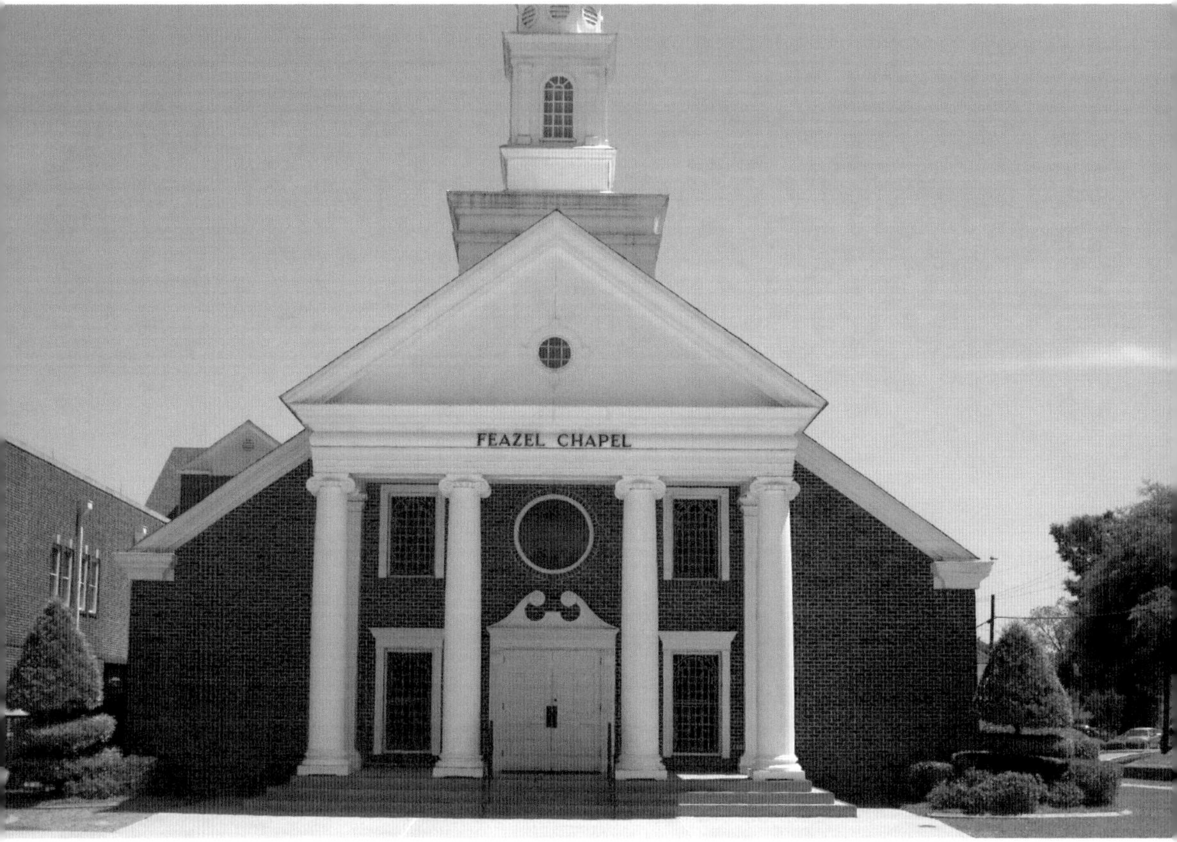

William C. Feazel

Born in Union Parish just east of Monroe only five years before the turn of the 20th century, William Crosson Feazel has the distinction of serving one of the shortest terms in US Senate history.

After finishing school, Feazel went into the energy business. In 1932, he won a seat in the Louisiana House of Representatives, serving four years before returning to the oil and natural gas business.

When John Overton, a US senator from Louisiana, died in office in 1948, Gov. Earl Long appointed Feazel to fill his seat. He was not in Washington, DC, long, though; Feazel merely kept Louisiana's senate seat warm long enough for Governor Long's nephew to win it in a special election held about seven months later. Following his brief stint in the Senate, he again turned to the oil and gas industry.

Feazel died in 1965 and is buried in West Monroe. (Photograph by Griffin Scott.)

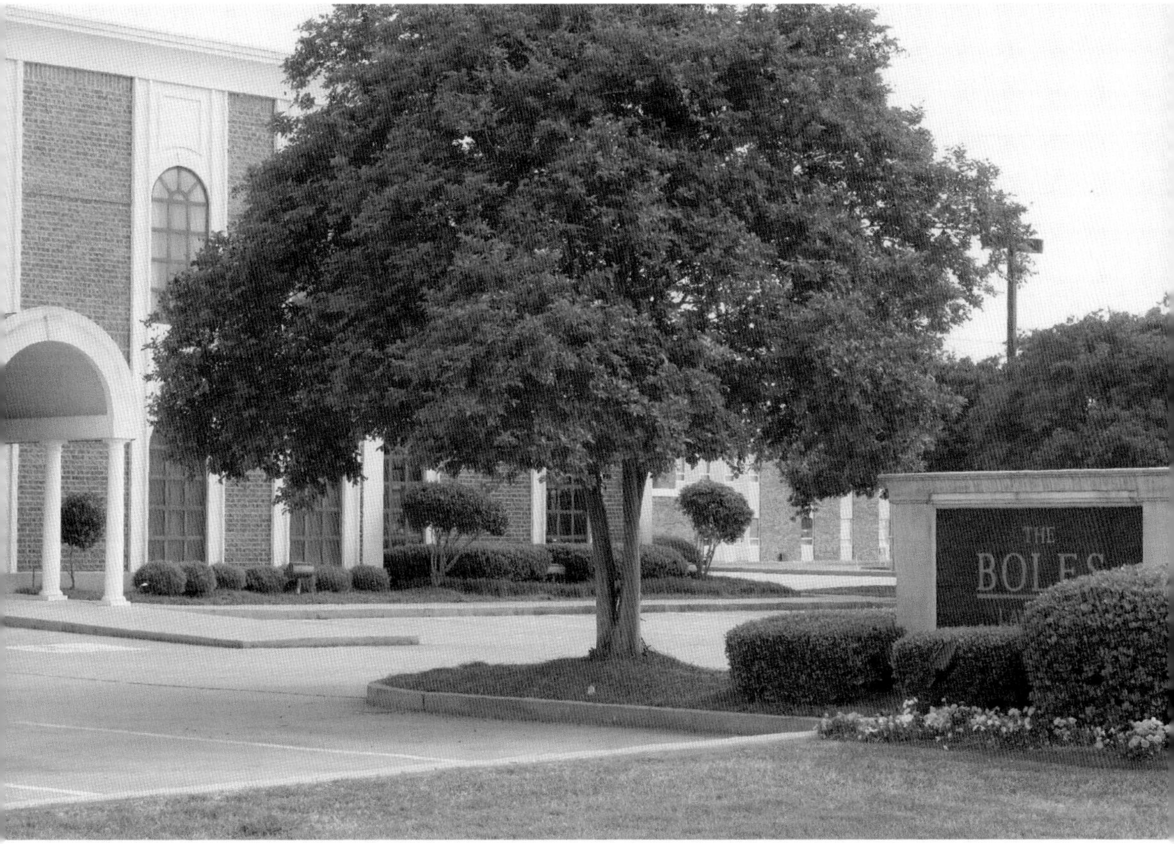

William R. Boles Sr.
At 24, an age when most young people are just starting their careers, William R. "Billy" Boles was a Louisiana state senator.

Born in Richland Parish just east of Monroe in 1927, Boles attended Northeast Louisiana University on a basketball scholarship before serving a hitch in the Navy.

He returned to northeast Louisiana, earning a bachelor's degree from Louisiana Tech University before going on to law school at Louisiana State University.

After serving a single term in the Louisiana Senate from 1952 until 1956, Boles returned to his private law practice and helped found some of the area's most successful banks, including what is now Regions Bank of North Louisiana. He died in 2008. (Photograph by Griffin Scott.)

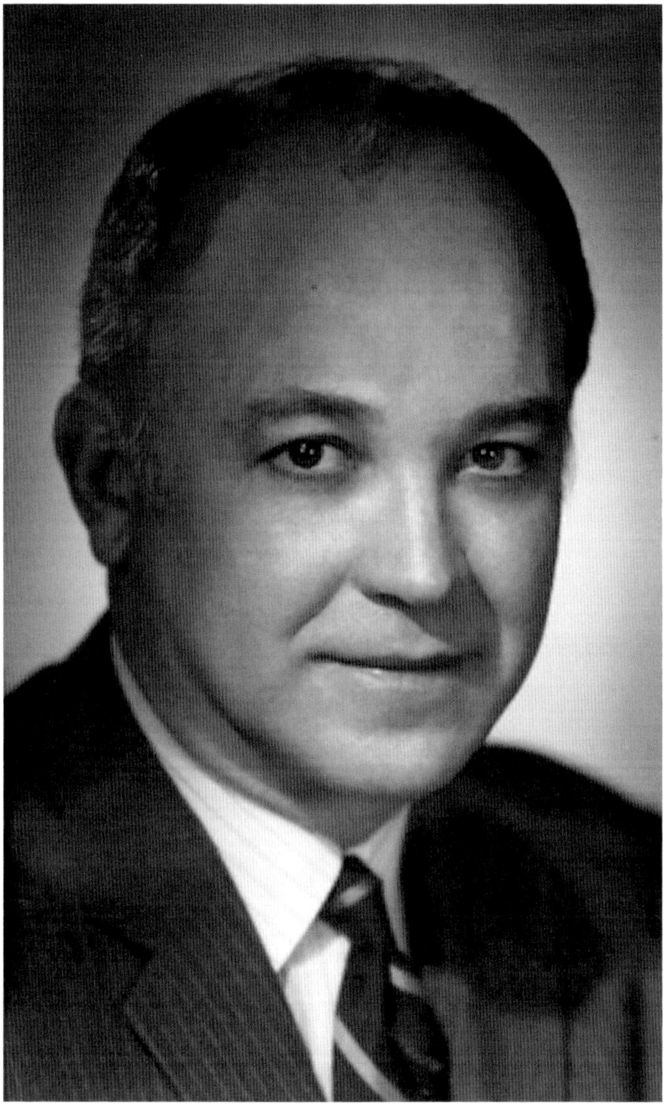

William Derwood Cann Jr.

When he was needed, William Derwood Cann Jr. answered the call for public service, first as a soldier and later as mayor of Monroe.

Born in 1919, Cann attended Northeast Louisiana University, followed by Louisiana State University. After graduating from college, young Cann joined the Army. At the time, World War II was raging. Commissioned as a second lieutenant, Cann became a paratrooper, then a unit commander, and saw action at major battles all over Europe. After the war, he stayed in the service until retiring as a lieutenant colonel in 1954.

Though he went on to enjoy innumerable successes in private business, Cann also sought opportunities to get involved in the community. Serving on a multitude of civic and nonprofit organization boards, including the YMCA and the United Way of Northeast Louisiana, he was also a member of the Monroe school board. When W.L. "Jack" Howard resigned in the middle of his fifth mayoral term, Cann was appointed interim mayor of Monroe, a post he served in briefly, from October 1978 until April 1979.

Cann died in 2010 at the age of 90 and is buried in Monroe. (Courtesy of Arabella Moore.)

CHAPTER NINE

Professional Athletes and Coaches

A wealth of hunting and fishing opportunities is a significant reason why Louisiana is known as the Sportsman's Paradise, but northeast Louisiana is also a hotbed of activity for other sports.

Football Friday nights are a phenomenon in the Louisiana Delta. Tens of thousands of fans pack stadiums across the region, like Rebel Stadium in West Monroe, where NFL stars Andrew Whitworth and Bradie James honed their gridiron skills. Richwood High School in southern Monroe produced NFL greats Sammy White and Joe Profit, while Pat Williams played his high school years at Wossman High School. Neville High School boasts Bubby Brister, while Ouachita Parish High School can claim Jonathon Wilhite. Rudy Niswanger was a Ouachita Christian Eagle, and Super Bowl champion Billy Joe Dupree started his sports career as a superstar at Richardson High School in West Monroe. Aeneas Williams, Johnny Robinson, and Stan Humphries round out the collection of Monroe's NFL legends.

When basketball season rolls around, high school gymnasiums are filled across the region. Paul Millsap played for Downsville High School near Monroe before joining the Louisiana Tech University Techsters and eventually playing in the NBA. In 1934, one of the greatest basketball players in history was born in West Monroe. William Felton "Bill" Russell was a five-time winner of the NBA's Most Valuable Player award and a 12-time all-star. Also an Olympian, Russell was part of the Gold Medal–winning team fielded by the United States in the 1956 Olympics. With Russell at center, the Boston Celtics utterly dominated the NBA for over a decade, winning an incredible 11 NBA championships. Russell was also the NBA's first African American coach.

Each spring, fans gather around the baseball diamonds of northeast Louisiana, where many future Major League Baseball players developed their boyhood dreams. Before he played for the California/Anaheim Angels, pitching ace Chuck Finley was a West Monroe High School Rebel. College baseball hall of famer Ralph "Road Runner" Garr played for Grambling State University before spending 13 seasons in the majors, and four-time all-star Ben Sheets spent his college years in a University of Louisiana at Monroe uniform.

Individual sports are not overlooked in this chapter of champions. Monroe's very own member of the PGA Tour, golfer Brian Bateman, is profiled, as is professional wrestler Cassidy Riley.

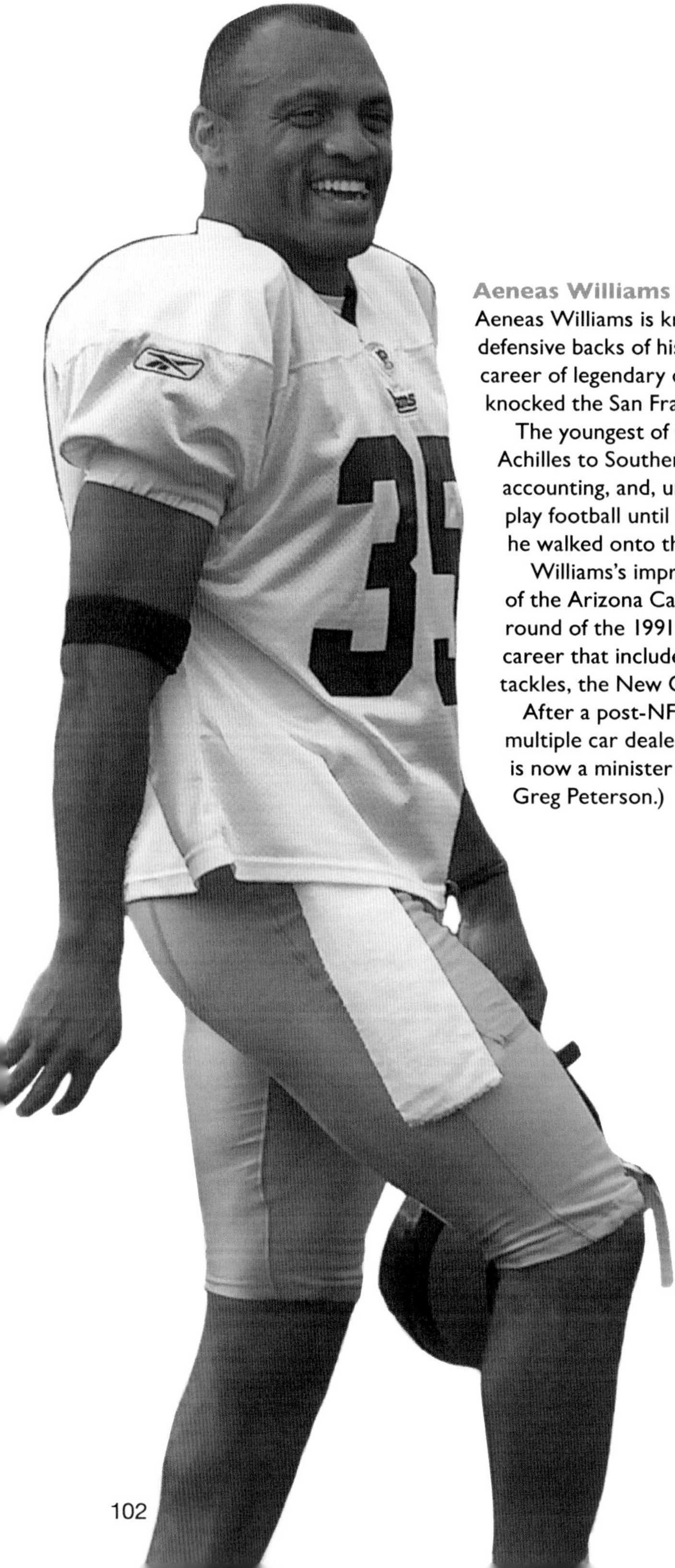

Aeneas Williams

Aeneas Williams is known to football fans as one of the best defensive backs of his time, the player who famously ended the career of legendary quarterback Steve Young with a hit that knocked the San Francisco 49ers legend out cold.

The youngest of three sons, Williams followed his brother Achilles to Southern University in Baton Rouge to study accounting, and, unlike many of his NFL peers, he did not play football until his senior year of graduate school, when he walked onto the Jaguar football team and became a star.

Williams's impressive skills on the gridiron caught the eye of the Arizona Cardinals, and he was drafted in the third round of the 1991 NFL draft. In 2005, after a long, successful career that included 14 seasons, 55 interceptions, and 692 tackles, the New Orleans native retired.

After a post-NFL career that included ventures into multiple car dealerships around his home state, Williams is now a minister in St. Louis, Missouri. (Photograph by Greg Peterson.)

Andrew Whitworth

NFL star and West Monroe High School product Andrew Whitworth now makes his home part-time in Ohio, where he has been a Pro Bowler at left tackle for the Cincinnati Bengals since graduating from Louisiana State University in 2006. But it is back home where the gentle giant makes his biggest impact.

He, together with his wife, Melissa Clark Whitworth (Miss Louisiana 2003), formed the Big Whit 77 Foundation, a nonprofit community organization so named for the six-foot-seven-inch player's nickname and jersey number. Big Whit 77 provides leadership training, scholarships, and mentoring opportunities to area youth and families, and also funds programs for gifted students and at-risk youth. Additionally, through its Open Arms grant program, Big Whit 77 provides funding to help families pay for the cost of adoption.

It is through these many charitable efforts that Whitworth, who credits his family upbringing and deep-rooted spirituality for his philanthropic nature, became a hometown hero.

Whitworth travels back to northeast Louisiana frequently, where he, Melissa, and their three children reside in the offseason. (Courtesy of the Big Whit 77 Foundation, Andrew Whitworth, and Melissa Clark Whitworth.)

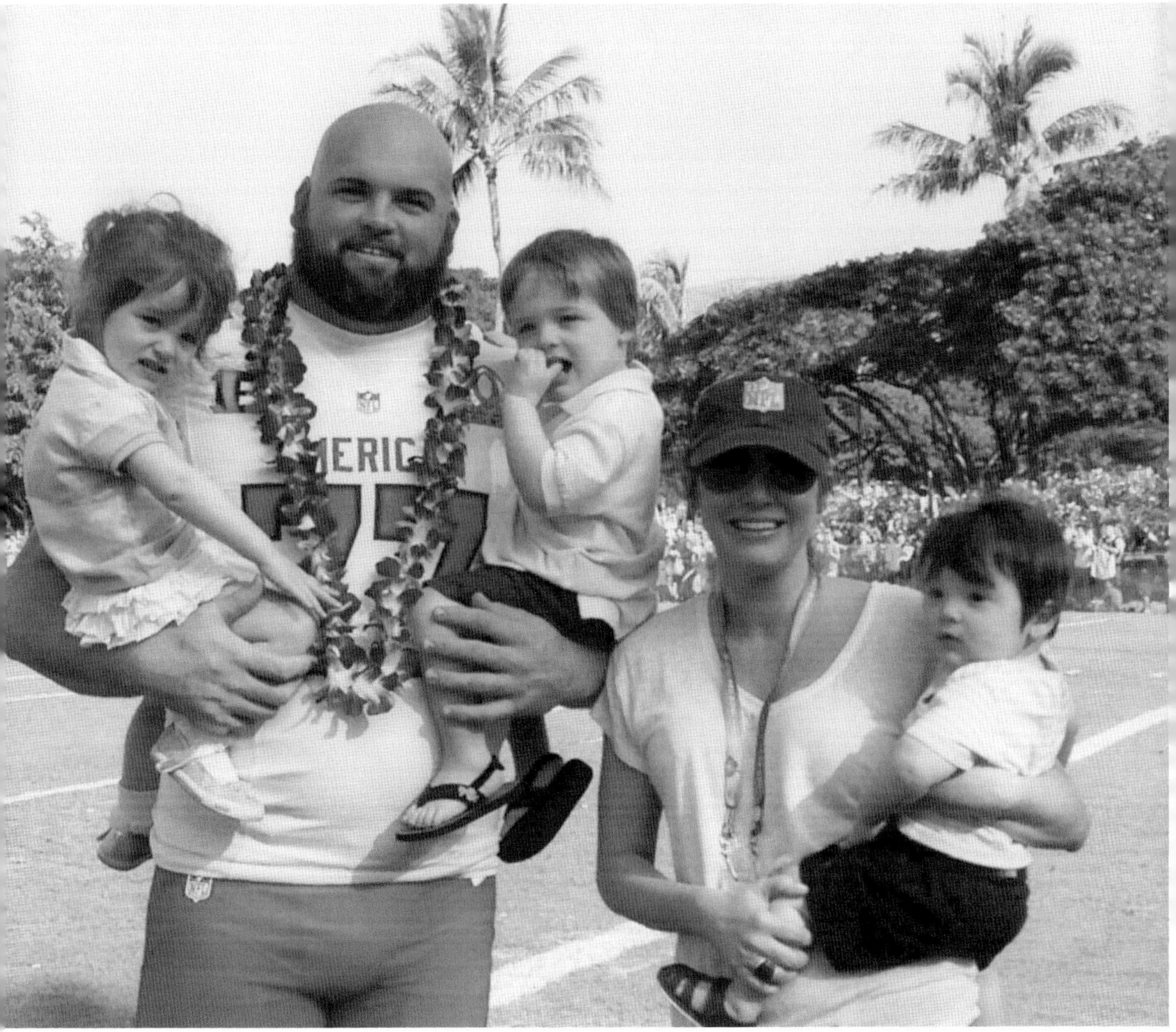

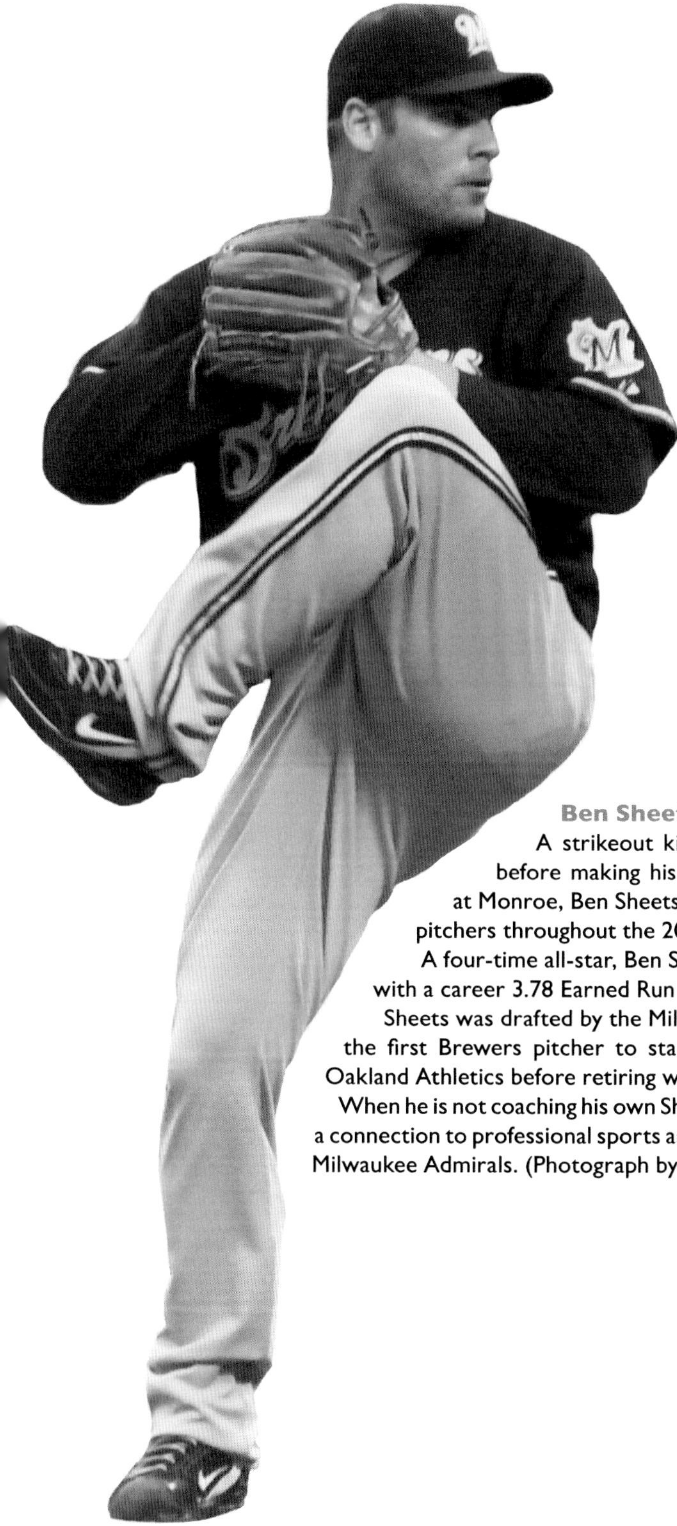

Ben Sheets

A strikeout king in Little League and high school baseball before making his college debut at the University of Louisiana at Monroe, Ben Sheets was one of Major League Baseball's premiere pitchers throughout the 2000s.

A four-time all-star, Ben Sheets compiled 94 wins in the Major Leagues, with a career 3.78 Earned Run Average and 1,325 strikeouts.

Sheets was drafted by the Milwaukee Brewers in 1999, and in 2008 became the first Brewers pitcher to start an all-star game. He later played for the Oakland Athletics before retiring with the Atlanta Braves in 2013.

When he is not coaching his own Sheets Academy baseball team, Sheets maintains a connection to professional sports as part owner of the American Hockey League's Milwaukee Admirals. (Photograph by Barbara Moore.)

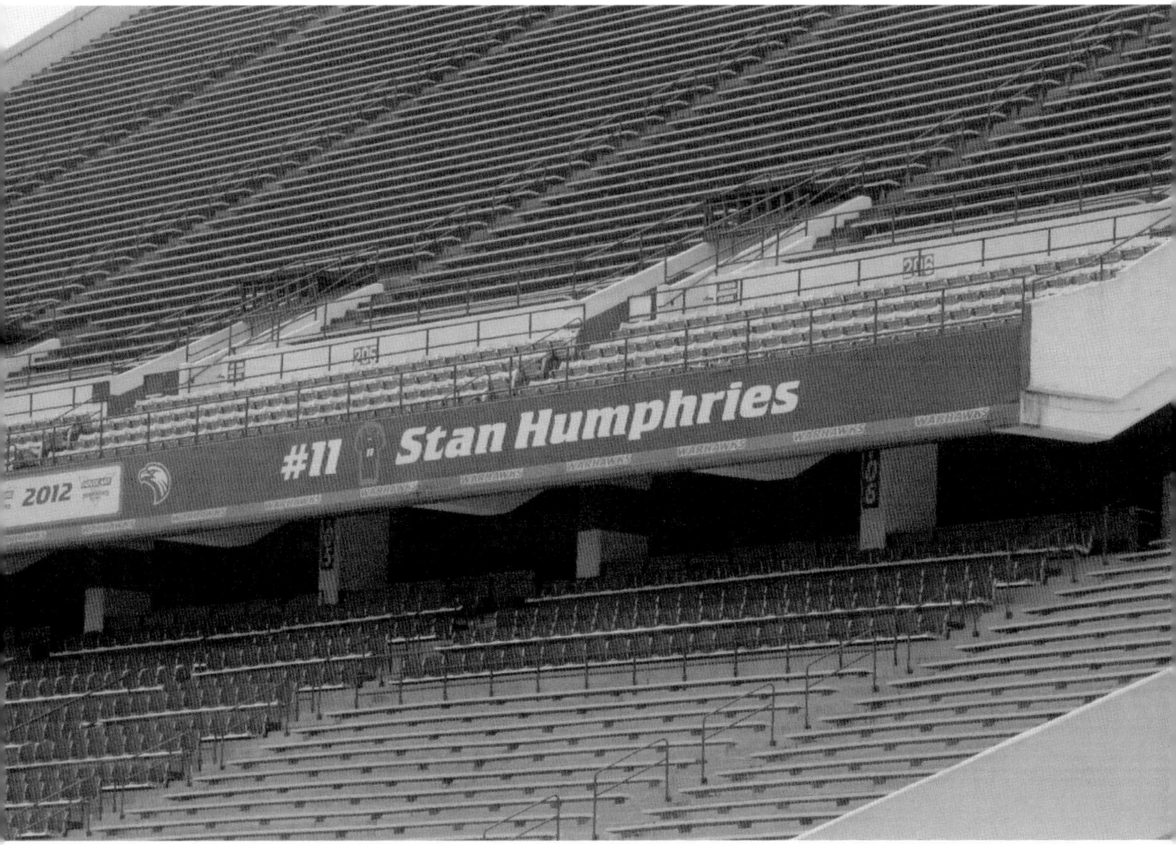

Stan Humphries

After leading the Northeast Louisiana University Indians to their sole national championship in 1987, quarterback Stan Humphries was drafted by the Washington Redskins, where he spent several seasons before moving west to play for the San Diego Chargers.

As a Charger, Humphries led his team to three playoff slots and their lone Super Bowl appearance to date, a losing effort against the San Francisco 49ers in 1995. (Photograph by Griffin Scott.)

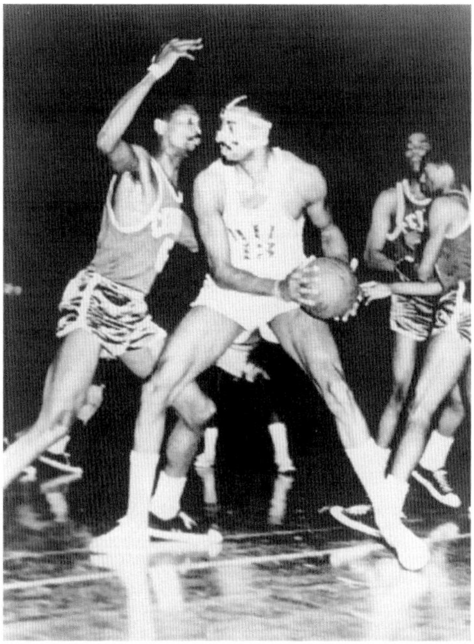

Bill Russell

Born in 1934 in heavily segregated West Monroe, sports and civil rights icon Bill Russell overcame innumerable obstacles to become the first African American NBA superstar, and later, the league's first black coach.

A lifelong Boston Celtic, Russell was named an NBA all-star 12 times and was awarded the coveted MVP award five times over the course of his playing career. In addition to being a natural addition to the NBA hall of fame, he is also an Olympic Gold medalist.

Russell is widely regarded as one of the most significant and talented professional athletes in history. He is pictured at left (with ball) and below at left (holding paper). (Left, photograph by the *New York World Telegram* and the *Sun* staff photographer; below, courtesy of the National Archives and Records Administration.)

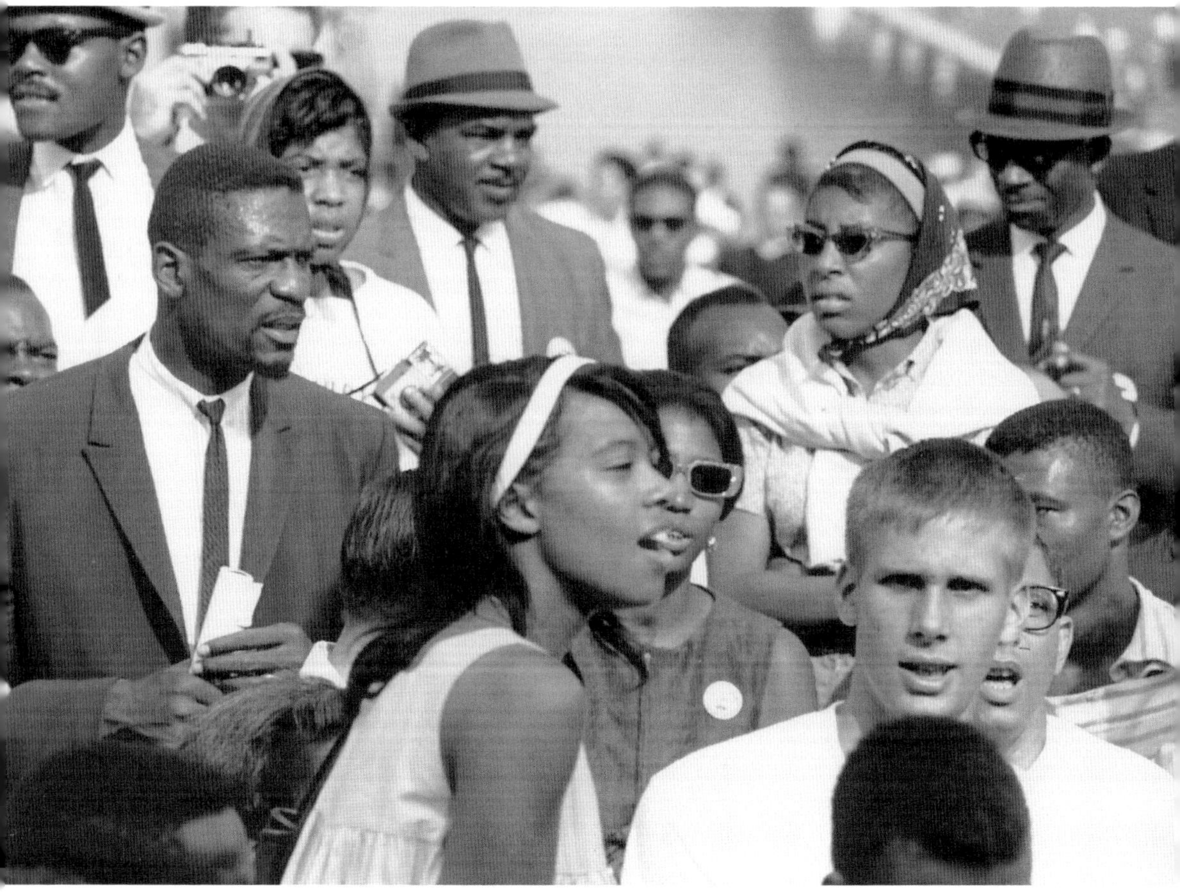

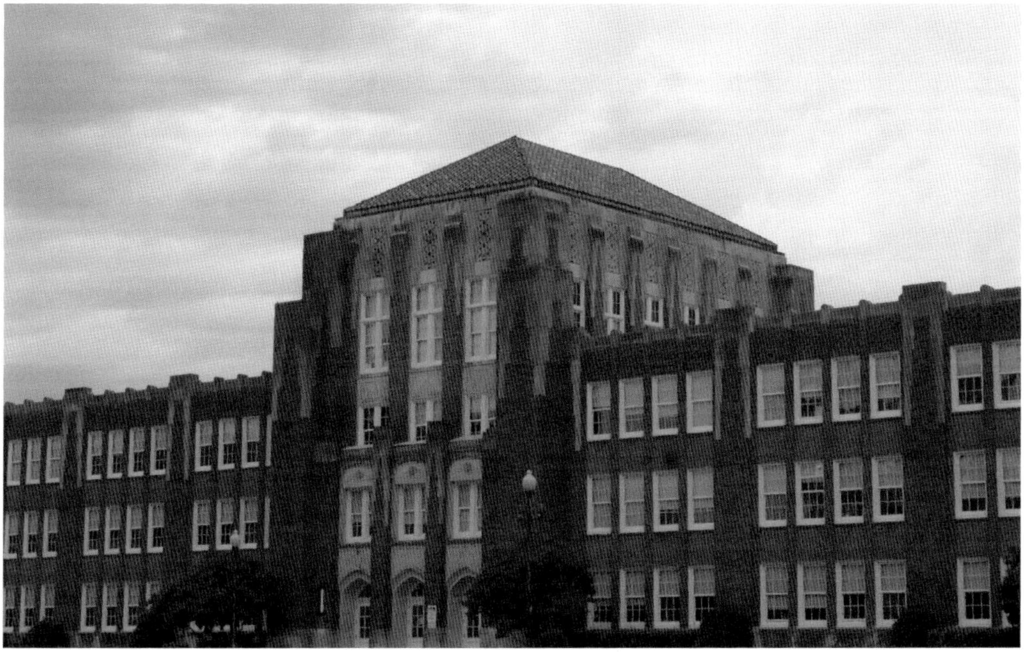

Bubby Brister

He was drafted by the Detroit Tigers baseball team following his senior year at Neville High School, but it was in the NFL, not the Major Leagues, where versatile athlete Walter A. "Bubby" Brister III would find sports acclaim.

Following an injury that ended his baseball career, Brister returned home and joined the football team at Northeast Louisiana University.

In 1986, Brister joined the professional football ranks when he was drafted by the Pittsburgh Steelers. He retired after 15 seasons in the NFL. (Both photographs by Griffin Scott.)

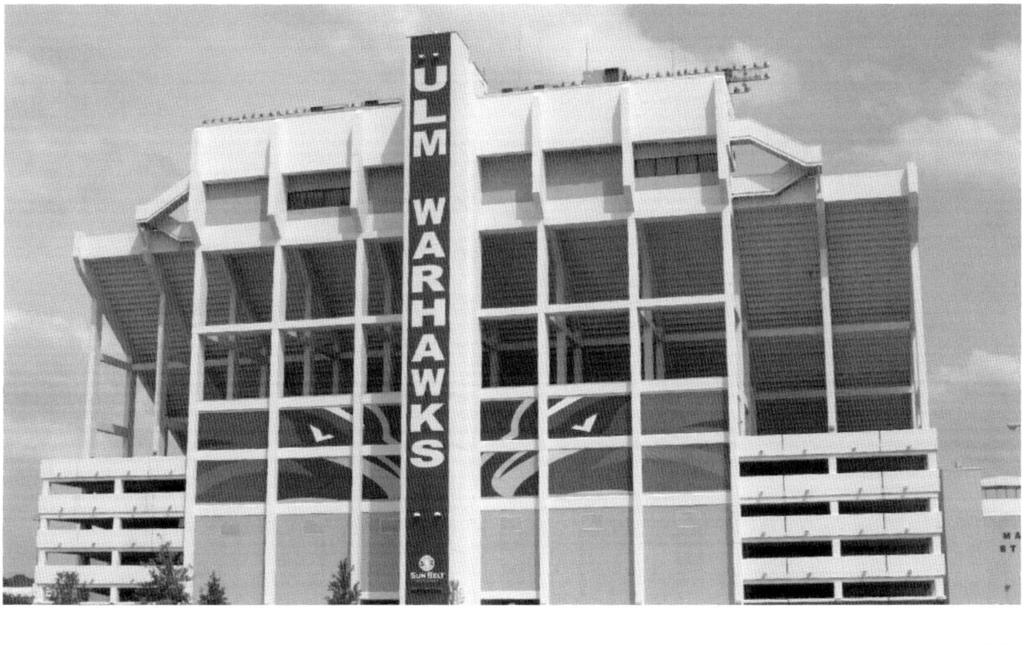

Bradie James

Like fellow NFL star and hometown hero Billy Joe Dupree, Bradie James found fame in a Dallas Cowboys uniform.

A ferocious linebacker, James played under legendary West Monroe High School coach Don Shows, winning a state championship in 1998 before going on to become a gridiron star at Louisiana State University.

Drafted by Dallas in the fourth round of the 2003 NFL draft, James spent nine years with the Cowboys before heading south to join the Houston Texans. Pictured below is the eastern end zone of West Monroe High School's Rebel stadium, where James honed his gridiron skills (Right, photograph by D.J. Judah; below, photograph by Griffin Scott.)

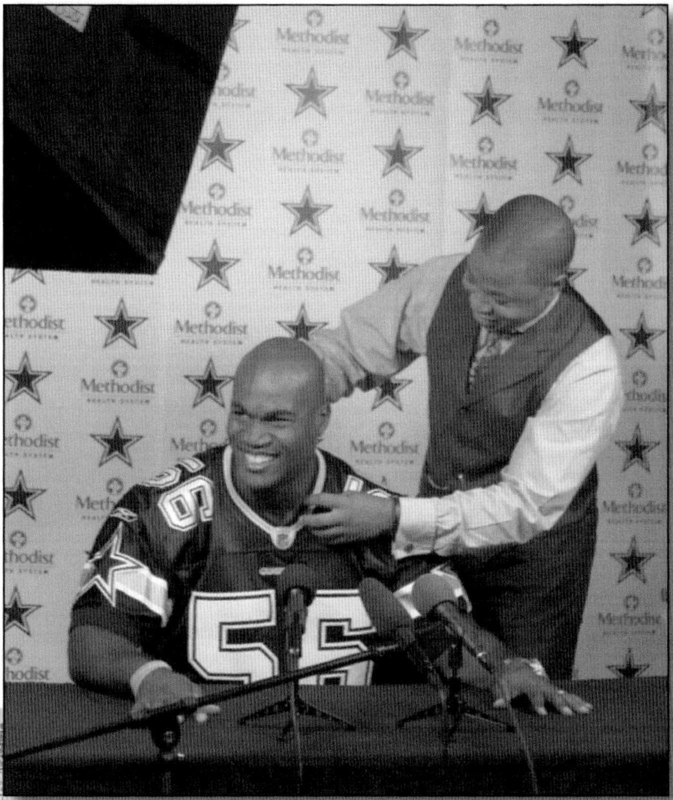

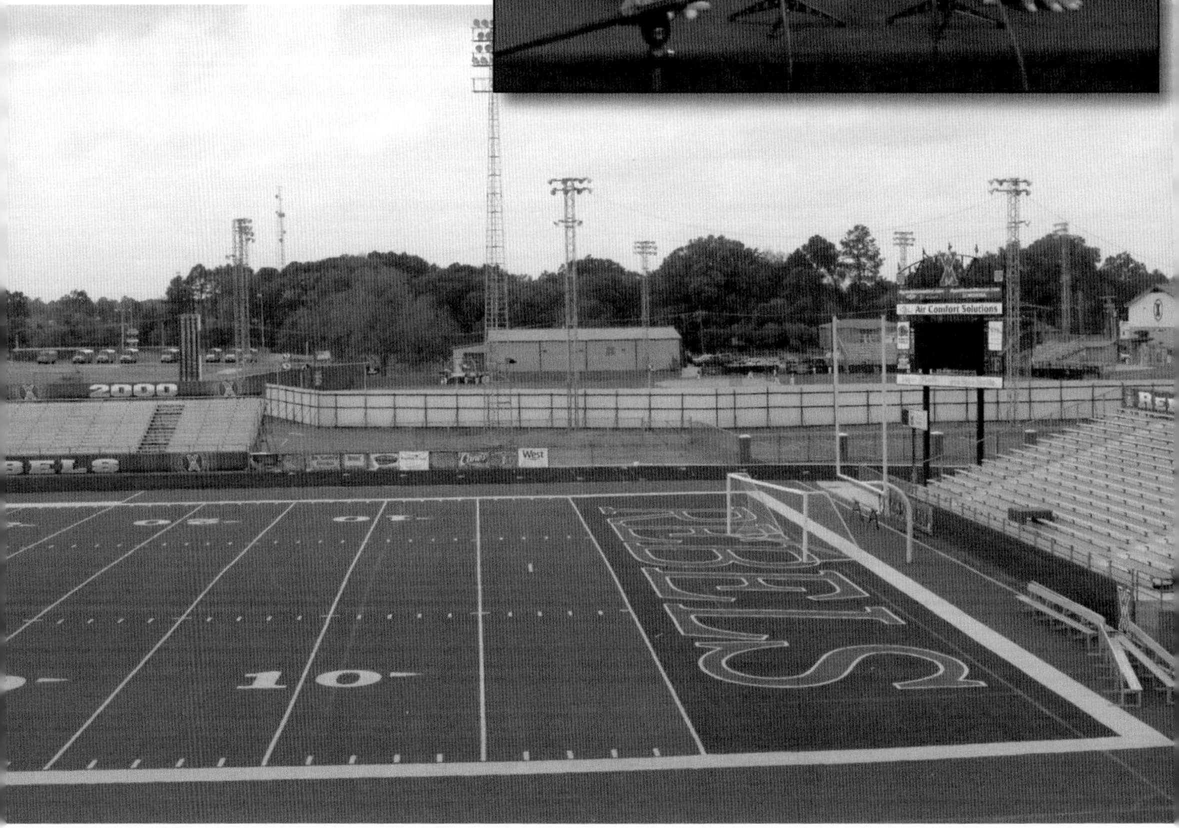

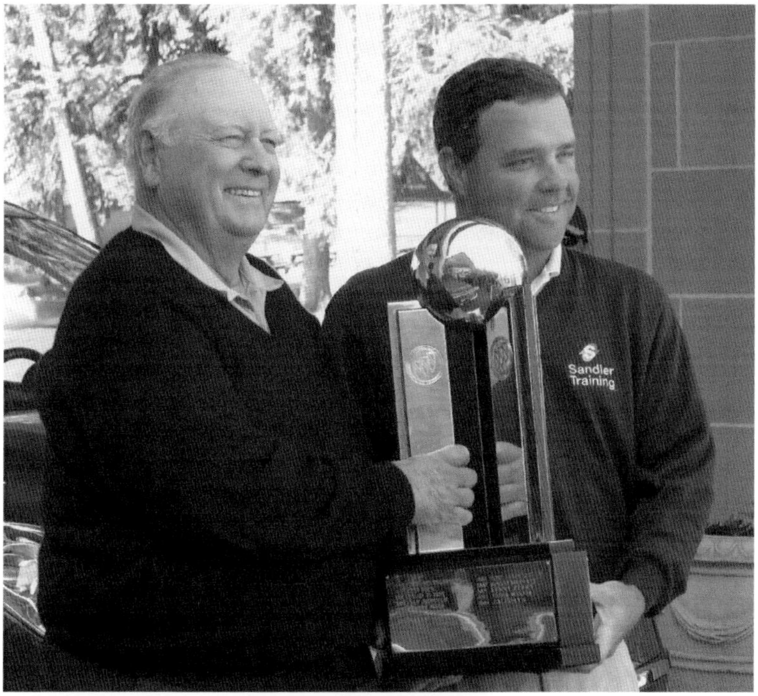

Brian Bateman
Although Monroe has been home to a host of professional football, basketball, and baseball stars, the city can also claim its very own Professional Golf Association champion in Brian Bateman (pictured on the right).

After joining the Nationwide Tour in 1997, Bateman won the Nike Carolina Classic in 1998. In 2002 he officially joined the PGA Tour, and in 2007, he won the Buick Open. (Photograph by Dave Hogg.)

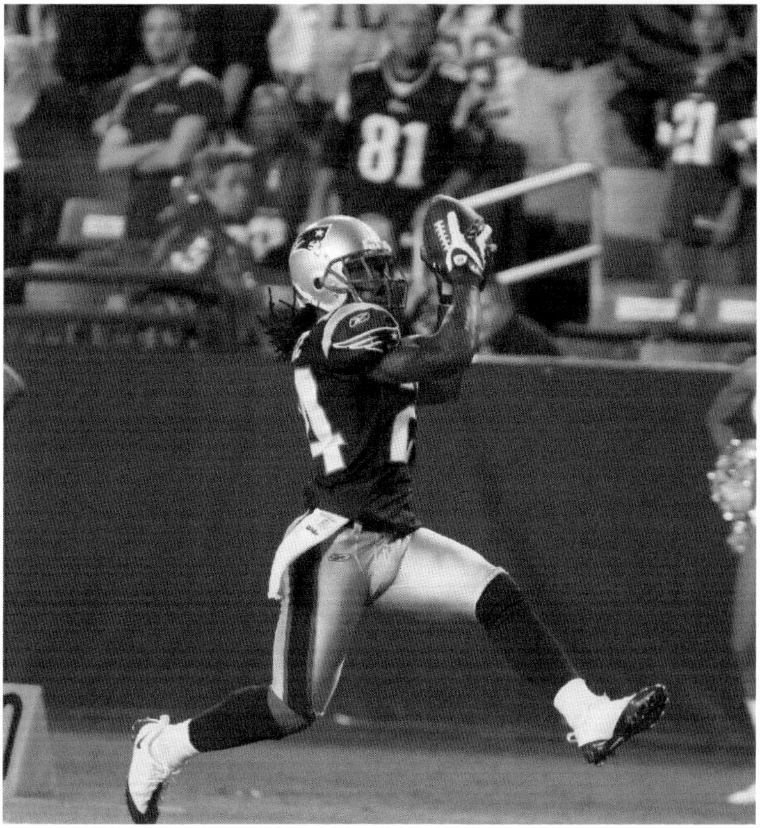

Jonathan Wilhite
Jonathan Wilhite spent several seasons in the bitter cold of the Northeast with the New England Patriots, but it was in the sweltering bayou heat of Louisiana where he earned his football stripes as a Ouachita Parish High School Lion.

After an impressive college career at Auburn University, Wilhite wound up in New England after being picked in the fourth round of the 2008 NFL draft. He has also played for the Denver Broncos and the Chicago Bears. (Photograph by Keith Allison.)

Chuck Finley (OPPOSITE PAGE)

Left-handed ace Chuck Finley signed with the California Angels in 1985 following a stellar high school and college baseball career in his native Monroe. A career milestone came in 1990 when he finished the season with a 2.40 ERA.

Finley made headlines off the diamond in 2002, when his then-wife, actress Tawny Kitaen, was arrested at the couple's Los Angeles home after assaulting the athlete.

Finley retired from professional baseball following a final season with the Cleveland Indians. In 2010, he was inducted into the Angels hall of fame. (Courtesy of Susan Cox.)

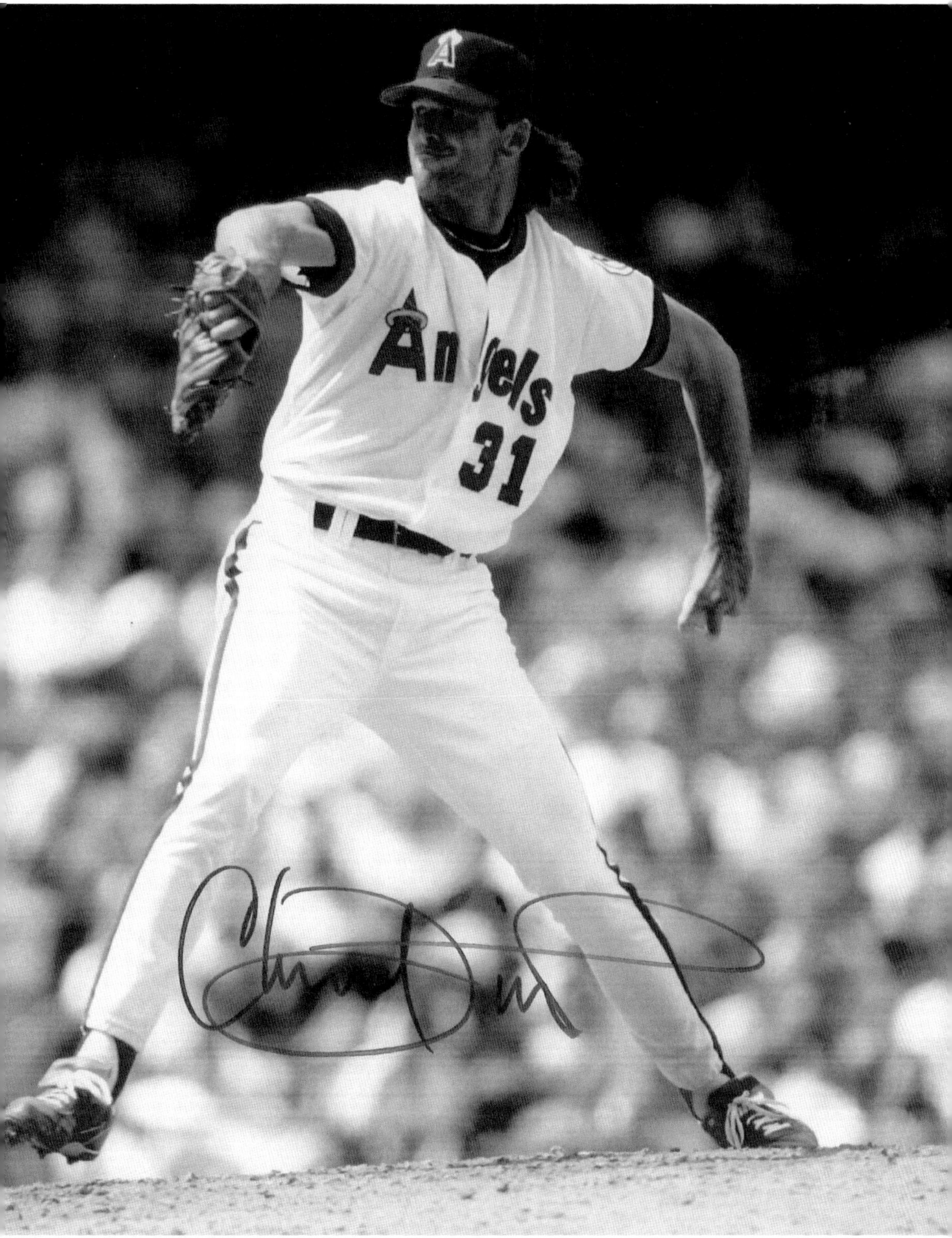
Angels
31

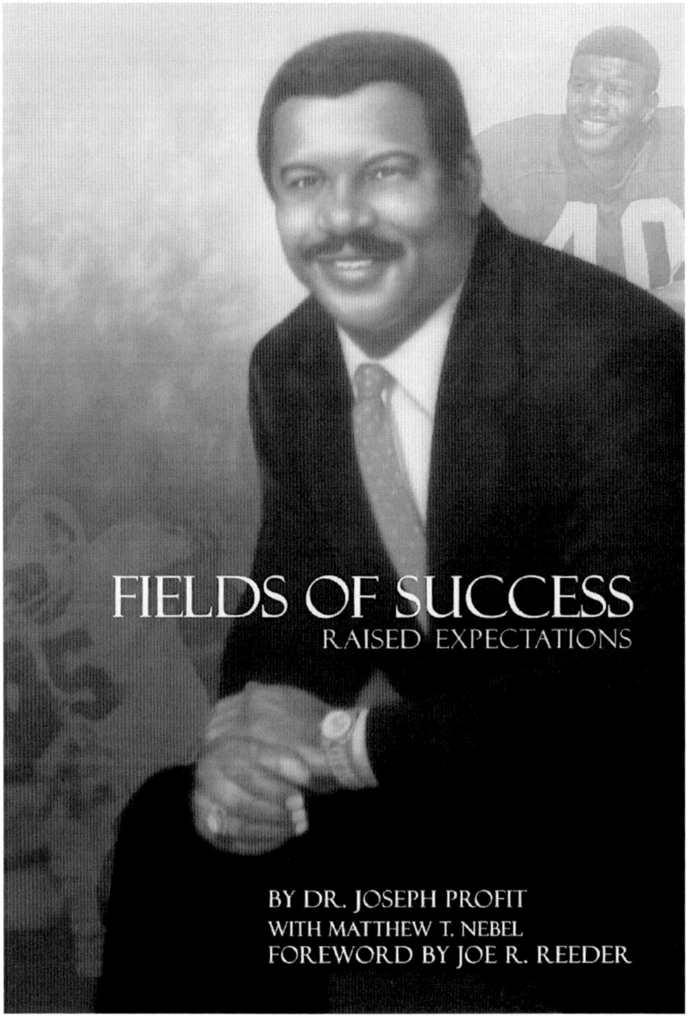

Dr. Joseph Profit

After a successful turn playing football for Richwood High School in Monroe, Dr. Joseph "Joe" Profit was one of the first African American players to become a star at a traditionally all-white college, Northeast Louisiana University.

The seventh player chosen in the 1971 NFL draft, Profit played with the Atlanta Falcons, the New Orleans Saints, and later, the Birmingham franchise of the World Football League during his professional football career.

In retirement, Profit became an entrepreneur, building a business resume as diverse as it is impressive, and perhaps even more impressive than his accomplishments on the field. His biography includes such highlights as starting a technology firm, founding *Inc.* magazine, holding top-secret government clearance as a defense contractor, and investing in numerous successful e-commerce ventures.

Named Entrepreneur of the Year in 1988, Profit was later inducted into the Business and Professional Hall of Fame in 1994, and the Louisiana Sports Hall of Fame just five years later. He has also served on federal boards at the request of the past five US presidents.

Always seeking new challenges and ever the trailblazer, he formed the nonprofit organization Youth United for Prosperity in 2005. Profit's autobiography, *Fields of Success*, was published in 2013. (Photograph by Amy Sliger.)

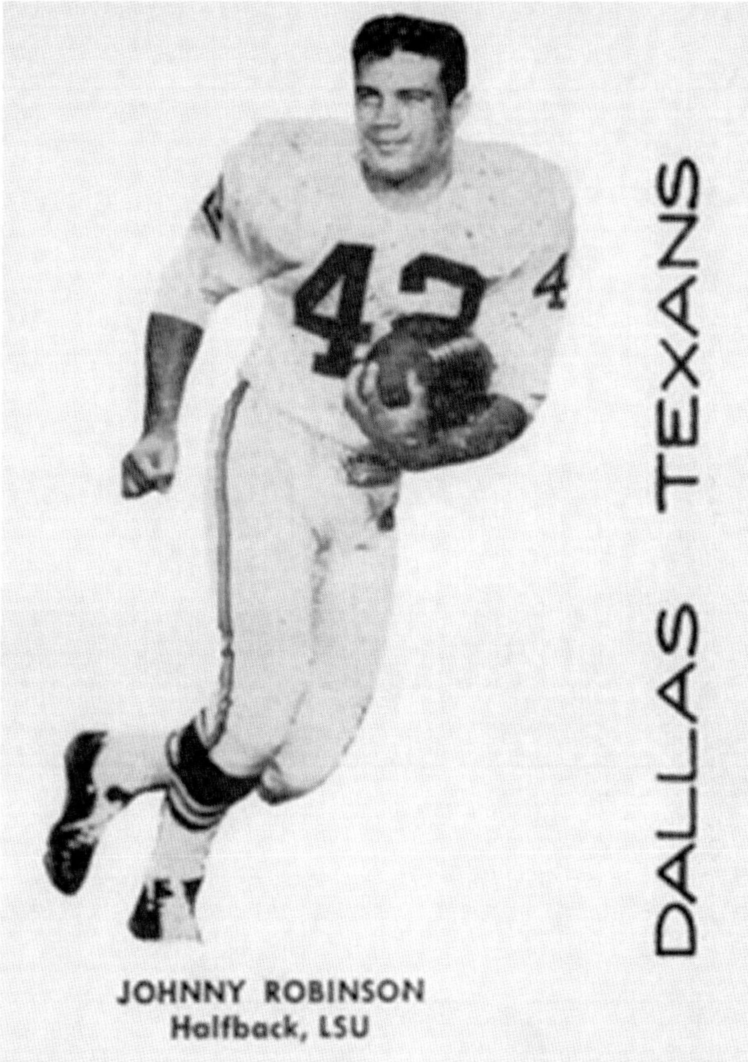

Johnny Robinson

Long before he was considered one of the greatest safeties in professional football, Louisiana sports legend Johnny Robinson was credited by fans and sportswriters alike as one of the best defensive players not inducted into the NFL hall of fame.

Robinson first earned prominence as a member of the famed Louisiana State University national championship team of 1958, sharing the backfield with Heisman trophy winner Billy Cannon. Drafted in the first round by the Dallas Texans in 1960, Robinson spent two seasons as a running back before moving to the other side of the ball and morphing into one of the greatest defensive backs to ever play the game.

In 1963, the team packed up and moved north to Missouri, where they reemerged as the Kansas City Chiefs. It was during Super Bowl IV that Robinson reached sports hero status, displaying strength and dedication by playing with three broken ribs, a parting gift from the American Football League championship game only one week before.

After the 1971 season Robinson retired to Monroe, where he now operates a home for troubled youth. (Courtesy of the Vintage Football Card Gallery.)

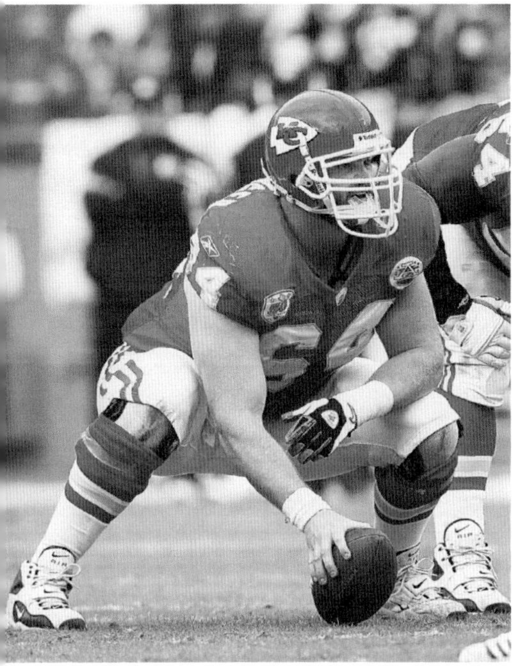

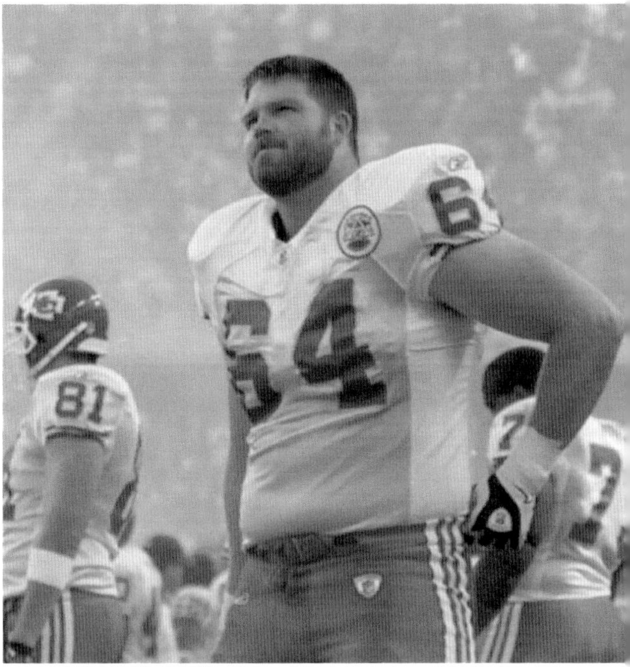

Rudy Niswanger

Protecting valuable assets is a specialty of Rudolph Nelson "Rudy" Niswanger. Born in Monroe in 1982, Niswanger played high school football for Ouachita Christian School, helping lead the team to a state championship.

Niswanger went on to have an outstanding college career at LSU and later played for the Kansas City Chiefs for five seasons.

After he was cut by the Detroit Lions in 2011, Niswanger went into private business as CEO of the Joe Gear Companies, a group of companies started by his family. (Both courtesy of Rudy Niswanger.)

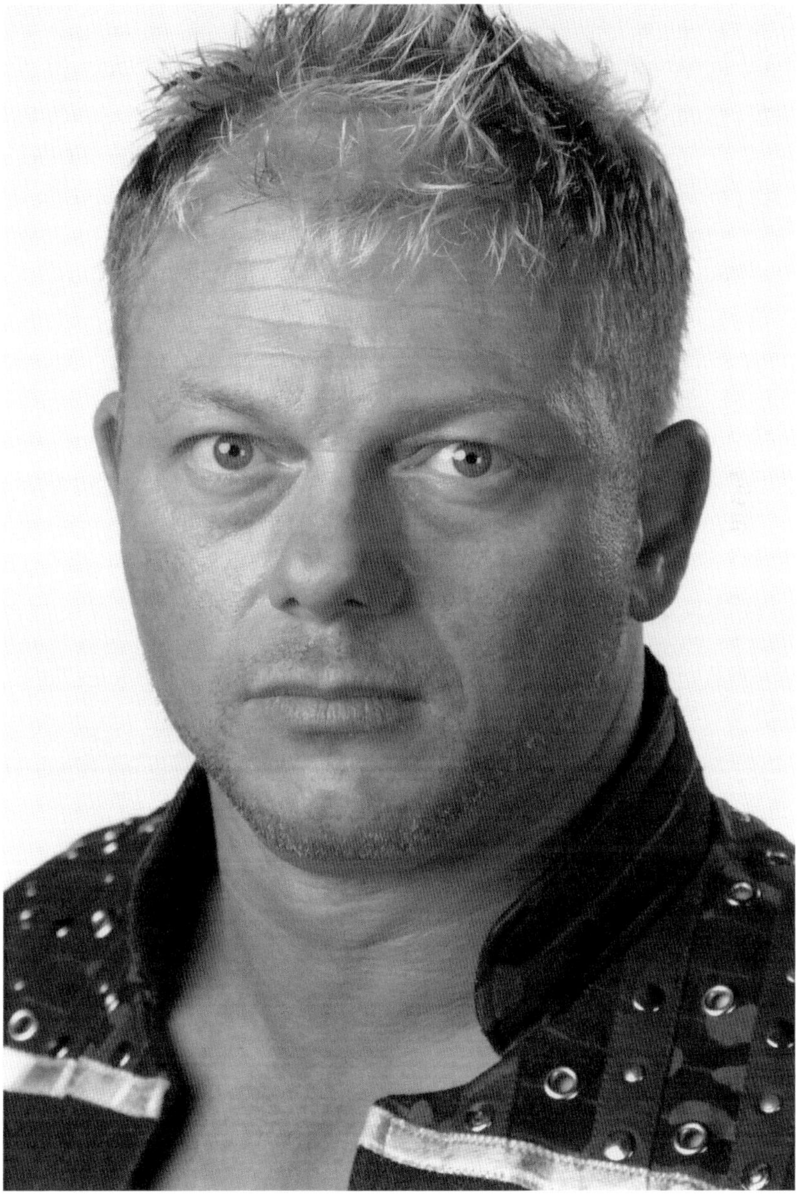

Cassidy Riley

It was in the early 1980s that six-year-old Cassidy Riley fell in love with professional wrestling after getting his young hands on a copy of a wrestling magazine. While still in his teens, Riley debuted on the professional circuit. Within a few years, he had worked his way to the top, with regular appearances for professional wresting entertainment companies Total Nonstop Action Wrestling and World Wrestling Entertainment.

Currently known as "the VIP," Riley is a professional wrestling chameleon, having gone through such monikers as "Cassidy O'Reilly," "Cass Reilly," "Hotshot Cassidy," and "Cassidy James."

His company, Southern Wrestling Superstars, which was featured on A&E's reality television hit *Duck Dynasty* in 2014, produces pay-per-view and DVD matches, and promotes professional wresting bouts across the South. (Courtesy of Cassidy Riley.)

Lenny Fant

At his 1998 funeral, coach Leonard O'Neil "Lenny" Fant's pastor described him as "an extraordinary, ordinary man." An Alabama native, Fant came to Louisiana via a basketball scholarship to Centenary College in nearby Shreveport.

After graduation, he coached at Delhi High School and several colleges before arriving at Northeast Louisiana State College in 1958. When Coach Fant hung up his whistle 22 years later, he left Northeast with a record of 326-221.

Fant coached his teams to seven conference crowns and three 20-win seasons, leading the school from the NAIA level to NCAA Division I, as well as a record stretch of 18 consecutive winning seasons. In 1979, his final season as head coach, Fant led his last team to a 23-6 record, earning the university its first NCAA postseason appearance.

All the young men who played for Fant were known by him as his "boys," a list peppered with numerous local luminaries, including former university president Lawson Swearingen, NBA star Calvin Natt, US Olympian Glynn Saulters, and the man who succeeded him as head coach, Mike Vining.

Longtime Monroe mayor Jamie Mayo remembers about Fant, "He cared about us after our eligibility ended. When I was first elected to the City Council, Coach Fant was one of the first people to call and congratulate me."

Fant was diagnosed with cancer in 1997, and passed away 18 months later. Though frail from his battle with the dreaded disease, he continued to support his beloved university, making appearances at games. A fighter right to the end, Fant participated in the American Cancer Society's Relay for Life just three months before his passing.

When he died in October 1998, thousands, including many of his former players, attended his funeral, held at the university's basketball coliseum, on the very court where the coach and his boys made so many memories, a facility that now bears his name.

Fant is a member of the Louisiana Sports Hall of Fame, the Louisiana Basketball Hall of Fame, the Centenary Hall of Fame, and, of course, the University of Louisiana at Monroe Hall of Fame. (Photograph by Griffin Scott.)

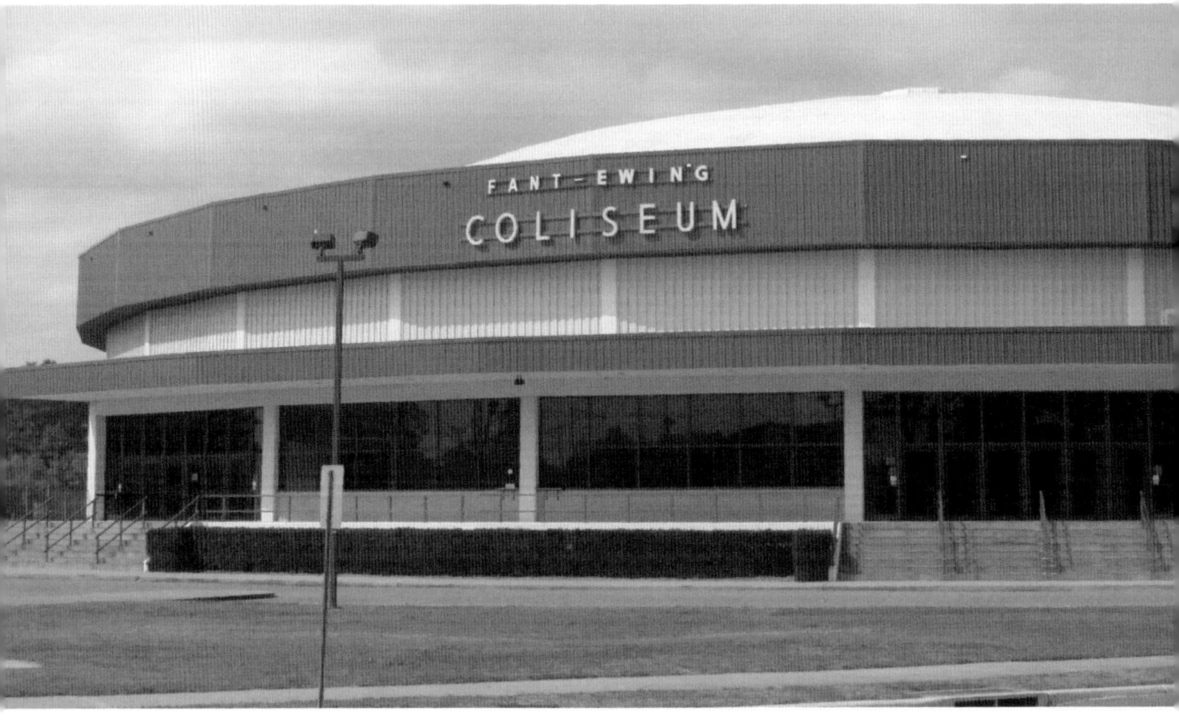

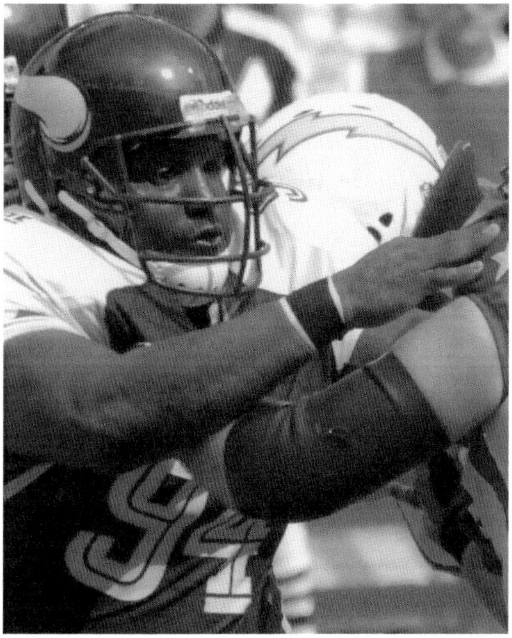

Pat Williams

Born in Monroe in 1972, NFL all-pro defensive lineman Pat Williams is a study in perseverance. After graduation from Wossman High School, where he lettered in football, basketball, baseball, and track, the multitalented Williams started out playing college ball at Navarro College before transferring to Texas A&M University. An academic issue caused him to lose his spot on the roster in 1994, and Williams was transferred to Northeast Oklahoma A&M College.

Undrafted in 1997, Williams signed with the Buffalo Bills, spending seven years with the team before moving on to the Minnesota Vikings, where he played another six NFL seasons.

Williams's most productive years were undoubtedly spent with the Vikings. He was named to the Pro Bowl for three consecutive years beginning in 2006, and, alongside teammate Kevin Williams, formed the so-called "Williams Wall," the backbone of one of the NFL's most dominant defenses. (Photograph by Michi Moore.)

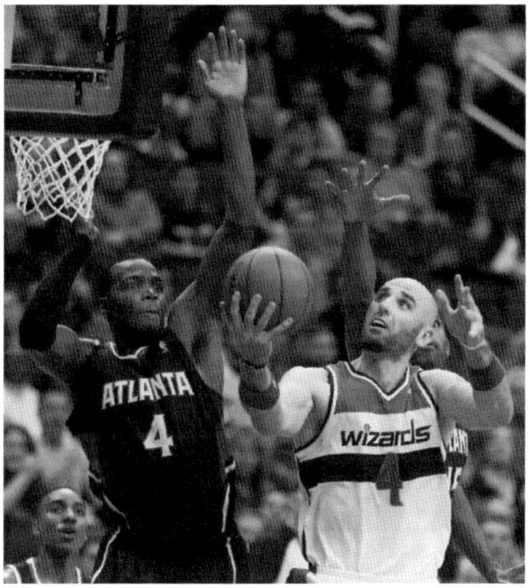

Paul Millsap

Although born in Monroe in 1985, Millsap (left) spent most of his childhood in Denver, Colorado, where, along with his four brothers, he dreamed of becoming a football star.

At age 14, Millsap's NFL dreams were stifled when his mother, Bettye, decided to move the family back to rural Louisiana from Colorado. With no football team to join, Millsap concentrated instead on basketball, setting courts on fire.

In 2006, Millsap was the 47th pick of the NBA draft, selected by the Utah Jazz, where he spent seven seasons.

He stays busy off the basketball court through his work with the Paul Millsap Foundation. He signed with the Atlanta Hawks in 2013. (Photograph by Keith Allison.)

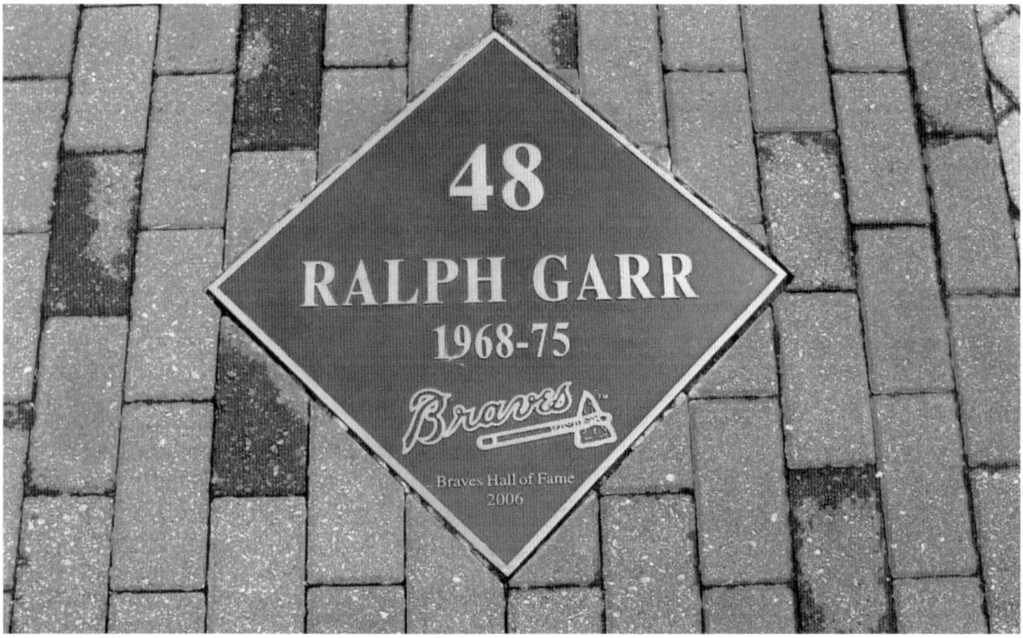

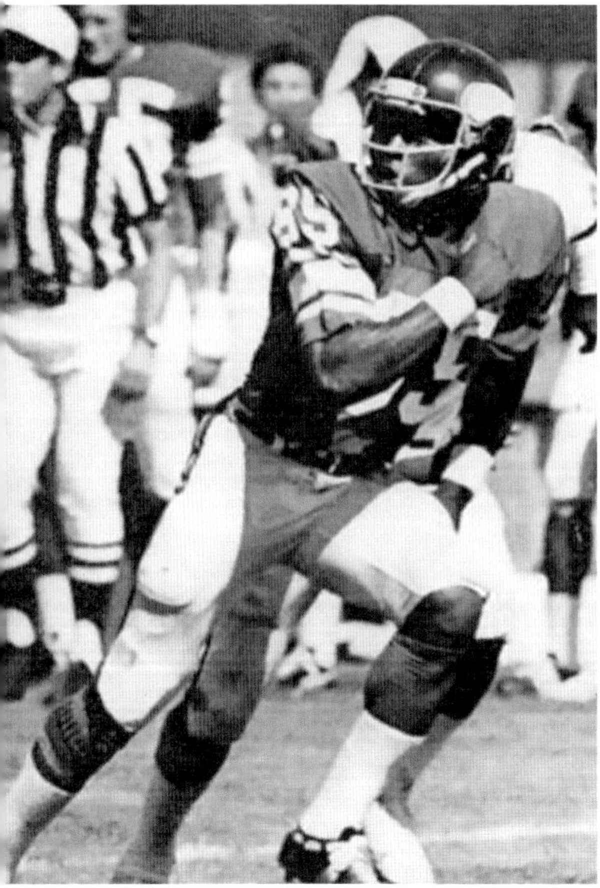

Ralph Garr

A prolific hitter who could also run like the wind, Ralph "Road Runner" Garr set a slew of records at Grambling State University before being selected by the Atlanta Braves in the 1967 amateur draft.

In 2013, he was inducted into the College Baseball Hall of Fame. (Photograph by Wally Gobetz.)

Sammy White

Wide receiver and two-time Pro Bowler Sammy White was a football and basketball star at Richwood High in Monroe. White went on to Grambling State University, and eventually the NFL, where he played with the Minnesota Vikings, the team he spent his entire professional career with. (Photograph by *Ebony* magazine, December 1976.)

CHAPTER TEN

Rebels and Villains

Just a few blocks from the Ouachita River, in one of Monroe's oldest cemeteries, stands a regal statue of one of Monroe's infamous notables, businessman Sidney Saunders. According to legend, Saunders, a 19th-century Monroe saloon proprietor, was secretly a brothel owner and married to a former prostitute. His death and the tale of the statue that serves as his tombstone are an intriguing mystery even today, over 125 years later.

Controversial Black Panthers cofounder Huey P. Newton was born in Monroe. A leading figure in the Black Power movement of the 1960s, Newton, who was named after Louisiana governor and "Kingfish" Huey P. Long, was a study in contradictions. He held a PhD and was a published author, but he was also convicted of murder after slaying a 17-year-old neighborhood girl over a perceived insult. In the end, Newton was a victim of violent crime himself, gunned down outside a West Oakland, California, crack house in 1989.

From 1947 until 1977, Otto Passman represented Monroe and the fifth district of northeast Louisiana in the US Congress. Passman was considered among the most powerful members of the House of Representatives before one of the biggest political scandals of the 1970s ended his political career and almost sent him to prison.

Hollywood star Ed Asner played former Monroe police officer Guy Banister in the Oliver Stone film *JFK*. After leaving Monroe, Banister spent 20 years as an agent with the FBI. He retired from the FBI, taking a position with the New Orleans police department, but was fired after pulling a gun in a bar and threatening a waiter. In 1964, shortly after President Kennedy was assassinated, Banister was running his own private detective agency out of New Orleans. Orleans Parish prosecutor Jim Garrison accused Banister and several other Big Easy figures of being co-conspirators with JFK's assassin, Lee Harvey Oswald. Banister never answered his accusers, and died only a few months later, in June 1964.

An alleged turn-of-the-20th-century pimp, a militant activist, a rumored "dirty" politician, and a man who may have been involved in the murder of a beloved US president; these are the rebels and villains of Monroe.

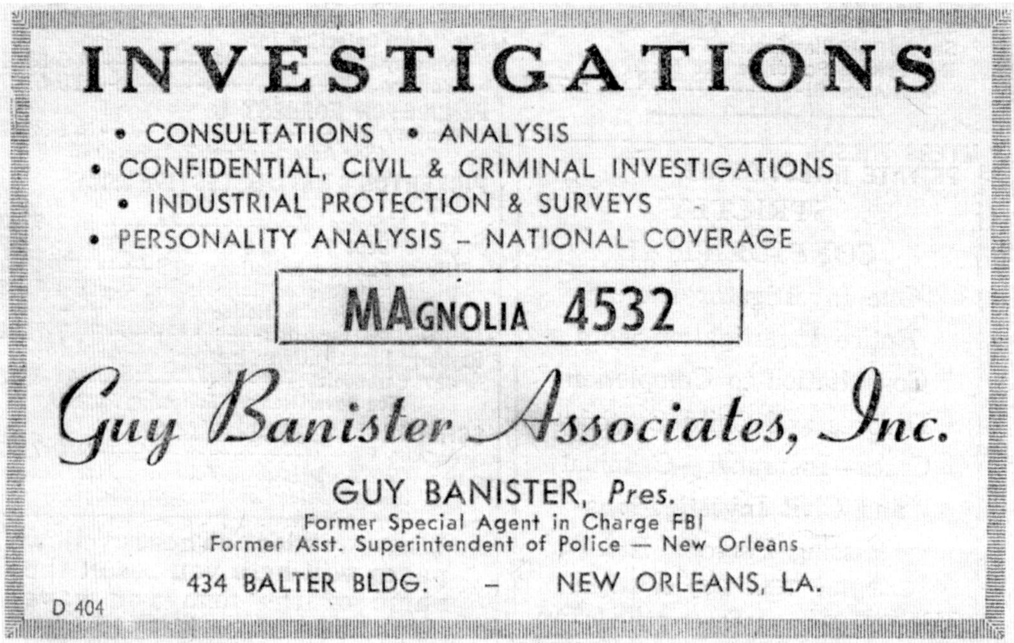

Guy Banister

Though his name is infamously connected to the Dallas assassination of Pres. John F. Kennedy, Guy Banister's roots began in Monroe. Born in 1901, Banister finished high school and studied at Louisiana State University, later returning to Monroe and serving on the city's police force before moving on to the FBI in 1934. After 20 years with the FBI, Banister retired. Returning to Louisiana, he joined the New Orleans Police Department, but was fired in 1957 for allegedly pulling a gun on a waiter in a Big Easy bar.

Following the notorious incident, he established a private detective agency, Guy Banister Associates. The tale of Banister's legend grows murky at this point. According to New Orleans district attorney Jim Garrison, himself a bullying demagogue or a brilliant investigator, Banister, working at the behest of the CIA and other government officials, conspired with New Orleans businessman Clay Shaw, Danny Ferrie, anti-Castro Cuban revolutionaries, the mafia, and Lee Harvey Oswald to assassinate President Kennedy. A subsequent trial ended in failure for Garrison.

Banister died of coronary thrombosis in 1964, only eight months after Kennedy's assassination, but his connection to the assassination has endured. In 1991, he was portrayed by Emmy Award–winning actor Ed Asner in director Oliver Stone's controversial film *JFK*. (Advertisement by Guy Banister Associates Inc., from the 1959 Yellow Pages.)

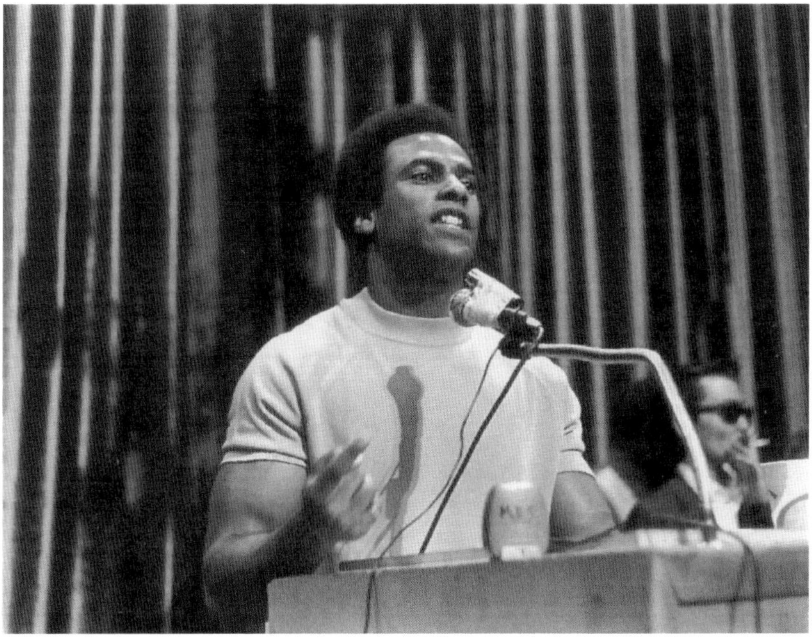

Huey P. Newton

People still disagree over whether Huey P. Newton was a villainous murderer or a revolutionary hero. In 1942, Newton, one of the city's most notorious sons, was born to sharecropper parents in Monroe. An accomplished man, Newton was a published author and political activist, and boasted impressive educational credentials, having earned a PhD from the University of California at Santa Cruz.

But he was also a convicted killer. First convicted of fatally shooting a 17-year-old neighborhood girl, Newton was later tried and convicted in the slaying of an Oakland, California, police officer, a charge that was later overturned and dismissed entirely.

Newton's storied career began around the time he met Bobby Seale. Together, the two men would make history. It was 1966, and Newton and Seale were students at Merritt College in Oakland, where they had displayed a burgeoning interest in activism. They had both served on the advisory board of the North Oakland Neighborhood Anti-Poverty Center. The civil rights and antiwar movements were exploding across college campuses nationwide, and it was against this backdrop that the duo founded the Black Panther Party for Self Defense. Seale proclaimed himself chairman, and Newton was minister of defense.

Like Newton, the Black Panther Party was either a great civic organization or a menace to society, depending on who one asks. The controversial group organized voter drives, marched on city halls to protest police brutality and political corruption, joined the growing chorus against war in Southeast Asia, and set up education programs for kids in low-income areas.

They were also alleged to be a violent, corrupt street gang underneath their political rhetoric, an image that Newton himself helped solidify. In 1982, Newton was arrested for embezzling funds from the Panthers in order to fund his drug habit. Soon after, the Black Panther Party disbanded.

On August 22, 1989, Newton's turbulent and often violent life came to an abrupt end when he was shot two times on a California street corner.

He has been mentioned in two dozen chart-topping songs by artists like Wiz Khalifa and Public Enemy. *The Boondocks* comic strip character Huey Freeman is based on him, and in 1996, the one-man play *A Huey P. Newton Story* was staged. In 2001, an award-winning film adaptation of *Story* was released, directed by Academy Award–nominated director Spike Lee.

Decades after his death, Huey P. Newton remains a controversial and popular figure. (Courtesy of the Richard Aoki Collection.)

Sidney W. Saunders (OPPOSITE PAGE)
The tale of Sidney W. Saunders is one of the most intriguing fables included in the chronicles of Monroe. Born in Mississippi in 1846, Saunders's family moved to Morehouse Parish when he was a young child.

He served in the Civil War and was wounded at the Battle of Vicksburg. Returning home to northeast Louisiana after the war, Saunders settled in Monroe and soon became a successful businessman running a saloon and grocery store.

Soon, the gifted entrepreneur found love (and controversy) with fellow Morehouse Parish native Annie Livingston. For reasons that have never become clear, Annie was rumored to be a prostitute of mixed race. Perhaps it stemmed from the gossip and tall tales that swirled around Saunders himself, as whispers around town suggested that he ran brothels and was a prodigious gambler. Saunders and Livingston had a child before they married, a son they named Willie St. John. The child died when he was only 13.

In 1888, a building owned by Saunders burned to the ground in a fire so intense it consumed several other nearby structures, and only an August rain prevented more widespread destruction. Following the incident, Saunders was accused of arson and insurance fraud and was set to stand trial when, in February 1889, he died at home from a bullet wound to the back of the head.

After his death was ruled a suicide, Saunders's siblings took Livingston to court, claiming the two were never married and that, as such, she was not eligible for a penny of Saunders's substantial fortune. When the dust settled, Livingston was able to produce a St. Louis, Missouri, marriage license dated 1875, entitling her to several thousand dollars in cash and property.

Livingston commissioned the construction of a magnificent monument, which also served as a small mausoleum, to be built in a Monroe cemetery. She had the remains of her son and her husband moved there, along with a collection of items that included Saunders's desk and Willie St. John's tricycle. Atop the monument is a statue of Saunders clutching a scroll containing the tragic couple's marriage license. Livingston directed the masons to orient his stone likeness toward downtown Monroe, forever gazing at the long-gone elites who looked down on their relationship.

She later remarried and moved to Texas, where she died in 1926 in an accidental fire. Livingston's remains were returned to Monroe, where she was interred with Saunders and their son.

Many decades later, in 2001, the mystery of Livingston and Saunders's relationship deepened further when researchers with the Ouachita Parish Public Library found a copy of the alleged St. Louis marriage license dated 1875, just as Livingston had always claimed. However, the license was not registered until 1889, four months after Saunders's alleged suicide. (Photograph by Griffin Scott.)

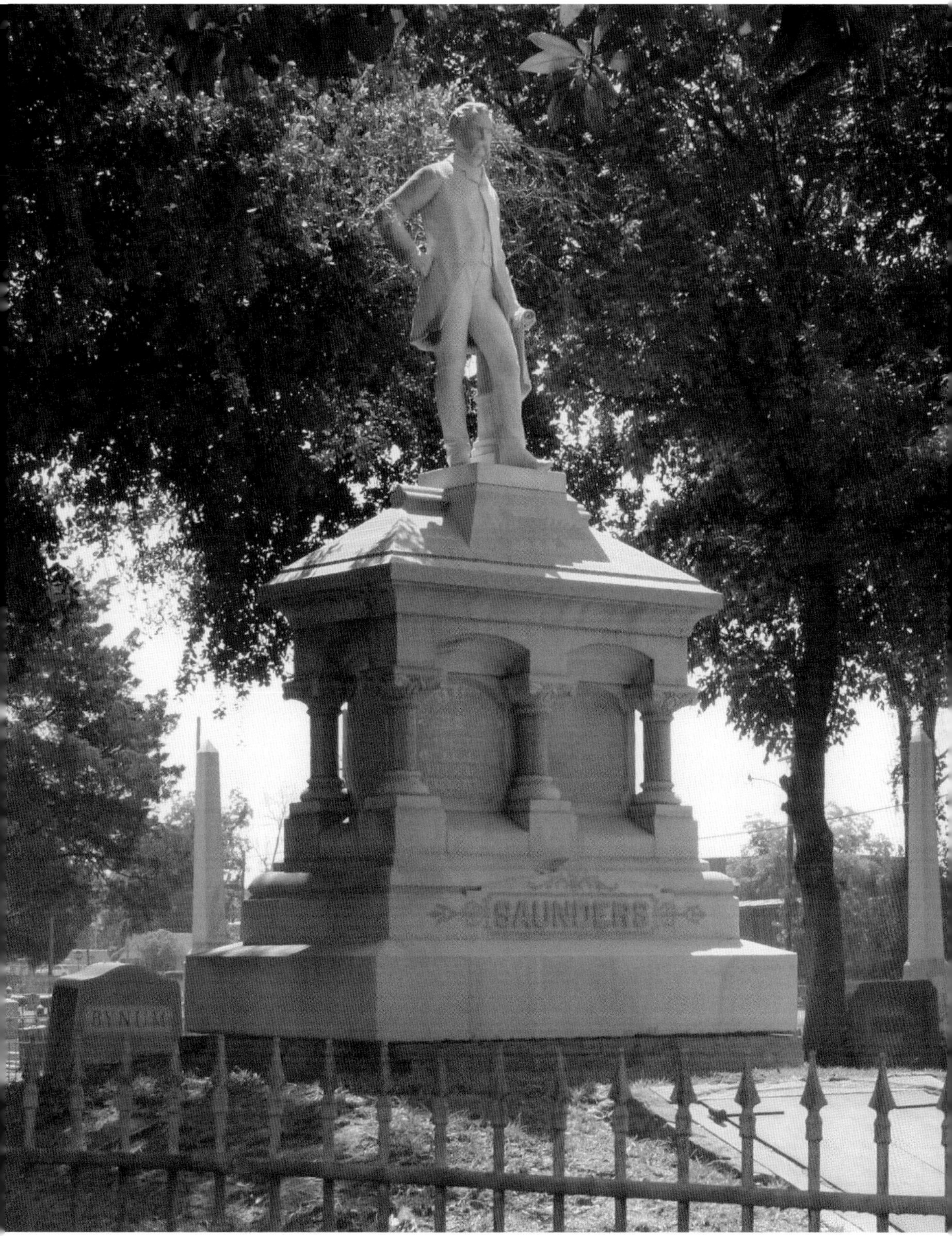
SAUNDERS

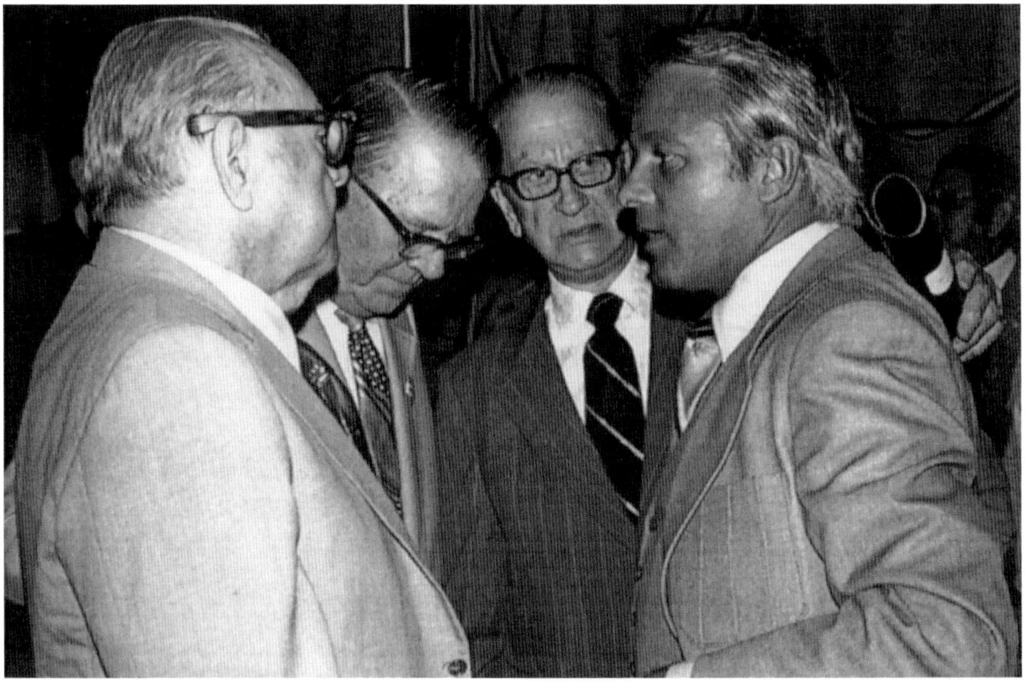

Otto Passman

Otto E. Passman served Monroe for 30 years in Congress before an international scandal helped prematurely end his political career.

In 1976, Passman (above, second from right) was accused of receiving extravagant gifts in exchange for favors in the Tongsun Park scandal. The controversy was known as "Koreagate." Passman was alleged to have received $213,000 from Park.

Two years later, the embattled politician was indicted for conspiracy, bribery, and tax evasion, but was vindicated when a Monroe jury took just 90 minutes to declare him not guilty of his alleged crimes. Following the trial, Passman never returned to the political arena. (Both courtesy of the Ouachita Parish Public Library.)

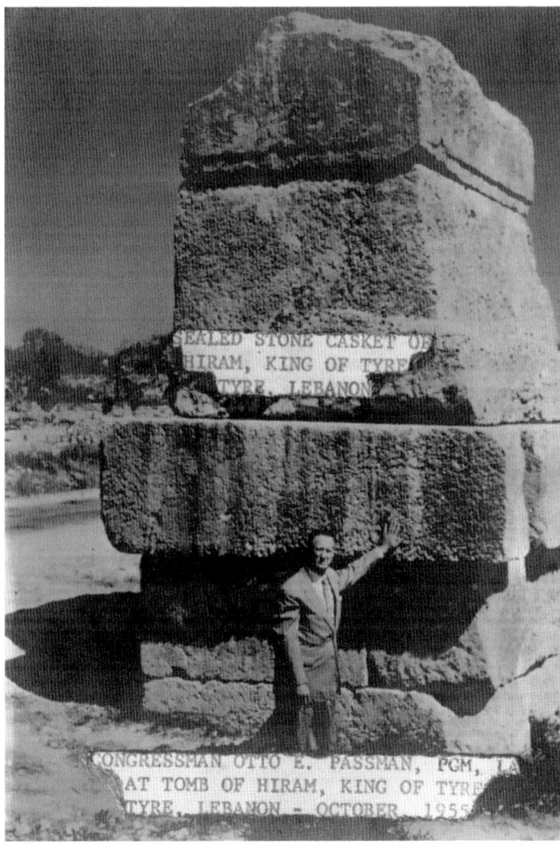

ABOUT THE OUACHITA PARISH PUBLIC LIBRARY

The Ouachita Parish Public Library is one of the finest library systems in the state. It features a treasure trove of local history in its genealogy and special collections department. In addition to being the keeper of the region's history, the Ouachita Parish Public Library Special Collections Department contains a collection of books by local authors, featuring rare titles from 1830 forward, and a repository of newspapers, from the *News-Star* to college and high school publications, as well as rare local photographs, archives, and artifacts.

For more information about the historical collections at the Ouachita Parish Public Library, contact Larry Foreman, head of Genealogy and Special Collections, in person at the main branch, located at 1800 Stubbs Avenue, Monroe, LA 71201, or by phone, at 318-327-1490, or visit the Ouachita Parish Public Library online at www.oplib.org.

INDEX

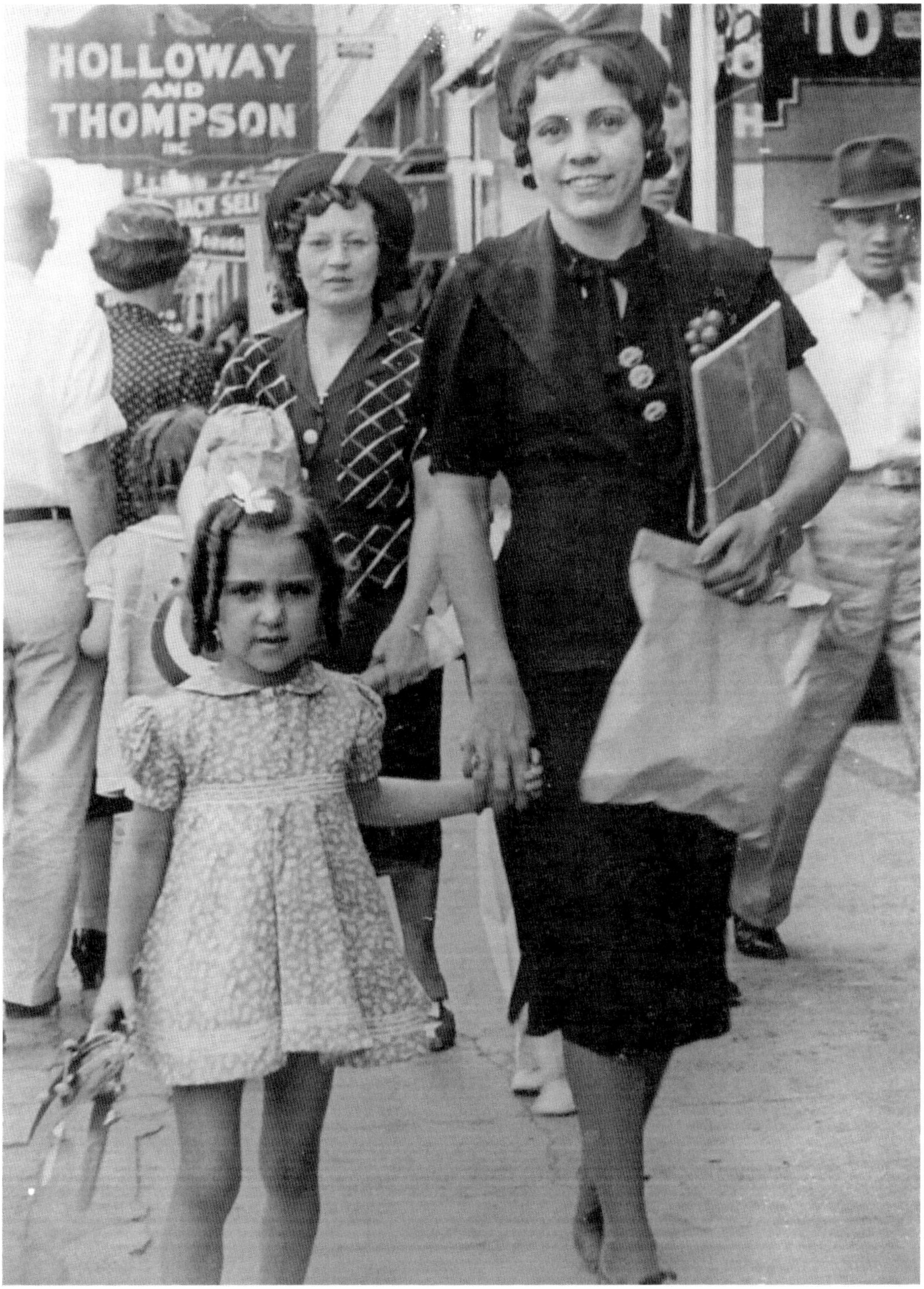

Downtown Monroe

Monroe shoppers convene in downtown Monroe around 1937. (Courtesy of Louise Khoury and the family of Mary Savana.)

LEGENDARY LOCALS

AN IMPRINT OF ARCADIA PUBLISHING

Find more books like this at
www.legendarylocals.com

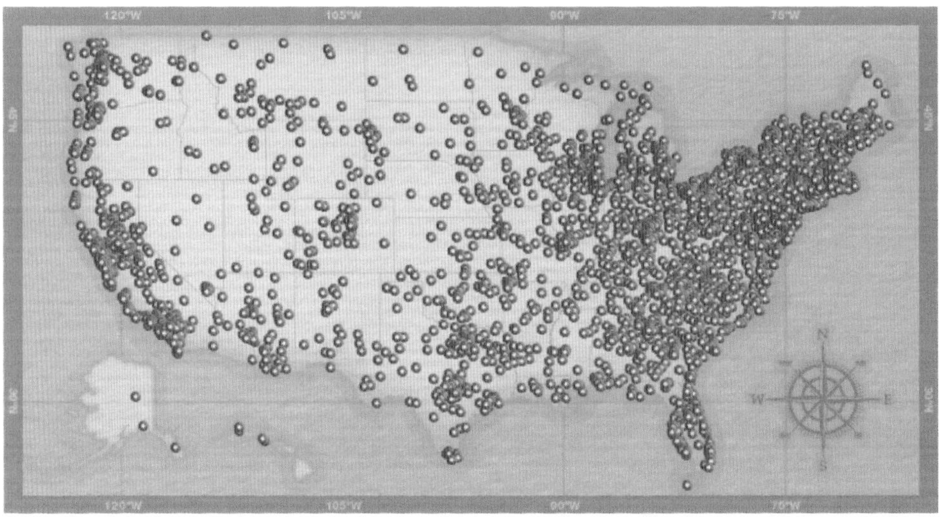

Discover more local and regional history books at
www.arcadiapublishing.com

Consistent with our mission to preserve history on a local level, this book was printed in South Carolina on American-made paper and manufactured entirely in the United States. Products carrying the accredited Forest Stewardship Council (FSC) label are printed on 100 percent FSC-certified paper.

MADE IN THE USA